Beyond Civil Rights

THE MOYNIHAN REPORT AND ITS LEGACY

Daniel Geary

UNIVERSITY OF PENNSYLVANIA PRESS

PHILADELPHIA

Published by
University of Pennsylvania Press
Philadelphia, Pennsylvania 19104-4112
www.upenn.edu/pennpress

Printed in the United States of America
on acid-free paper
1 3 5 7 9 10 8 6 4 2

Library of Congress Cataloging-in-Publication Data
ISBN 978-0-8122-4731-2

For my parents, Susan and William Geary

CONTENTS

INTRODUCTION

Crisis of Equality

In his 2006 bestseller *The Audacity of Hope,* Barack Obama praised the Moynihan Report, which famously predicted that female-headed families would impede African American progress after the passage of civil rights legislation. Obama repeated a common account of the controversy sparked by the 1965 report: "Moynihan was accused of racism . . . when he raised alarms about the rise of out-of-wedlock births among the black poor." Responding to the most famous criticism of the report—that it "blamed the victim"—Obama portrayed the uproar against Moynihan as a telling example of how "liberal policy-makers and civil rights leaders had erred" when "in their urgency to avoid blaming the victims of historical racism, they tended to downplay or ignore evidence that entrenched behavioral patterns among the black poor really were contributing to intergenerational poverty."[1]

By suggesting that African Americans take responsibility for their social advancement, Obama drew on a powerful interpretation of the Moynihan Report: urging racial self-help. "[A] transformation of attitudes has to begin in the home, and in neighborhoods, and in places of worship," he argued.[2] As the first black president, Obama continued to echo the Moynihan Report. In 2014, he launched My Brother's Keeper, a program that identified lack of father figures as a central problem facing young men of color. His comment in an interview that year strikingly recalled the report's analysis of a "tangle of pathology," interconnected social ills afflicting African Americans: "There's no contradiction to say that there are issues of personal responsibility that have to be addressed, while still acknowledging that some of the specific pathologies in the African-American community are a direct result of our history."[3]

Responding to Obama's comment, prominent African American commentator Ta-Nehisi Coates was outraged that the president pointed his finger at African Americans rather than at institutional barriers to advancement. "I can't think of a single credible historian of our 500-year tenure here," he retorted, "who has concluded that our problem was a lack of 'personal responsibility.'"[4] Six months earlier, however, Coates had appealed to an alternate interpretation of the Moynihan Report, one that advocated "national action" to address black male unemployment. To Coates, "Moynihan powerfully believed that government could actually fix 'the race problem'" through jobs programs designed to make "more [black] men marriage-material."[5] A half-century after its publication, the Moynihan Report remains a contested reference point for debating the causes and cures of African American inequality. The controversy endures because it elicits competing explanations for why African Americans, despite ostensibly having equal civil rights, experience a standard of living significantly lower than that of other Americans.

Officially titled *The Negro Family: The Case for National Action*, the report was colloquially named after its author, Daniel Patrick Moynihan, then a member of President Lyndon Johnson's administration. Moynihan wrote at the dawn of a new era in American race relations: landmark legislation in 1964 and 1965 ended Jim Crow segregation, granted formal equality to African Americans, and discredited overt arguments for white supremacy. Yet Moynihan's opening sentence warned, "The United States is approaching a new crisis in race relations." The crisis, he wrote, resulted from African American demands that went "beyond civil rights" to include economic "equality."[6] Moynihan responded to civil rights leaders who had long advanced economic reforms designed to ensure a basic standard of living for all Americans. The 1963 March on Washington, after all, was for "jobs and freedom." Yet Moynihan worried that achieving full racial equality would be hindered by what he viewed as the "crumbling" and "deteriorating" structure of many African American families reflected in high numbers of out-of-wedlock births and female-headed families. Family structure stood at the heart of what he notoriously labeled a "tangle of pathology" evident in high rates of juvenile delinquency, drug abuse, and poor educational achievement among African Americans. Moynihan's thesis produced conflicting notions about how to combat racial inequality. For liberals, it suggested the need to provide jobs for black men to stabilize families. For conservatives, however, it suggested the need for racial self-help: for African American leaders to morally uplift blacks by inculcating family values.

The Moynihan Report sparked an explosive debate at the intersection of competing conceptions of race, gender, and poverty. The political dispute over the document was actually a short-lived affair. Moynihan finished the report in March 1965. In June, it served as the basis for a major speech by President Johnson. In August, it became public. By November, the Johnson administration had disowned it in the face of mounting criticism. From the left, critics charged Moynihan with "blaming the victim": by shifting attention to African Americans' alleged family problems, he overlooked the institutions that oppressed them. Though the report lost direct relevance for public policy after 1965, intellectuals and political activists hotly debated it well into the 1970s. In the mid-1980s, the report witnessed a political and media revival that never fully dissipated. Even today, as Obama's and Coates's remarks suggest, it remains a litmus test for revealing an individual's political beliefs.

Beyond Civil Rights diverges from prevailing accounts of the Moynihan Report controversy that focus on establishing the document's intended meaning. Some scholars claim the report was a conservative document that reinforced racist stereotypes. Others defend it as a quintessentially liberal document, arguing that critics simply misunderstood it. In contrast, I argue that the report had multiple and conflicting meanings. It produced disparate reactions because of internal contradictions that reflected those of 1960s liberalism and because of its contentious assumptions about race, family, poverty, and government. Instead of focusing solely on Moynihan's intentions, this book explains why and how the report became such a powerful symbol for a surprising range of groups including liberal intellectuals, Southern segregationists, civil rights leaders, Black Power advocates, feminists, neoconservatives, and Reaganite conservatives.

One prominent interpretation finds that the Moynihan Report pioneered using images of "matriarchal" African American families to undermine the welfare state, an effort that accelerated during the 1980s and 1990s with Republican attacks on welfare recipients, usually pictured as African American single mothers. For example, scholar Roderick Ferguson writes that the report "facilitated a conservative blockade of social welfare policy" through its "pathologizing of black mothers."[7] Historian Alice O'Connor depicts the report as a prime example of how liberal social science generated conservative welfare reform.[8] However, the report was not inherently conservative. Ferguson and O'Connor conflate the report, a product of 1960s liberalism, with the late twentieth-century attack on welfare led by conservative Republicans.

By contrast, in the 1960s, many interpreted Moynihan's emphasis on "social pathologies" to indicate the need for unprecedented "national action." Civil rights leader Martin Luther King, Jr., and socialist Michael Harrington both hailed the report; seeing it as inherently conservative makes it impossible to understand why.

Another common interpretation takes the Moynihan Report as an unequivocally liberal document. This view, first advanced by Lee Rainwater and William Yancey in *The Moynihan Report and the Politics of Controversy* (1967) and stated most recently in James Patterson's *Freedom Is Not Enough* (2010), correctly notes that Moynihan called attention to black family structure to push for jobs programs and other measures to benefit African Americans.[9] Interpreting the report as unambiguously liberal fails to explain its immediate attraction to 1960s conservatives such as William F. Buckley and long-term appeal to neoconservatives and Reaganite conservatives. Moreover, even the report's liberal call for job creation sprang from assumptions that struck 1960s liberals, radicals, and their present-day heirs as "conservative." These included viewing African American culture as pathological, defending the patriarchal family, and relying on technocratic expertise rather than grass-roots activism to generate reform.

Patterson is the most recent historian to misinterpret the dispute over the report as a simple case of "misunderstandings and misrepresentations."[10] The controversy resulted not from critics' misunderstanding of Moynihan's reformist intentions, but from the report's ambiguities that allowed multiple interpretations. Misrepresentations fed the debate, as they do in any significant controversy. But they did not occur solely on one side. If opponents sometimes missed Moynihan's liberal intentions, he and his supporters often ignored the substance of their criticisms by reducing them to assertions that Moynihan was a "racist," a charge few critics actually made. Viewing the controversy through Moynihan's perspective, Patterson distorts critics' views and overlooks important groups that challenged the report, such as African American feminists, who were its most thorough critics and among the most influential. Patterson and others also misstate the extent to which Moynihan suffered from the controversy: Nicolas Lemann's claim that the report stands as the "most refuted document in American history" is vastly exaggerated.[11] In fact, for fifty years, the report has received overwhelmingly positive media coverage. Far from damaging Moynihan's career, the report launched him to a prominent professorship at Harvard University, a top post in Richard Nixon's administration, and a long career in the Senate representing New York.

Liberals nostalgic for a mid-1960s moment when government officials con-templated ambitious programs to redress African American inequality have been especially drawn to the idea that the Moynihan Report was misunder-stood. For them, the report marked a lost opportunity for reforms that might have been enacted but for the unfortunate response the report generated.[12] Conservatives similarly explain the controversy as a misunderstanding by treating left-wing critics' attacks as irrational. For them, the Moynihan Re-port controversy marked the onset of "political correctness." Conservatives claim criticism of the report by civil rights leaders and liberals suppressed an honest discussion about race.[13] In their view, Moynihan's critics convinced African Americans to perceive themselves as victims without responsibility for moral failings and civil rights leaders wrongly focused on criticizing Moynihan instead of exhorting blacks to strengthen their families.[14] There is no necessary contradiction between conservatives' advocacy of racial self-help and liberals' support for government efforts to redress inequalities. How-ever, in national political debate, conservative appropriations of the Moynihan Report to call for racial self-help denied national responsibility for persistent anti-black racism and gross economic inequality.

Rehashing the same arguments over the Moynihan Report's meaning brings us no closer to understanding the dispute. Indeed, the controversy was more historically significant than the document itself. It never was a two-sided contest between Moynihan and his left-wing critics, as it has been portrayed. Rather, it was a multi-cornered affair that cannot be reduced to a divide be-tween liberals and conservatives or between liberals and radicals. Moynihan had defenders as well as critics among liberals, civil rights leaders, Black Power advocates, and conservatives. To provide a definitive account of the contro-versy, this book draws on extensive archival research, mostly in previously unused sources, and interviews with surviving participants. It explains the reactions of all major participants in the controversy, not just Moynihan's. Analyzing contradictions and flaws in arguments on all sides reveals the de-bate's complexity and offers a history without heroes or villains.

The controversy ranged so widely because it affected so many communi-ties of discourse. The report connected academic research, public policy, and public debate. The controversy fed back into each of these arenas with continuing reverberations for the others. Because the report drew heavily on social science, the dispute rebounded into academic disciplines where its policy relevance infused scholarly debate with political significance. Media discussion inflamed criticism from intellectuals and political activists. The controversy's impact also reached well beyond Moynihan's elite circles. Hundreds of Americans wrote directly to Moynihan to share their views.

The controversy is best understood as a struggle to define the meaning of a highly publicized but unclear document. Participants fought to establish interpretations of the report that served their larger aims. The report's ambiguity proved useful for Moynihan, who sought acclaim across the political spectrum, and for the Johnson administration, which adopted the civil rights movement's rhetoric about economic equality but failed to endorse measures such as the $100 billion Freedom Budget advocated by civil rights leaders. The report's ambiguity helped it become a crucial text in American political culture, functioning like what cultural critic Raymond Williams termed a "keyword," a familiar term that articulates social ideals but is open to diverse and conflicting interpretations.[15] The character and impact of political ideas are often defined less by their inherent logic than by the struggle of forces that claim, contest, and modify them. Thus, examining the meanings Americans made of this single document illuminates broad transformations in American political culture.

What lent the report its enduring salience was its maddening inconsistency on key issues. Was family instability primarily cause or consequence of racial inequality? Were the "social pathologies" of African Americans race-specific, rooted in the history of slavery and racial discrimination, or were they class-specific, based on the overconcentration of African Americans among the urban poor? Was patriarchal family structure naturally superior, or did racial minorities simply have to conform to mainstream nuclear family norms if they wished to advance? Moynihan also articulated two distinct notions of "equality." On one hand, equality meant a guaranteed basic living standard for all Americans. On the other, equality meant "equal results"—a class distribution among African Americans that matched other American ethnoracial groups.

How Moynihan framed African American inequality proved especially contentious because it involved several divisive issues in the post-civil rights era. The controversy reveals how discussions of race and class have remained deeply intertwined in American discourse. The report became a touchstone for discussing the merits of the liberal welfare state and Johnson's Great Society programs. Partly because of its inconsistencies, the report served multiple political perspectives. Focus on male unemployment's destructive effects on families indicated the need for an activist state to surpass the limited antipoverty measures enacted by Johnson and ensure full male employment and a guaranteed annual income. However, emphasis on how family structure determined economic success suggested that poverty resulted from the poor's flawed cultural values. Especially since the 1980s, conservatives have cited the report to argue that poverty is best solved not by economic redistribution but by moral revitalization, particularly the restoration of patriarchal nuclear families.

Though the controversy framed American race relations in black and white, it held implications for other ethnoracial groups. For example, Moynihan's proposal that African Americans should receive "equal results" extended to other racial minorities, justifying affirmative action programs initially designed for blacks that benefited other nonwhite groups. The debate over the report became linked to the similar and contemporaneous concept of a "culture of poverty," a term made famous by anthropologist Oscar Lewis's depictions of Mexican peasants and Puerto Ricans.[16] The report was also based on Moynihan's particular understanding of race, which emerged from co-authoring an influential 1963 study of New York City ethnic groups, *Beyond the Melting Pot*, which analogized African Americans to European immigrant groups. The book concluded that the success of any group depended on sociological characteristics, especially family structure. Moynihan, an Irish-American, frequently compared African Americans to nineteenth-century Irish immigrants to the United States.

A document born of a liberal mindset that valued the perspective of trained elites, the report generated challenges to established experts' claims to understand African American life. Many African Americans criticized the Moynihan Report as yet another case of white domination of the study of African Americans. The Black Power movement attacked Moynihan, demanding control over how African Americans were represented. The related Black Sociology movement called for the "death of white sociology" and contended that Moynihan's depiction of African American culture as "pathological" falsely presumed the superiority of "white" middle-class American norms. Black Feminists thought the report promoted racist stereotypes of black women. They targeted not only white liberals such as Moynihan but also African American men who wanted to restore black male authority in the family.

Gender ideals were barely contested in the report's initial reception, but assumptions about family roles of men and women were always integral to the report. Like most postwar liberals, Moynihan defined economic equality in terms of the "family wage"—the ability of male breadwinners to provide for their families. The second wave of feminism rose in the years immediately after the report, so that by the late 1960s, debate about the report became explicitly as much about gender as about race. Second-wave feminists, white and black, challenged its patriarchal norms. The controversy became embroiled in growing debates over middle-class values and the nuclear family, the superiority of which were contested by the counterculture and gay liberation movement as well by second-wave feminism.

The combustibility of Moynihan's assumptions about race, gender, and government was clearest in reactions to his most concrete policy for African American advancement: recruiting more black men into the military. The proposal fit a liberal strategy to provide jobs to male breadwinners to stabilize African American families and communities. It also reflected a belief that success in American society required middle-class values presumed lacking among African Americans. In the army, Moynihan alleged, black men would learn "discipline." The proposal also reflected Moynihan's belief that African American men suffered from a "matriarchal" culture. The military would provide them with "an utterly masculine world . . . a world away from women, a world run by strong men of unquestioned authority."[17] Moynihan's suggestion, advanced during the rapid escalation of the Vietnam War, met opposition from several fronts. Even though many Black Power advocates agreed with Moynihan's patriarchal ideals, they rejected military service as participation in an American imperialism that targeted nonwhites abroad just as it oppressed nonwhites at home. Men involved in the antiwar and countercultural movements rejected Moynihan's equation of masculinity with submission to hierarchical discipline. Feminists viewed the plan as a brief for patriarchy. One mocked Moynihan for assuming "women are so terrible that it is a fantastic relief to get away from them." "Never mind that the service is experiencing explosive racial problems," she continued, "it is still better than being around women."[18]

Though the Moynihan Report controversy involved leftists and conservatives, it proved especially significant for liberals, who could not resolve the crisis of equality. Liberalism is defined here as a political ideology committed to reducing social and economic inequality within a capitalist, formally democratic system and to securing equal rights for ethnoracial minorities.[19] An important constituency in the Democratic Party, liberals dominated mid-twentieth-century intellectual discourse. Attaining economic equality for African Americans, unlike securing legal and political rights, exposed the limits of postwar liberalism, divided liberals, and enabled challenges to liberalism to surface with new intensity.[20]

The Moynihan Report controversy is sometimes mistakenly viewed as emblematic of a postwar liberal consensus that suddenly unraveled during the late 1960s.[21] Rather than demonstrating a liberal consensus, the initial range of reactions to the document reveals an ideological diversity that predated the controversy. Far from a stable consensus, postwar liberalism itself contained diverse and conflicting strands. The report reflected these contradictions and typified a postwar liberal mindset that recognized structural economic barriers to African American achievement yet was committed to meritocratic notions that individuals and ethnic groups succeeded based on ability to compete in an open marketplace. The race-based economic inequality Moynihan identified was so entrenched in American society that readers could conclude either that government needed to enact radical reforms advocated by civil rights leaders or that it was incapable of addressing the problem. The report contained both the seeds of left-wing challenge that deepened liberals' war on poverty and a neoconservative attack on the welfare state. Just as the Moynihan Report did not solely involve race, postwar liberalism did not become embattled only because of its commitment to African American equality, which was equivocal in any case.[22] Rather, several forces converged to contest core postwar liberal assumptions articulated in the Moynihan Report such as: the government's ability to allieviate economic inequality without reforming corporate capitalism, the cultural assimilation of ethnoracial minorities, the desirability of male-headed families, the efficacy of social engineering by experts and government officials, and the superiority of middle-class American values.[23]

One way to track the controversy's impact on liberalism is to examine the trajectory of the report's author. In the late 1960s, Moynihan became one of the most prominent "neoconservatives," a set of postwar liberals who moved right. The report contained a thread of neoconservatism in its suggestion that government might be unable to solve a problem rooted in family structure. Neoconservatives spun that into a blanket challenge to liberal social engineering. The controversy itself played a key role in pushing Moynihan and other neoconservatives to the right. Ultimately, Moynihan concluded that those who most forcefully called for racial equality—radical African Americans and their allies—were responsible for the racial discord of the late 1960s. In a notorious 1970 memo to President Nixon, in whose administration he then served, Moynihan advised a policy of "benign neglect" for discussing race. Moynihan and other neoconservatives anticipated conservatives' appropriation of the report, which accelerated during the 1980s. Thus, late twentieth-century conservatism emerged not only as a reaction to postwar liberalism, but also as a development from it.[24]

Because African Americans, despite considerable progress, have yet to achieve equality by any definition, the report retains its relevance.[25] The controversy has significantly influenced how Americans discuss racial equality. Many ideas central to racial discourse in twenty-first-century America can be traced to the Moynihan Report controversy. The debate defined the image of an African American urban "underclass" with deviant cultural values commonly referenced by Obama and others. Justifications for affirmative action emerged from the report's contention that African Americans deserve and require special preferences, as did the competing notion that African Americans benefit most from class-based programs for the poor and working class. Criticism of the report helped generate multiculturalism by challenging the document's racial paternalism, asserting the positive value of a distinctive African American culture, and demanding that racial minorities be allowed to define themselves. Refuting the report's assumption that anti-black racism would no longer hinder African American progress after civil rights helped establish the concept of "institutional racism" which recognizes persistent systemic racism. Finally, conservatives drew on the report to claim that that only individual achievement and racial self-help, not the welfare state, could lead to African American progress.

By pointing to cultural deficiencies among African Americans, the report explained without recourse to now-discredited notions of biological inferiority how racial inequality persists even if race supposedly no longer matters. Its call to go "beyond civil rights," intended to highlight economic inequality, misleadingly implied that full legal and political equality had already been achieved. Hence many used the report to complement the dominant American ideology of the post-civil rights era: a willfully naïve color-blindness that suggests that racism no longer significantly factors in American life.[26] The illusion of color-blindness allows Americans to overlook such contemporary realities that disproportionately affect African Americans as mass incarceration, blatantly unjust police violence, and even disenfranchisement.

Today, a report written to convince the Johnson administration to go "beyond civil rights" is used to rationalize that civil rights legislation *alone* could overcome centuries of injustice toward African Americans. This irony is one of many revealed by the history of the Moynihan Report dispute, in which racial inequality was entwined with questions of class, gender, social expertise, and the role of government. The astonishingly wide-ranging and long-running controversy over Moynihan's views of African American families offers a revealing illustration of how Americans have discussed the tangled aspects of persistent African American inequality from the civil rights era to the present day.

CHAPTER 1

The Liberal Mindset

Could anyone have imagined that Daniel Patrick Moynihan would make his name with a report about black families? He had no long-standing interest in the subject. He was not an acknowledged expert on race; paradoxically, writing the report made him one. He worked for the U.S. Department of Labor, an agency hardly associated with research on race or the family.

Until the civil rights movement forced African American inequality onto the national agenda, it was not a central issue for Moynihan or many other Northern liberals. Yet, when the civil rights movement's cresting tide pushed policy-makers to address racial inequality, Moynihan felt he understood the issue in ways other Johnson officials did not. His childhood experience of economic insecurity was unusual in elite policy-making circles. Moynihan felt his "personal history" of being raised in a "broken family" with economic hardship allowed him to understand African Americans who came from "mostly the same world" as he did.[1] His Catholicism further led him to see economic inequality as a social injustice and prompted his belief that "family interests were perhaps the central objective . . . of social policy."[2] Moynihan's particularly strong commitment to the male breadwinner family model led him to view its absence as a crucial marker of social inequality.

The Moynihan Report reflected its author's distinctive perspective. It also embodied a broader liberal mindset. Moynihan brought to the report typical postwar liberal assumptions about employment, family, individual achievement, social expertise, and poverty. The report's heavy use of statistics suggested a technocratic faith in the ability of elites to engineer solutions to social problems. The major problem identified—the lack of African American male breadwinners—pointed to a pervasive liberal commitment to providing men a family wage so that mothers of young children could avoid wage labor. This gender ideal was integral, not incidental, to mid-century liberalism.

While other liberals shared Moynihan's concern with poverty, Moynihan feared that Lyndon Johnson's War on Poverty lacked the jobs and income redistribution programs needed to truly combat economic inequality. By writing his report, Moynihan sought to capitalize on the rising political salience of African American inequality to persuade Johnson to expand his antipoverty policies. However, Moynihan's concern with economic inequality clashed with another intellectual strand present in the report: the framework of race relations he developed working with influential sociologist Nathan Glazer on *Beyond the Melting Pot* that suggested that American ethnic groups' success owed to deeply rooted cultural institutions such as family structure. Here deviation from the nuclear family norm was a cause of economic inequality rather than an effect, casting doubt on whether government action could improve African Americans' economic standing and implying instead the need for racial self-help. The tension between this cultural explanation for racial inequality and Moynihan's desire to extend the family wage to African Americans produced the report's inherent ambiguity.

Moynihan of the Moynihan Report

"I grew up in Hell's Kitchen. My father was a drunk. I know what this life is like." So Moynihan told the *New York Times* shortly after controversy over his report exploded.[3] Moynihan claimed that his personal background offered him insight into lower-class African American families that civil rights leaders from secure middle-class families lacked. Sympathetic press accounts related certain facts of Moynihan's background to enhance his intellectual authority on African American families: he had risen out of poverty, been raised by a single mother, and understood discrimination as an Irish Catholic. According to *Life*, "Moynihan knows firsthand about poverty, minority groups, and broken families. His grandfather was an Irish immigrant, and his father left their New York City home when Pat was a boy." Moynihan's early years were often fitted into a classic American rags-to-riches tale of how he "pulled himself out of the ghetto."[4] The *New York Times Magazine*, for example, profiled "Moynihan of the Moynihan Report" in a 1966 article. "Some contemporary Horatio Alger," it declared, "could scarcely have concocted a more classic up-from-poverty story than that of Daniel Patrick Moynihan." The article recounted his father's abandonment of his mother and their children; moves with his family to "every slum neighborhood in Manhattan";

shining shoes as a boy in Times Square; and college matriculation after Moynihan realized that university education was not just for (in his words) "sissy rich kids." To affirm comparisons between Moynihan and poor African Americans, the newspaper ran a photograph alongside its profile of Moynihan. It depicted a black shoeshine boy working at the corner of Forty-Third and Broadway where, it claimed, "Moynihan [once] plied the same trade."[5]

Press profiles gave the misimpression that Moynihan was raised in poverty, when in fact he hailed from a comfortably middle-class family that fell on hard times during the final years of the Great Depression. Daniel Patrick, best known as "Pat," was born on March 16, 1927, to Margaret and John Moynihan. John was the son of an Irish immigrant from County Kerry, but Margaret came from a German American Protestant family. She converted to Catholicism to marry John. Throughout his life, Pat accentuated his Irish identity and barely mentioned his German roots. For he and other whites of his generation, ethnic identity was partly a matter of *choice*; not so for African Americans, for whom racial identity was ascribed. Though Moynihan did help his mother run a bar in the rough Manhattan neighborhood of Hell's Kitchen in the late 1940s, he was not raised there, as the *New York Times* reported. In fact, shortly after Moynihan's birth in Tulsa, Oklahoma, the family settled in a pleasant New Jersey suburb when John Moynihan took a position as an advertising writer in New York City. The public image of Moynihan forged during the controversy over *The Negro Family* elided such details and falsely equated his experience to those of poor African Americans.

Nevertheless, there can be little doubt that Moynihan's concern for African American families emerged from his traumatic childhood experience of economic and family insecurity. One can trace the report's focus on "family instability" to the pivotal event of Moynihan's childhood: his father, an alcoholic, abandoned his family in 1937. Pat never saw him again. Without the father's income, the family fell out of the middle class. Moving to successively poorer areas in New York City, Moynihan and his brother shined shoes to earn money. Moynihan transferred from parochial school to public school. This experience of economic decline later enabled Moynihan to empathize with African Americans whose families, he claimed, were broken up by poverty. Ironically, the policy he advocated in *The Negro Family*—creating jobs so that men could serve as breadwinners—would not have helped his family in the late 1930s. Moynihan experienced economic insecurity because his family depended so much on his father's income that his absence was catastrophic.[6]

How Moynihan and his family recovered from this trauma left him with an enduring faith in the ability of government to offer possibilities for social advancement. As Moynihan recalled in 1964, "the luckiest thing that ever happened to me was the Second World War."[7] The war lifted the nation out of the Great Depression and the Moynihan family out of poverty. Margaret Moynihan, after a brief and unsuccessful second marriage motivated by the need to find another male provider, found work as a chief nurse in a war production plant. She was one of millions of American women who landed well-paid jobs during the war. After graduating first in his high school class in 1942, Pat worked on the docks as a stevedore. He attended City College of New York for a year before enlisting in naval officer training school in March 1944. As Moynihan recollected, he owed his college education to the fact that "the U.S. Navy needed officers and was willing to pay to educate them."[8] He received his B.N.S. in 1946 from Tufts University through the Reserve Officer Training Corps (ROTC) program. Moynihan served actively in the navy until 1947 and in the reserves for several years thereafter; he achieved the rank of lieutenant. His experience left him certain that military service could advance the opportunities of young men.

Moynihan's support for the liberal welfare state tracked national support for Franklin Roosevelt's New Deal during a foundational period for twentieth-century American liberalism. His demographic characteristics perfectly embodied the New Deal coalition: urban, Catholic, ethnic, and economically insecure. At age ten, Moynihan distributed pamphlets for Roosevelt's 1936 reelection. Roosevelt campaigned that year on the success of his New Deal reforms, which had installed new financial regulations, established a social security system of old age pensions and unemployment insurance, and provided jobs for unemployed Americans through public works programs. He targeted the nation's financial elites who resisted his programs as "economic royalists" and won in a landslide. From an early age, Moynihan strongly backed labor unions, whose membership grew rapidly during the years of his adolescence and which provided crucial political support for New Deal reforms. He later recalled that for a young man of his generation "the most attractive, personally satisfying, and useful job he could hold would be to work for a union."[9] For a brief time as a young man, Moynihan was even attracted to socialist ideas that surpassed New Deal reforms. He later claimed to have voted for Socialist Party presidential candidate Norman Thomas.[10] Moynihan's high-school yearbook lampooned his political sentiments. In a feature that pretended to glimpse graduates' future, a fortune-teller prophesied: "Now

I see Pat Moynihan. He is president of a bank. He is cussing out the labor unions and the durn radicals."[11]

Moynihan's experiences after leaving the navy affirmed his belief in liberal government programs. In addition to offering favorable home and business loans, the 1944 GI Bill provided veterans such as Moynihan with free university educations. After finishing his B.A. in 1948, he pursued a Ph.D. at the Tufts University Fletcher School of Law and Diplomacy, where students trained primarily for careers in government. In 1950, Moynihan received a Fulbright grant to study at the London School of Economics. He told a friend that between his GI Bill benefits and the Fulbright grant, he would make about 21 British pounds a week, three times the average weekly earnings of a British worker. The opportunity, he knew, was "unbelievably good."[12] Moynihan's time in England deepened his commitment to liberal welfare policies, which he saw executed on a broader scale than in the United States. He praised the British Labour Party for constructing a substantial public welfare system following the war. For example, it established the National Health Service to provide free universal health care. Moynihan reported to an American correspondent, "I have been hugely impressed by the socialist movement [which] has brought real democracy to the English people."[13]

Though Moynihan hoped to bolster the U.S. welfare state, his ambitions were tempered by his embrace of the postwar U.S. social order from which he had received tangible benefits. Despite his youthful flirtation with socialism, Moynihan disliked left-wing radicalism and strongly supported the Cold War fight against Communism. While in England, he defended the American war effort in Korea in an exchange with venerable British socialist G. D. H. Cole, a leader of the Labour Party's left wing. In a 1951 letter to the socialist magazine *New Statesman and Nation*, Moynihan asserted the fundamentally positive role of American influence in the world, ridiculing Cole's "assumption that the United States offers no more hope to the world than does Soviet Russia."[14]

Moynihan's sentiments reflected Cold War liberalism's shift to the center. In 1948, New Dealer Henry Wallace ran a third-party campaign to challenge incumbent president Harry Truman and his Cold War policies. A group of Cold War liberals successfully rallied to reelect Truman and discredit Wallace, forming the Americans for Democratic Action (ADA), which became a key intellectual organ of postwar liberalism. Moynihan would become a member. ADA leader Arthur Schlesinger, Jr., redefined liberalism as a "vital center." While committed to further reforms in the New Deal tradition,

ADA liberals disassociated themselves from more radical policies earlier enter-
tained by New Dealers who challenged corporate capitalism more directly.
The postwar Red Scare placed intense pressure on left-leaning liberals and
Cold War critics to distance themselves from any positions that reeked of
radicalism.[15]

Moynihan's doctoral dissertation, which he initially came to England to
research, reflected his embrace of this "vital center" liberalism. Temperamen-
tally, Moynihan proved better suited to politics and intellectual journalism
than to traditional academic scholarship. He seems to have lost interest in
his dissertation, not completing it until 1960. Friends reported finding that
note cards in Moynihan's dissertation file contained cocktail recipes. Nevertheless, his thesis, a dry historical account with only a few rhetorical flour-
ishes that later characterized Moynihan's writing style, offers insight into the
development of his liberal mindset.[16] Moynihan traced American involvement
with the International Labour Organization (ILO), a social reform organization that promoted international labor standards. His celebration of the ILO
reflected his advocacy not only of liberal internationalist institutions such as
the United Nations, of which the ILO was a forerunner, but also of a regu-
lated form of capitalism: "In essence the idea of international labor legislation is one of reform as against revolution. It proceeds from the assumption
of the legitimacy of capitalist concern with competition."[17]

Having lost interest in his academic work, Moynihan became involved
in New York state politics after returning to the United States in 1953. After
serving in Averill Harriman's 1954 campaign for the New York governorship,
Moynihan joined his administration, eventually becoming Harriman's
executive secretary. Moynihan married one of Harriman's aides, Elizabeth
Brennan, in 1955. They had three children together. Moynihan's pride in his
ability to provide for his family, as his own father had failed to do, likely led
him to sympathize with African American men unable to do the same.

When Harriman lost his bid for reelection in 1958, Moynihan was appointed assistant professor of political science at Syracuse University.[18] There
he began writing for major journals of opinion, which were enjoying a golden
age of influence. His first pieces appeared in *The Reporter*, edited by Irving
Kristol, later a leading neoconservative. Moynihan also wrote for magazines
such as *Commonweal* and *Commentary*, drawing on experience in government and his academic training. Moynihan developed a style that was witty,
accessible, provocative, and full of literary and historical allusions. It was
perfectly calculated to appeal to his educated middle-class readership.

By 1960, Moynihan was on his way to a successful career in public affairs. In addition to his burgeoning profession as a writer, his political experience and connections positioned him well for a job in the federal government after John F. Kennedy's election in 1960. Moynihan flourished because of his personal qualities. He was intelligent, charismatic, and ambitious. But he was also fortunate to grow up during a period that offered extraordinary opportunities for individual advancement to white men. Like many Americans of his generation, Moynihan benefited enormously from the long economic boom that began with World War II and from government programs that offered him a free education.

Moynihan's background left him with distinct notions of inequality, family, and government, but offered him few direct experiences of African American life and hardly prepared him to understand racism. Ultimately, it led him in two directions regarding African American inequality. He keenly appreciated the important role that government programs had played in his advancement. When he obtained a position of power, he argued that similar opportunities should be extended to African Americans, who were systematically excluded from liberal social programs of the 1930s and 1940s that had benefited Moynihan and other whites. Nevertheless, Moynihan's belief in his Horatio Alger story led him to equate falsely his experience with those of poor African Americans and ignore systemic barriers to African American advancement. For example, under redlining practices in place until 1968, advantageous mortgages backed by the Federal Housing Authority were denied to African Americans, limiting their ability to acquire equity and ensuring residential and educational segregation. As a result, most African American war veterans could not benefit from the GI Bill's housing loans.[19] Moynihan was concerned that African Americans were poorly prepared for economic success, but his overriding concern to improve employment and family stability so that lower-class African Americans could better compete overlooked that opportunities were not the same for blacks as they had been for him.

Justice, Stability, and Expertise

"Growing up in the New Deal, I had come to equate taking a job in the Federal government with entering the ranks of a political movement intent upon establishing social justice and stability in the United States and throughout the world." So wrote Moynihan in 1960 shortly before he joined the Kennedy administration. "The challenge to my generation," he continued, "was not the political one of determining objectives . . . but the technical one of achieving them."[20] Moynihan's statement embodied a mindset typical of liberal policy-makers and intellectuals of the period. They merged technocratic belief in the efficacy of government action based on scientific knowledge with an idealistic desire to extend economic security to all Americans.

The early 1960s marked the high point of liberal belief in the application of social science to policy-making, an assumption later contested in the Moynihan Report dispute. Early 1960s liberals believed that government could act on the basis of sound scientific knowledge. After the New Deal, most American liberals presumed that the federal government would lead in developing and applying social knowledge. Bolstered by the postwar expansion of American universities and expanding research funds, American social scientists developed new research techniques and bodies of knowledge. The Kennedy administration actively touted its reliance on academic experts and intellectuals. Moynihan, a lowly assistant professor of political science at Syracuse University, joined more prominent academics in the Kennedy administration such as Harvard historian Arthur Schlesinger, Jr., and economist John Kenneth Galbraith.

Moynihan's commitment to applying expert knowledge to government was evident in the work on traffic safety that first brought him public notoriety. His widely read 1959 article in *The Reporter*, "Epidemic on the Highways," drew on his earlier experience in New York government. He argued that officials should gather scientific knowledge to prevent traffic accidents systematically rather than blame bad drivers. "Instead of approaching the problem as one of preventing disease," Moynihan complained, "we generally approach it as one of punishing wrongdoing." Traffic safety, Moynihan declared, was "in the first instance . . . simply a problem in social science."[21] Moynihan's faith in expert knowledge went hand-in-hand with his belief in government's remit to regulate business in the public interest. The automobile industry's prioritizing of profits over safety demonstrated the need for government to protect citizens against the excesses of industry. In classic muckraking style, Moynihan exposed the dangers of unsafe automobile design to arouse public opinion to push for government action.[22] (Moynihan later hired Ralph Nader as a research assistant at the Department of Labor. Nader's famous 1965 book, *Unsafe at Any Speed*, endorsed a "rational quest for safer automobiles" and helped lead to Congress passing the 1966 Vehicle

National Traffic and Motor Safety Act, which mandated many of the safety features of automobiles that drivers today take for granted.[23])

Many early 1960s liberals agreed with President Kennedy that government had become so complicated that managing national affairs required expert knowledge: "most of the problems . . . we now face are technical problems, are administrative problems. They are very sophisticated judgments which do not lend themselves to the great sort of 'passionate movements' which have stirred the country so often in the past. Now they deal with questions which are beyond the comprehension of most men."[24] In a 1965 article, "The Professionalization of Reform," Moynihan celebrated a new development in which experts and government officials pushed for social reforms that previously required active social movements or pressure groups. While Moynihan expressed some concerns for decreased democratic participation and political passion, he largely endorsed the professionalization of reform as a "profound promise of social sanity and stability."[25] The application of expert knowledge by government officials would allow the "creation of a society that can put an end to the 'animal miseries.' "[26] Moynihan claimed that the benefits of professionalization of reform were clearest in economics, which provided knowledge to government officials to maintain continuous economic growth and reduce unemployment. He predicted that government collection of social statistics would allow officials to successfully intervene in other areas of American society.

To institute social reforms, Moynihan looked not to a popular social movement but to government experts such as himself. The War on Poverty, he argued, reflected "the growing capacity of government to respond on its own to new information and new circumstances." It was "a rational rather than a political event," originating in the ideas of intellectuals and policy-makers.[27] Believing in the power of rational administration, Moynihan, like other liberals, saw poverty as a "manageable problem" now that "the nation is learning to run its economy."[28] Thus, Moynihan declared that poverty could be eliminated without a "social revolution."[29] He affirmed his faith in the American nation: "I think we have produced the best social system the world has so far seen despite the obvious fact that it can be improved."[30] Early 1960s liberals could stress the technical nature of political problems because they felt Americans shared a political consensus on the necessity of government action to regulate capitalism, generate economic growth, and ensure prosperity.

Assurance in the ability of experts and policy-makers to resolve social problems gave liberals confidence that they could solve even complicated and deeply rooted problems such as African American inequality. However, it also implied that social problems were best solved by experts and that social reform should proceed without undue disruption.[31] The dispute over *The Negro Family* revolved partly around Moynihan's liberal beliefs that social reform could be engineered from above and that social stability was equally important as social justice.

Liberals' faith in the basic soundness of the American postwar social and political order assured them that racial integration required no fundamental changes to American society. However, the early 1960s belief in liberal consensus proved unfounded. Moynihan's existence in a liberal policy-making and intellectual bubble fostered a false belief that Americans had left behind what he dismissed as the "stupid controversies that afflict most peoples."[32] He was unprepared for the ideological conflict his report triggered.

Full Employment and the Family Wage

In the liberal mindset, complacency with consensus conflicted with more idealistic hopes, a tension reflected in the contrast between Kennedy's cautious policies and his soaring rhetoric. Many liberals inside and outside the Kennedy administration viewed the New Deal project of building a welfare system as incomplete. This feeling was perhaps strongest in the Department of Labor. It was significant that Moynihan worked there, for he could just as easily have gotten a position in the Department of State (given his training at the Fletcher School) or the Department of Transportation (where he believed his strong stance on traffic safety activated automobile interests to block his appointment). Moynihan's post at Labor directly led him to develop the strong interest in unemployment that underlay *The Negro Family*.

Under Kennedy and Johnson, the Labor Department articulated the views of organized labor, a key component of the liberal coalition. In the postwar period, unions compromised with corporations to provide their workers higher wages, better benefits, and protection from arbitrary managerial actions on the shoproom floor in exchange for leaving the basic tasks of management to companies and acceding to demands for increased productivity. Unions provided benefits to their members but fell well short of earlier hopes that organized labor might play a determinative role in American economy and society. Nevertheless, organized labor in the early 1960s still pushed for government reforms to benefit all workers.[33] Perfectly representing postwar

organized labor was Kennedy's secretary of labor, Arthur Goldberg, a lawyer rather than a fiery orator on the 1930s model of labor leader. Goldberg, a
mentor to Moynihan, sought to protect union gains from a business onslaught
already evident by the late 1950s and worked to extend benefits to the many
American workers who lacked union representation.[34]

Moynihan's stint at Labor strengthened his commitment to the liberal goal
of "full employment": using government policy to provide wage work to all
who sought it. The Full Employment Act of 1946, one of the last bills of the
New Deal era, set a target unemployment rate of below 3 percent, but it lacked
enforcement mechanisms. In 1960 unemployment stood at 5.5 percent, and
it reached nearly 7 percent the following year. During Moynihan's tenure, the
Department of Labor's major goal was to reduce unemployment. The department even favored public works programs along the lines of the New Deal
Works Progress Administration, which had employed millions of Americans
during the Great Depression. Kennedy's economic package instead featured
tax cuts to stimulate the economy and reduce unemployment indirectly by
fostering economic growth. The Moynihan Report invoked family breakdown
to dramatize the costs of high unemployment among African American men
in order to make Labor's case for direct employment measures.

Moynihan saw unemployment as a family issue because the liberal commitment to full employment entailed strong assumptions about ideal families and gender roles. Liberals sought to universalize the "family wage" model
in which male breadwinners received wages adequate to support wives and
children. Male wage-earners were the primary beneficiaries of New Deal-era
social programs, including old age pensions, unemployment insurance, and
the GI Bill. Few liberals in the early 1960s questioned the fact that employers
offered male workers higher wages and greater job security because they saw
men as primarily responsible for supporting their families and believed
women's domestic duties took precedence over wage-earning. In truth, the
male-breadwinner/female-homemaker model never accurately described
many American families, particularly those outside the affluent upper and
middle classes. Most working-class women worked out of economic necessity. By the early 1960s, family wage ideology was at odds with women's increasing participation in the workforce. Twice as many married women were
employed in 1960 as in 1940.[35] Nevertheless, the male-breadwinner family
remained a powerful ideal. Liberals such as Moynihan sought to extend the
family wage model to all Americans especially those African Americans to

whom it had been denied because of discrimination, poverty, and racially exclusive New Deal programs.[36]

Moynihan's passion for full employment also originated from a rarely discussed source: Catholic social teaching, which strongly linked male employment and family responsibilities. The election of the nation's first Roman Catholic as president in 1960 signaled the increasing public prominence of Catholics in an American nation that once considered itself Protestant. Moynihan attended Catholic school as a boy but had since operated mainly in non-Catholic institutions. Writing about his Catholicism in 1960, Moynihan quipped, "while I am reasonably strict in my observances, I am . . . more of a buttress to the church than a pillar, in that I support it from outside."[37] He advocated church modernization as part of the Second Vatican Council (1962–1965) and challenged church stances on birth control, divorce, and censorship. During his years in the Department of Labor, Moynihan often addressed Catholic gatherings. Government officials believed Moynihan well suited to engage Catholic constituencies, and church leaders recognized Moynihan as a well-placed Catholic. Moynihan held particularly strong ties to Catholic social welfare organizations. He served on the board of the National Catholic Social Action Conference and delivered the keynote address at its 1964 meeting.[38]

Moynihan was influenced by a strand of Catholic social teaching that employment and wages should be determined by family needs not market mechanisms alone. John XXIII's 1961 papal encyclical *Mater et Magistra* ("Mother and Teacher") reinforced this view. It endorsed "the rights and duty of each individual normally to provide the necessities of life for himself and his dependents," highlighted the social obligations of property-holders, and advocated workers' rights to earn just wages.[39] The pope proclaimed that men were morally entitled to "receive a wage sufficient . . . to fulfill family responsibilities properly."[40] *Mater et Magistra* outraged American Catholic conservatives. Writing in *National Review*, William F. Buckley quipped, "Mother, yes; teacher, no."[41] But it delighted Catholic liberals. Moynihan frequently cited *Mater et Magistra* to argue for full employment, as in a 1964 address at the Harvard Divinity School: "It is clearly time to develop a socially acceptable concept of full employment for this nation that does not . . . depend solely upon supply and demand in the market place . . . I am inclined to think that my own church . . . has been more involved in this problem . . . than some of the other churches."[42]

Catholic social teaching provided Moynihan a moral vocabulary to attack economic inequality. "Men without work," he maintained, "are deprived of an essential condition of human dignity."[43] Moynihan's assertion of employment as a fundamental human right led him to challenge a prominent strand of liberalism that suggested widespread economic prosperity could be engineered solely through macroeconomic policy that would generate economic growth and provide employment through market mechanisms, a philosophy that had undergirded the Kennedy-Johnson tax cuts. Moynihan instead suggested that government had a direct social responsibility for providing men with jobs: "Pope John . . . [said] labor is 'both a duty and a right of every human being.' If that is so—if labor is a right—does it not follow that the rights of the hard-core unemployed are being transgressed? And if such is the case, is it not a question of social justice . . . ?"[44] Moynihan adopted Catholic social teaching's emphasis on the male-headed family rather than the individual as the basic unit of society. It was a man's right to provide for his family, a woman's right to focus on her maternal obligations, and a child's right to be raised in a stable, secure family with appropriate role models. Moynihan perceived men's inability to serve as breadwinners as the central injustice of economic inequality. Thus, it is hardly surprising that he framed racial inequality as the inability of black men to support families.

The family wage ideal obviously held clear gender expectations. Moynihan believed that women with young children should stay home, as did his own wife Elizabeth with their three children. However, he supported women working at other stages of their lives. In a 1964 speech he opined, "Apart from a rich uncle . . . a young man could have no greater fortune than a willing young woman whose education and training will give her the general intelligence and adaptability to go back to work in her 40's. If she is a surgeon, so much the better for all concerned. But if she only knows how to type—well, one species there never is enough of is good secretaries."[45] Moynihan recognized women's value in the workforce, while presuming that most would be confined to stereotypically female occupations. He also described a woman's income as supplementing her husband's wages and assumed that most women would not earn income during their twenties and thirties—an economically unrealistic scenario for many American families and one that would make it challenging for women to pursue careers as doctors or other professionals. Other statements from the period reflect Moynihan's gendered notion of individual opportunity. In one speech, he celebrated American society as offering "equal opportunity for most, with most boys getting a reasonably fair chance to be president of a corporation, or even a country, and most girls, if not endowed to be Hollywood queens, at least destined to be surrounded by appliances and married to junior executives."[46]

Moynihan's particularly strong attachment to the male-breadwinner norm explains why the Moynihan Report became such a strong target for feminists. However, most liberals in the early 1960s accepted the family wage ideal. Even some feminists did, as evident in the deliberations of the President's Commission on the Status of Women (PCSW), appointed by Kennedy in 1961, which offered its final report in 1963. Eleanor Roosevelt chaired the commission, but its architect was Esther Peterson, head of the Department of Labor Women's Bureau. Moynihan was Department of Labor liaison to the commission and assisted Peterson. The belief of most commission members that women workers needed to be treated differently because of their family responsibilities compromised their ability to make a strong statement against sexual discrimination. Peterson, in fact, organized the commission to sidetrack growing momentum for the passage of the Equal Rights Amendment, which would have declared gender discrimination unconstitutional but in so doing would have invalidated laws protecting women workers from long hours and difficult working conditions. The Commission's final report endorsed the notion that men held primary responsibility for supporting their families. Proposals for aiding women workers were counterbalanced by its endorsement of "the fundamental responsibility of mothers and homemakers and society's stake in strong family life."[47] The commission's promotion of the family wage helps explain why Moynihan was blindsided by feminist criticisms of *The Negro Family*.

The Commission's deliberations also foreshadowed strains that soon divided liberals over the family wage. The Commission helped stir second-wave feminism by focusing attention on women workers and catalyzing formation of networks among women activists and officials. A few Commission members objected to family wage ideology. For example, Caroline Ware and Elizabeth Wickenden advocated measures to support poor single mothers so they could adequately maintain their families. They felt that single-parent households were viable and that the male-breadwinner model was simply unrealistic for many poor Americans.[48] Tellingly, Ware and Wickenden were among the earliest critics of the Moynihan Report.

Moynihan advised Peterson that he did not wish to see the commission promote the entrance of greater numbers of mothers of young children into the workforce. Referring to his "R[oman] C[atholic] objection to the widespread notion that women can and *ought* to work," Moynihan stated that he "would like to see a country and an economy in which men made enough money that their women can stay home and raise their families." To Moynihan, more women in the workplace would undermine efforts to combat class and racial inequality. He speculated, "day care centers institutionalize the colored maid and subsidize the middle-class households that enjoy such luxuries."[49] Moynihan's understanding of economic inequality was particularly male-centered. Unlike women activists involved with the PCSW, many of whom later became outspoken critics of the family wage, Moynihan paid little attention to problems of women workers, such as unequal pay, sexual discrimination, and lack of childcare. In general, he discounted social policies that did not primarily aid male breadwinners. He was contemptuous of the woman-dominated profession of social work, deriding efforts to combat poverty with "welfare work."[50]

Moynihan especially disliked the most prominent New Deal program targeted at women: Aid to Families with Dependent Children (AFDC). Popularly known as "welfare," AFDC provided money to single mothers. Unlike programs benefiting male wage-earners, which were universal entitlements, AFDC was needs-based. Recipients were stigmatized. Though AFDC received little public attention during the first two decades of its existence, it became a major public issue by the early 1960s and a target for conservative critics of the liberal welfare state. Moynihan supported welfare as a temporary relief measure, noting that his own mother accepted public assistance during the 1930s. However, he deeply disliked long-term reliance on welfare. He caused a stir when he reportedly said in a 1964 speech that welfare was "rotting the poor."[51] Moynihan wanted women on welfare to be financially supported by husbands, not by the government. Unlike conservative opponents of welfare, Moynihan wanted to provide all men with the possibility of supporting their families. He felt that increasing public opposition to welfare could be channeled to support liberal measures to ensure full employment.[52] In 1964, he wrote, "[Welfare] must not be allowed to become the economic system of a permanent subculture. Men need jobs, families need fathers, communities need independence."[53] Nevertheless, his willingness to stigmatize welfare, and by implication its recipients, reinscribed the racial and gender exclusions built into the two-tiered American welfare state that, as historians have shown, offered universal benefits for wage-earners (disproportionately white men) and less generous means-tested programs for others (disproportionately female and nonwhite).[54]

In family wage ideology, liberal economic ideas merged with a notion of family that, starting in the late 1960s, rapidly came to be seen as conservative. The Moynihan Report's embodiment of that ideal made it a potent symbol of patriarchal values. In New Deal liberalism and Catholic social teaching, men's family responsibilities made their employment a social necessity that could not be left solely to the vagaries of the marketplace. Moynihan pushed intently for full employment when he joined a taskforce to plan the War on Poverty that embodied the mindset of early 1960s liberals even as it demonstrated differences among them.

The War on Poverty

Moynihan first concentrated attention on African Americans in the context of liberal efforts to alleviate economic inequality that culminated in Lyndon Johnson's War on Poverty. Concerns about poverty percolated among liberal journalists, intellectuals, and policy-makers during the Kennedy administration. *The Other America*, the surprise 1962 bestseller by socialist Michael Harrington, exposed material deprivation in the United States previously invisible to middle-class Americans. Like Moynihan, a one-time drinking buddy, Harrington drew on Catholic social teaching.[55] The President's Commission on Juvenile Delinquency and Youth Crime, established in 1961, experimented with approaches to urban poverty and drew on theories of leading liberal social scientists.

Moynihan helped identify poverty as a major American social problem by writing a 1963 report on armed forces draft rejects, *One-Third of a Nation*. Moynihan seized on a news report that the Selective Service pre-induction exam disqualified a large percentage of draft registrants for military service. Employing a strategy similar to that he would deploy with *The Negro Family*, he opportunistically sought to use this issue to highlight male unemployment. Enlisting the aid of secretary of labor Willard Wirtz, who succeeded Goldberg in the position earlier that year, Moynihan convinced the president to create a taskforce to investigate the issue. On September 30, 1963, Kennedy formed the Taskforce on Manpower Conservation and instructed it "to prepare a program for testing, guidance, training, and rehabilitation of youths found disqualified for military service." Kennedy worried, "Today's military rejects include tomorrow's hard-core unemployed." Wirtz headed the taskforce; Moynihan was its secretary. Moynihan took on the primary task of analyzing data on draft rejects and proposing policies.[56] Moynihan could propose the study because he had an unusual amount of bureaucratic independence in his new position as assistant secretary of labor, to which he was appointed in March, 1963. Moynihan oversaw the Office of Policy Planning and Research, tasked with developing new policies. This position gave him a platform to initiate studies and programs of particular interest to him that would bring him to the attention of more senior officials.[57]

The report's title, *One-Third of a Nation*, harkened back to Franklin Roosevelt's statement about "one-third of a nation ill-housed, ill-clad, ill-nourished," suggesting a political return to questions of economic inequality ignored since the New Deal. Its name also referred to its finding that approximately one-third of eighteen-year-old men would not qualify for military service under the Selective Service exam, with roughly equal numbers disqualified for health and mental reasons. Moynihan interpreted individual failures on the exam as a broader failure of American society. Most draft rejects, he maintained, were "victims of inadequate education and insufficient health services." He contended that those deemed unfit for military service would struggle to find other employment: they "face a lifetime of recurrent unemployment unless their skills are significantly upgraded." Moynihan worried that poverty damaged the life chances of young men and thus undermined individual advancement based on merit. Those who failed the test had inadequate opportunities, having simply "inherited their situation from their parents." Anticipating the Moynihan Report's concern with social stability, Moynihan also worried about the dangers of a large group of men "not equipped to play their role in society."[58]

One-Third of a Nation typified how early 1960s liberals approached poverty. It advocated greater social research, recommending that all young men be tested for military service when they registered for the draft at eighteen (rather than after they were drafted). This change would allow the government to identify candidates for training and education and direct them to relevant programs for assistance. Rather than directly providing jobs or income, the government would help train them to compete successfully for employment. The goal was to make draft rejects into "effective and self-supporting citizens."[59] Evidence in the report that draft rejects welcomed opportunities for upgrading skills suggested that they valued gainful employment. Moynihan hoped to offer the benefits of postwar affluence to those who "missed out on the American miracle."[60] Providing the economy with more skilled workers would also create a broader social benefit. Though framing its conclusions in terms of class rather than race, Moynihan recognized that disproportionate numbers of exam failures were African American. Liberal antipoverty discourse, while often avoiding explicit discussion of race, commonly noted the disproportionate representation of African Americans among the poor; African Americans were frequently identified as an untapped human resource in the broader postwar debate about manpower needs.[61]

A telling feature of Moynihan's liberalism was that he tackled youth unemployment and poverty by focusing on the military draft. Cold War liberals frequently tied reform programs to national defense. Accordingly, *One-Third of a Nation* couched training programs for young men who failed the service test in terms of military preparedness as well as poverty reduction. The idea of soldiering as a means of social advancement and a marker of full citizenship was particularly popular in American culture during the period between World War II and the Vietnam War. Moynihan keenly felt the importance of military service to his own success. Focusing on draft rejects demonstrated the male-centered approach to social reform embodied by Moynihan and other liberals. Since only men registered for the draft, the policies suggested in *One-Third of a Nation* would do nothing to identify and upgrade women's job skills.

Presented to President Johnson on January 1, 1964, *One-Third of a Nation* was used by government anti-poverty planners. Moynihan served on the poverty task force Johnson created shortly following Kennedy's assassination in November 1963. That group developed the central legislation of the War on Poverty: the Equal Opportunity Act, passed by Congress in August 1964. The bill included jobs training and education programs such as the Jobs Corps and Head Start, reflecting *One-Third of a Nation*'s concern that too many young people were unprepared to compete in the labor market. The bill's most innovative and ultimately controversial aspect was grants to community action programs developed by local organizations with input from the poor themselves.[62]

Like Moynihan, War on Poverty planners aimed to extend the family wage and targeted their programs at male workers.[63] Against Moynihan's preferences, however, the War on Poverty eschewed direct job creation and income transfers. As planner Adam Yarmolinsky recalled, policy-makers focused on "preparing people for jobs" instead of "preparing jobs for people."[64] They adopted this approach largely because they believed that combating poverty could be achieved without structural economic reform by simply training poor people to take advantage of existing opportunities. The public works and income redistribution programs favored by Moynihan would have been expensive and have alarmed corporations and wealthy elites. Planners were constrained because Johnson devoted a relatively small amount of the federal budget to the War on Poverty: $1 billion, or about 1 percent of the total budget, an amount clearly inadequate to eradicate U.S. poverty. Johnson wanted to keep the federal budget below $100 billion because of his political deal with Congress to enact the Kennedy-Johnson tax cuts. These cuts were designed to stimulate the economy, but they primarily benefited wealthy and middle-class Americans and corporations. Despite Johnson's rhetoric, helping the poor was not at the center of his political agenda. Johnson wanted to fight poverty, but he wanted to do it on the cheap and without alienating economic elites.[65]

The Johnson administration's anti-poverty commitment nevertheless provided an opening for policy-makers to propose more ambitious programs. The task force considered measures more extensive than those it adopted. Some members, including Moynihan, advocated direct job creation. Moynihan's boss, Willard Wirtz, advised Johnson, "Without question, the biggest single immediate change which the poverty program could bring about in the lives of most of the poor would be to provide the family head with a regular, decently paid job."[66] Wirtz and Moynihan helped convince Office of Economic Opportunity (OEO) head Sargent Shriver to present to the president the case for a public works program to be funded by a cigarette tax. However, Johnson's aversion to new taxes ensured that the War on Poverty included no measures for direct job creation.

Despite losing this battle, Moynihan continued to advocate more substantial efforts to combat poverty. He argued that community action would prove of limited utility and that economic growth alone would be insufficient because of the effects of "automation": technological innovations in production that generated wealth yet created unemployment. He stressed the crucial role of "the original anti-poverty movement in this nation," trade unions. He also emphasized more systematic issues: "Our social insurance system is unfinished; our wage system is unbalanced and incomplete; our employment nexus . . . is frighteningly inadequate." He concluded, "Trying to cure poverty without attending to these matters, is treating the symptoms and not the disease."[67] However, Moynihan proved an opponent of the War on Poverty's most radical feature: its galvanizing effect on grassroots activism among the poor. In his prominent 1968 book, *Maximum Feasible Misunderstanding*, Moynihan criticized community action programs designed to include "maximum feasible participation" of the poor. Though Moynihan favored more extensive antipoverty measures, his commitment to top-down social engineering left him wary of the War on Poverty's democratizing effects.[68]

Moynihan wrote *The Negro Family* to convince Johnson to institute jobs and income redistribution programs that he had been reticent to adopt. Just a few days after Johnson's landslide election in 1964, Moynihan wrote a memo to Wirtz that outlined the political strategy of focusing attention on African American families to press the president to escalate the War on Poverty. He complained that the Equal Opportunity Act "had not a nickel in it for job creation" and that Johnson's tax cut "worsened income distribution in America, rather than improved it." "[O]nly our howling and bitching," he contended, had led to the act's inclusion of the Job Corps. Moynihan outlined an ambitious series of measures to alleviate economic inequality modeled on Northern European welfare systems: "[They] have abolished poverty and we have not." He advocated extending the minimum wage to agricultural workers, expanding unemployment insurance benefits, encouraging union organization by repealing the provision of the Taft-Hartley Act that allowed states to pass "right-to-work" laws, and instituting a national thirty-five-hour work week with four-week paid vacations. Most originally, Moynihan advocated a plan for "income distribution." Moynihan was an early advocate for a Guaranteed Annual Income, an idea that gained currency throughout the 1960s to provide a minimum standard of living. His preference for a family allowance on a European and Canadian model that based payments on family size reflected Moynihan's Catholicism: the family was the basic social unit and larger families needed additional support.[69]

Moynihan hoped to leverage the growing political salience of African American inequality to convince Johnson to back full employment and family allowances. He advised Wirtz that Labor needed to "repackage" its arguments to offer "the administration and the nation solutions to problems they know they wish to solve." He asserted, "I think we can make a case that a solution to the racial problem absolutely requires a solution to the Negro unemployment problem." The most poignant illustration of social inequality's negative effects Moynihan could imagine was "that unemployment is destroying the Negro family structure."[70] Here, Moynihan urged exploiting concern with racial inequality to combat class inequality. However, Moynihan was also developing a contradictory viewpoint: an understanding of American race relations that suggested that economic inequality resulted from the different internal characteristics of ethnoracial groups.

Beyond the Melting Pot

In *One-Third of a Nation*, Moynihan treated African Americans simply as a subset of the poor, and neglected racist structures that had left them especially impoverished. However, the Moynihan Report did draw on a particular understanding of racial inequality that he gained from his experience writing *Beyond the Melting Pot*. Accounts of the Moynihan Report's origins have strangely neglected Moynihan's role in writing this influential 1963 book about the role of ethnicity in American life. *Beyond the Melting Pot* suggested that race-based socioeconomic inequalities resulted from ethnic groups' cultural attributes, including family structure. Writing it led him to see that African Americans suffered more than just acute class inequality and suggested the need for policies specifically targeted at them. It also introduced Moynihan to nascent neoconservative ideas that undermined his social-democratic emphasis on government assurance of basic living standards for all Americans.

The primary author of *Beyond the Melting Pot* was Nathan Glazer, a leading sociologist and public intellectual and the author most cited in the Moynihan Report. Glazer was a prominent member of a group of predominantly Jewish thinkers known as the "New York Intellectuals." Though many New York Intellectuals had been Marxists in their youth, most renounced their radicalism in the 1940s. They played a key role in defining American liberalism in the Cold War period. Many became university professors; Glazer taught at the University of California, Berkeley, and later at Harvard. New York Intellectuals were known for their vigorous style of argumentation and ability to reach a broadly educated public outside academia through journals such as *Partisan Review, New Leader,* and *Commentary* (where Glazer had once been an editor). Glazer correctly anticipated that *Beyond the Melting Pot* would similarly reach such an audience.[71]

In its origins, *Beyond the Melting Pot* straddled the worlds of academia and journalism. Glazer successfully applied for funds from the New York Post Foundation for a project, "The Peoples of New York," a series of articles about what happened to the second generation of migrants to New York City. The project also had an academic sponsor: the recently created Harvard-MIT Joint

Center for Urban Studies, which Moynihan later directed. Glazer's project proposal articulated sociological explanations for differences among the city's ethnic blocs. Though Glazer originally intended to write about several New York City ethnic groups, including its Chinese, Japanese, and "Slavs," *Beyond the Melting Pot* ultimately studied five: African Americans, Jews, Irish, Italians, and Puerto Ricans. By emphasizing "real differences between groups," Glazer challenged common understandings of the immigrant experience that stressed individual assimilation and adaptation to American norms. "Each group has certain characteristics," Glazer explained, "given by its special history, and affected by the special characteristics of the society it enters, what it does and what is done to it." While the book discussed New York City, its conclusions applied more broadly to the whole United States, or at least to its cities.

Glazer originally planned to recruit a representative of each ethnicity to write a chapter on his own group. Glazer himself would write the essay on Jews. Each essay would be published in the *Post*, and they would be collected together as a single book.[72] As it turned out, the *Post* disliked Glazer's approach and ran only one essay. Meanwhile, Glazer could not find collaborators who met his specifications: members of New York City ethnic groups who shared his sociological perspective. The exception was Moynihan, whom Glazer recruited to write the chapter on the Irish. (Irving Kristol was the matchmaker who introduced Moynihan to Glazer. Kristol edited *The Reporter*, to which Moynihan frequently contributed, and had known Glazer since their days as undergraduate socialists at the City College of New York.) Responding enthusiastically to Glazer's invitation, Moynihan affirmed his Irish credentials: "I grew up in a neighborhood so completely Irish, that I didn't really learn I *was* Irish until I joined the Navy." However, he expressed some trepidation about writing the chapter because he was "not a sociologist."[73] Through writing *Beyond the Melting Pot*, Moynihan familiarized himself with sociological approaches to race and family that proved vital elements of *The Negro Family*. As Glazer's sole collaborator, Moynihan's involvement in *Beyond the Melting Pot* deepened over time. Not only did he write the Irish chapter, he also wrote most of the book's conclusion.

The book contested the notion that immigrant groups assimilated into American culture. "The point about the melting pot," wrote Glazer and Moynihan, "is that it did not happen."[74] To be sure, they argued, immigrant groups were altered by moving to New York City. However, they did not amalgamate into a homogeneous culture but retained distinctive identities that

combined past histories with adaptations to their new environments. Glazer
and Moynihan advanced a pluralist vision of American life. There was, they
argued, "some central tendency in the national ethos which structures
people, whether those coming in afresh or the descendants of those who have
been here for generations, into groups of different status and character."[75]

Glazer and Moynihan's pluralism differed from the cultural pluralism advocated earlier in the twentieth century and the multiculturalism that followed. The purpose of *Beyond the Melting Pot* was not to celebrate the rich
tapestry of cultures in New York City, although the authors clearly appreciated the city's diversity. Their perspective was more akin to the political pluralism that dominated postwar American political science, which viewed
politics as a struggle between various pressure groups. New York politics,
Glazer and Moynihan argued, could largely be understood as contests between alliances of different ethnic blocs: "ethnic groups in New York are also
interest groups."[76] *Beyond the Melting Pot* envisioned New York and the nation as marked by competition among different ethnicities for status and resources. In the United States, the authors argued, ethnic conflict generally
replaced class conflict: "In a democratic culture that has never much liked to
identify individuals in terms of social classes, and does so less in the aftermath of the radical 1930s and 1940s, the ethnic shorthand is a considerable
advantage."[77] Though Glazer and Moynihan knew that New York City ethnic groups had varying class compositions, they emphasized ethnicity over
class as a deciding factor in American society, thus bolstering a broader American tendency to discuss class in racial terms. This perspective contradicted
Moynihan's full employment liberalism, which saw race primarily in class
terms.

Beyond the Melting Pot examined how sociological characteristics produced different outcomes for distinct ethnic groups. Its main goal was to explain "widely varying patterns of achievement in areas such as education,
business, and politics."[78] To this end, the authors provided an unsparing look
at the weaknesses of each group. In their introduction, they warned their readers about their "harsh judgments" and begged "the understanding of those
who will be offended."[79] Influenced by the "culture and personality" school,
a prominent group of twentieth-century anthropologists, Glazer particularly
emphasized the effects of various family structures. For example, he concluded
that overprotective Jewish parenting produced "more neurosis . . . but less psy-
chosis," while "the problems of the Italian children [at school] stemmed from
a too strong, too rigorously ordered family, which did not value education."[80]

Beyond the Melting Pot rejected biological explanations for differences in group success in favor of anthropological, sociological, and historical ones. Nevertheless, its approach suggested that differences among ethnicities were significant and deep-seated. While writing the book, Moynihan even pondered whether there might be a biological basis for such differences. He asked Glazer, "do we think races are different? Do Chinamen incline to do things differently than Sicilians? Dogs do, don't they? Almost all the other breeds and species of animals have different characteristics. Are there not such differences among men, or are we essentially of the same stock and therefore of one breed?"[81] Moynihan's questions reflected his inexperience with racial issues that writing *Beyond the Melting Pot* helped rectify. *The Negro Family* explicitly rejected biological explanations for racial inequality. However, his questions suggest a possible affinity between sociological accounts emphasizing the strong nature of ethnic group differences and biological racism. In fact, some of the Moynihan Report's critics charged that it offered a new sociological guise for racist generalizations.

Beyond the Melting Pot is best remembered today for resuscitating discussion of white ethnic groups. It contributed to the "ethnic revival" of the 1960s and 1970s, a movement that emphasized cultural differences between white ethnics and WASPs (white Anglo-Saxon Protestants).[82] Most chapters analyzed white ethnics: the Irish, the Italians, and the Jews. At its time of publication, however, when African American equality was the central national question, *Beyond the Melting Pot* was most noted for its chapter on African Americans. Though written entirely by Glazer, its influence on Moynihan was apparent. Responding to one of Glazer's drafts in 1961, Moynihan enthused, "I have just finished the Negro chapter and would shout 'Hallelujah!' were it not for fear of offending [Nation of Islam leader] Elijah Muhammad and his band." However, Moynihan predicted, "we are going to make some enemies."[83] Indeed, Glazer's chapter proved controversial in ways that foreshadowed the uproar over *The Negro Family.* Glazer wrote as a liberal who favored equal rights for African Americans, but challenged what he saw as unfounded liberal optimism that civil rights reforms would put blacks on par with other groups economically.

Glazer viewed African Americans through the lens of European immigrant experience. "These Americans of two centuries," Glazer wrote, "are as much immigrant as any European immigrant group, for the shift from the South to New York is as radical a change for the Negro as that faced by earlier immigrants."[84] In the early 1960s, white liberals commonly compared the experiences of black migrants to northern cities to those of European immigrants. There was a long scholarly tradition of doing so. The Chicago School of Sociology treated blacks who flocked to Chicago in the Great Migration of the early twentieth century as another new arrival in the city akin to Poles, Jews, and Italians. Analogizing African Americans to European immigrants suggested the degree to which social thought had proceeded beyond scientific racism, since the very comparison denied biological differences between whites and blacks.

In *Beyond the Melting Pot*, the analogy fulfilled several functions. It offered the Jewish Glazer and the Irish Moynihan credibility to discuss African Americans as members of a fellow ethnic group. Glazer never found a suitable African American to write the chapter on their group, so he positioned himself as the next best thing. Similarly, in later writings, Moynihan repeatedly drew on his Irish identity as a source of his expertise about African Americans. He frequently analogized the problems of discrimination, poverty, crime, and family instability faced by African Americans in the 1960s to those faced by Irish Americans a century earlier. In *Beyond the Melting Pot*, he discussed the "wild Irish" immigrants of the nineteenth century who "poured into the city to drink and dance and fight in the streets."[85] In *The Negro Family*, he briefly compared these "wild Irish" to African American migrants in Northern cities as groups who suffered because of abrupt adjustments to an urban life for which they were unprepared.[86] Using stereotypical terms for Irish and African Americans, he even proclaimed in a 1967 *Time* interview, "Paddy and Sambo are the same people."[87]

Glazer contended that racial discrimination against African Americans was different in degree, but not in kind, to the serious prejudice previously faced by many European immigrants. He overlooked that African Americans had long faced a level of discrimination in employment, housing, and other areas of economic and social life never confronted by whites. Moreover, New York had a well-established black community long before Europeans started pouring through Ellis Island. There was a sleight-of-hand in suggesting that blacks were migrants to Northern cities and then using New York to stand in for the United States as a whole, making it appear as if African Americans were newcomers to modern American society. It suggested that Northern whites were racially innocent and ignored the systemic racism faced by African Americans. While mentioning housing discrimination, Glazer and Moynihan, for example, ignored the effects of the Cross-Bronx Expressway, built between 1948 and 1972 for the benefit of affluent white suburban commuters, which destroyed working-class neighborhoods and facilitated residential segregation. This absence of understanding how institutionalized racism fostered African American inequality in the North also marked the Moynihan Report and fueled criticism of it.

Beyond the Melting Pot suggested a model of ethnic competition that implied African American self-help as the primary solution for overcoming historic inequalities. Glazer argued that since American society comprised different ethnic groups, African Americans could not expect to assimilate *as individuals* into white American society; no ethnic group could. In a pluralist and heterogeneous society, Glazer argued, black social advancement depended on rising as a group. Yet Glazer was pessimistic that African Americans could compete with other ethnic groups. Glazer highlighted problems Moynihan also identified in *One-Third of a Nation*, especially noting that many African Americans lacked marketable job skills in an economy with increasingly fewer industrial jobs for unskilled or semiskilled workers. Lack of skills and education among African Americans, Glazer argued, meant that removing racial discrimination would not sufficiently alleviate black unemployment: "there are today problems in finding enough colored Americans with the motivation, training, and ability to fill the opportunities that are available."[88] Like Moynihan and typical of liberals, Glazer worried in particular about black *men*. "In a peculiar way," he wrote, "the problem of the Negro in America is the problem of the Negro men more than the Negro women."[89]

Glazer argued that internal weaknesses in the black community underlay black men's lack of competitiveness. Noting that African Americans valued education more than most other groups, Glazer explained their relatively poor educational achievement in terms of "the home and family and community—not in its overt values, which . . . are positive in relation to education, but in its conditions and circumstances."[90] He pinpointed allegedly weak family structures of African Americans in which, he argued, "the heritage of two hundred years of slavery and a hundred years of discrimination is concentrated."[91] Glazer cited statistics of higher rates of female-headed families and higher rates of out-of-wedlock births among African Americans. Black boys in particular, he argued, suffered from lack of adult male role models. This discussion of black families was hardly new in *Beyond the Melting Pot*. However, the book pioneered identification of family weakness as a sociological explanation for the poor socioeconomic status of African Americans. Strong families, Glazer argued, allowed other groups, such as Jews, to advance rapidly in socioeconomic status even in the face of prejudice. Weak families, he suggested, prevented blacks from making similar progress.

Glazer identified other elements of African American culture that created competitive disadvantages. Unlike immigrant groups who shared common traditions such as language, he argued, African Americans lacked a distinct cultural tradition to ensure stronger group cohesion. In a passage that later became notorious among Black Studies scholars, Glazer wrote, "it is not possible for Negroes to view themselves as other ethnic groups viewed themselves because—and this is the key to much in the Negro world—the Negro is only an American, and nothing else. He has no values and culture to guard and protect."[92] Glazer's denial of African Americans' shared and distinctive cultural heritage was also articulated by other mid-century liberals. In *An American Dilemma*, Gunnar Myrdal described black culture as a "pathological" variant of "the general American culture."[93] African American sociologist E. Franklin Frazier also insisted on the essential Americanness of African American culture, fearing that to stress distinctive characteristics would play into the hands of white racists. In *Beyond the Melting Pot*, the view that "the Negro is only an American" emphasized both the particular challenges of black social advancement and the need for African Americans to follow the autonomous self-help model of European immigrant groups. In the rarely quoted continuation of the passage cited above, Glazer wrote, "He [the Negro] insists that the white world deal with his problems because, since he is so much the product of America, they are not *his* problems, but everyone's. Once they become everyone's, *perhaps he will see that they are his own too.*"[94]

Translating Glazer's sociological analysis into a political stance revealed the complexities of his argument. Glazer saw clearly that removing racial discrimination alone would not lead to African American equality: "The strictly legal approach to discrimination will have to be supplemented with new approaches."[95] Directly anticipating the Moynihan Report, *Beyond the Melting Pot* shifted focus from the direct effects of racism toward internal characteristics of the black community, prominently including family structure. African Americans, Glazer argued, were unprepared to take advantage of opportunities created by the removal of barriers of racial discrimination. Though he argued that African Americans could only advance through racial self-help, he believed that internal weaknesses would block their advancement. "Negro communal organization is weak," he claimed, "and insufficient to make much impact on the great needs of the poorer and disorganized part of the community."[96] It was "not likely that we will see a massive self-help effort."[97]

At times, Glazer suggested that the "exceptional concentration of problems in the Negro community" required a special effort by all Americans to aid African Americans. At one point, he opined, "while the problems of other groups are in large measure their own, the problems of the Negro community become the problems of all of us."[98] Glazer's analysis could be used to argue the need for programs specifically targeted at African Americans to bolster their competitiveness. In the end, though, Glazer stressed the necessity of racial self-help. Problems of family disorganization, crime, juvenile delinquency, and educational achievement, he argued, could best be met by private black organizations. The most important tasks of racial advancement were ones "that conceivably no one but Negroes can do."[99] Glazer praised the Nation of Islam for its ability to convince poor blacks to adopt "middle-class patterns." If only the Nation of Islam could be stripped of its black nationalism, it seemed to Glazer exactly the kind of organization needed. "This is indeed a nationalist and racist movement," he wrote, "but it is surprising how much of Horatio Alger there is in it, too."[100] Even before the passage of national civil rights legislation, Glazer advanced the argument, later a staple of neoconservative discourse, that African American leaders needed to turn away from political activism and toward racial self-help: "Succeeding . . . the period of protest, one can detect the need for a period of self-examination and self-help, in which the increased income and resources of leadership of the group are turned inwards."[101] By arguing both that racial self-help was the necessary route to African American equality, and that African Americans were ill-equipped to take it, Glazer offered a powerful rationalization for the persistence of African American inequality after civil rights.

Reviews of *Beyond the Melting Pot* commented mostly on its chapter on African Americans in ways that anticipated responses to the Moynihan Report. The book was widely heralded; it was nominated for the National Book Award and won the 1964 Anisfield-Wolf Award for best book on race relations. It was not a bestseller, but it did sell a respectable 50,000 copies by 1966. Many reviewers noted the authors' Jewish and Irish identities as sources of their authority on the subject. Writing in the *New York Times*, prominent Harvard immigration historian Oscar Handlin promoted the utility of the book's pluralist framework for understanding African Americans: "The Negroes are not a minority who confront a homogeneous majority, but an exceptionally visible and underprivileged group whose fate is intertwined with that of many others."[102] *Time* highlighted black family problems: "Through no fault of their own, the years of slavery shaped the Negro character in a way that contributes to their difficulties."[103] Others endorsed Glazer's calls for black self-help in ways that anticipated how conservatives embraced the Moynihan Report. The *Jewish Advocate* concluded, "It is obvious that the Negroes need to help themselves and will have difficulty finding the strength to do so."[104] *U.S. News and World Report* accepted the validity of Glazer's comparison of African Americans to other ethnic groups. The lack of blacks in leadership roles in New York City, it argued, could not be blamed on racism alone: "Other immigrant groups—notably Japanese, Jews, and Puerto Ricans—have also faced frustrations in breaking into the U.S. labor market, but have managed to acquire higher educations and have been ready when opportunities opened."[105] Mary McGrory, a journalist who later played a key role interpreting the Moynihan Report as advocating racial self-help, reviewed the book for the *Washington Star*. Writing just days after white supremacists bombed an African American church in Birmingham, Alabama, killing four girls, McGrory opined, "a little more self-help and a little less self-pity may be the answer for their [Negroes'] troubled existence."[106]

The Moynihan Report was decisively influenced by its comparative ethnic framework that treated family structure as a decisive variable in a group's success. In a memorandum to President Johnson summarizing the report, Moynihan compared African Americans to Japanese Americans, a surprising analogy for Moynihan given his typical focus on European immigrants. "A quarter-century ago," he wrote, alluding to World War II internment, "Japanese Americans were subject to the worst kind of racial discrimination and mistreatment." He attributed the recent success of Japanese Americans (and Chinese Americans, with whom he conflated them) to the fact that "Japanese and Chinese have probably the most close knit family structure of any group in America." Moynihan invoked Japanese Americans as proof that "the color problem" was not "insoluble." But invoking Japanese Americans as a model minority group, a common postwar stereotype of Asian Americans, undercut his argument. By contending that family structure was a primary cause of a group's success, he suggested that African Americans, whose "weak" family structure his report detailed, had deeply rooted sociological characteristics that would prove exceedingly difficult for government to rectify. "Negroes today," Moynihan told Johnson, "are a grievously injured people who in fair and equal competition will by and large lose out."[107]

The Moynihan Report did not advance Glazer's argument about the primary necessity of racial self-help. Moynihan was more confident than Glazer that government policies could rectify the social inequalities faced by African Americans.[108] Moynihan was more inclined to see the presumed "exceptional weaknesses of the Negro community" as reason for a special effort to aid African Americans. Nevertheless, Glazer's overall approach to race profoundly influenced Moynihan. Moynihan accepted the validity of the European immigrant-black analogy, viewed African Americans' inability to compete with other groups as their central problem, and saw family instability as a central explanation for racial inequality. From these premises, it was easy to conclude that the problems of black socioeconomic inequality were either intractable or could only be addressed by African Americans themselves. The ideas Moynihan took from *Beyond the Melting Pot* thus conflicted with his urgent case for national action to create jobs for black men.

CHAPTER 2

Negro Equality—Dream or Delusion?

"Negroes must be free in order to be equal and they must be equal in order to be free. . . . Men cannot win freedom unless they win equality."[1] So declared African American labor leader A. Philip Randolph in 1944. Randolph's March on Washington movement during World War II was the inspiration for the 1963 March on Washington for Jobs and Freedom. Hundreds of thousands of mostly black protestors came to the nation's capital to claim civil and economic rights. Marchers' signs called for "jobs for all" and "decent pay," expressing the civil rights movement's long-standing demand for economic equality. The "dream" Martin Luther King, Jr., shared with protestors that day envisioned not only freedom from racial discrimination but also economic justice for all Americans.[2]

Moynihan sympathized with the march, but did not attend. Fearing traffic, he drove to the office early that day. In the car, he was surprised to hear an old minstrel song, "Old Black Joe," on the radio. When he discovered deserted government offices, he was disappointed: "The Federal civil service had learned that the Negroes were coming to Washington to demand jobs and freedom, and they abandoned the city. They stayed home in the suburbs."[3] Moynihan relayed the civil rights movement's economic demands to other federal officials. Marshaling statistics as well as the work of African American scholars E. Franklin Frazier and Kenneth Clark, Moynihan wrote *The Negro Family* to convince White House officials of the need for a new step in the path to African American progress, one focused on economic "equality" rather than political "liberty."[4] With the signing of the 1964 Civil Rights Act and the imminent passage of the 1965 Voting Rights Act, Moynihan concluded that civil rights were nearly achieved. An alternate title Moynihan considered for his report was *After the Barriers Are Down*.[5] Nevertheless, Moynihan's conception of African American equality differed from that of the civil rights movement. He aligned himself with white liberal intellectuals who in the early 1960s advocated government action to address the economic dimensions of racial equality. Unlike civil rights leaders who favored more extensive transformations of American society and economy, liberals such as Moynihan focused on upgrading African Americans' skills so they could compete in the marketplace.

Civil rights leaders and liberal intellectuals frequently viewed the creation of male-headed nuclear families as vital to African American economic progress. In a 1964 speech, Moynihan implied that racial equality required not only jobs but also stable heterosexual unions: "last August's [civil rights] March on Washington was for both jobs and freedom. The two go together in our society, just as inextricably as the relationship in the song that talks about love and marriage . . . you can't have one without the other."[6] While black family structure often figured in discussions about achieving racial equality, the Moynihan Report made family the *central* terrain of this debate.

The effects of highlighting family depended on whether family was presented as a consequence of economic inequality or as its cause. Did Moynihan point to damaged black families to illustrate the need to tackle black male unemployment? Or did he assert that family instability was the "master problem" facing African Americans? While the former view underpinned new government programs aimed at bolstering the economic position of black men and their families, the latter suggested the limited utility of government action. Even as Moynihan's report spurred Lyndon Johnson to offer a major address that endorsed affirmative measures to secure African American economic advancement, it undercut the rationale for such programs. Another of the report's alternate titles, *Negro Equality: Dream or Delusion?*, reflected its contradictory mix of optimism about the potential for "national action" to achieve full racial equality and pessimism that deep-rooted family problems would inevitably inhibit African American advancement.

Jobs and Freedom

In recent years, historians have rediscovered the substantial economic programs of civil rights organizations. However, they often neglect how white liberals responded to such economic demands, mistakenly interpreting liberals as committed to color-blind policies.[7] Moynihan, because of his commitment to full employment, understood that African Americans demanded economic equality in addition to the dismantling of Jim Crow segregation. In a March 1964 speech, Moynihan emphasized the same point made by historians today: "the sudden escalation of the civil rights movement in the spring and summer of 1963 had put the specific issue of economic and social equality at the center of national politics . . . .They marched for *Jobs* and Freedom on August 28, 1963."[8] Moynihan wrote *The Negro Family* in part to alert White House officials: "The Negro revolution, like the industrial upheaval of the 1930s, is a movement for equality as well as liberty."[9] Nevertheless, his interests differed from those of the civil rights movement, which had long confronted the race-based economic inequalities that Moynihan only grasped because of the political pressure the movement generated. As Moynihan candidly acknowledged in a rough draft of *The Negro Family*, federal government support for black rights emerged "primarily as a result of Negro militancy."[10]

The economic demands of the civil rights movement were not novel, though Moynihan and other liberals often portrayed them as such. For decades, civil rights organizations advocated federal policies to improve the economic position of African Americans through full employment and universal social insurance. In the 1930s and 1940s, African American protest organizations in the North and South made economic demands central to their programs. They allied themselves with industrial unions, New Deal reformers, and a vibrant socialist movement. In the 1950s, many civil rights organizations muted economic demands as the national political climate turned hostile to radical economic ideas during McCarthyism. The National Association for the Advancement of Colored People (NAACP), for example, concentrated instead on attacking legal discrimination, particularly in the Jim Crow South, reflected in its victory against segregated schools in the Supreme Court's *Brown v. Board of Education* decision of 1954.[11]

By the early 1960s, black leaders increasingly linked demands for civil rights and economic equality. In some cases, this trend reflected the continued influence of activists of an earlier generation. The principal organizer of the March for Jobs and Freedom was Bayard Rustin, a socialist and close associate of A. Philip Randolph. In a widely noted 1965 article, "From Protest to Politics," published while Moynihan was drafting *The Negro Family* and cited in it, Rustin offered his vision of the black freedom struggle's "next stage." Its focus was "not *civil rights*, strictly speaking, but social and economic conditions." Confronting "economic relations," Rustin reasoned, required "government action—or politics." Though Rustin agreed with Moynihan on the need for a next stage in the movement focused on economic issues, his proposals were more far-reaching and his conception of "politics" entailed a broad popular mobilization distinct from liberal social engineering. Rustin called for an interracial coalition of African Americans, labor unions, and middle-class white liberals—groups strongly represented at the 1963 March on Washington. He envisioned policies that far surpassed Johnson's War on Poverty. "What is the value of winning access to public accommodations," he asked, "for those who lack the money to use them?"[12]

Though economic equality was always a key component of Martin Luther King, Jr.'s vision, he most outspokenly linked civil and economic rights in the final years of his life. He was assassinated in 1968 supporting a Memphis sanitation worker strike. In his 1964 book, *Why We Can't Wait*, King forcefully stressed connections between "bigotry and economic exploitation." He noted, "Negroes are still at the bottom of the economic ladder. They live within two concentric circles of segregation. One imprisons them on the basis of color, while the other confines them within a separate culture of poverty." King called for legislation modeled on the GI Bill to offer financial support to all disadvantaged Americans but especially to benefit African Americans. He also advocated "special, compensatory measures" for African Americans as restitution for the long "appropriation of the labor of one human being to another."[13]

King's proposals were partly modeled on those of another civil rights leader, Whitney Young of the National Urban League. In 1963, Young called for a "Domestic Marshall Plan" to assist African Americans to close the economic gap with whites. A career social worker, Young became executive director of the Urban League in 1961 and quickly moved the half-century-old organization into the center of civil rights activity. As a Northern, urban organization headed by middle-class African Americans and funded by white philanthropists, the League had long been concerned with problems of poor blacks in cities. As part of its mission, it always lobbied for improved social services for the poor, but Young's 1963 plan was far more ambitious.[14]

Though Young strongly backed desegregation in the South, he worried that blacks might end up with "a mouthful of rights and an empty stomach."[15] The average African American family, he noted, earned only 55 percent of what the average white family earned.[16] Young's plan called for a ten-year, $145 billion "crash program" to upgrade education, housing, and health for all Americans. By cleverly comparing his plan to the Marshall Plan for U.S. aid to Western Europe after World War II, Young asserted that "special, emergency aid" for needy groups was an American tradition. He proposed measures that targeted African Americans in addition to universal benefits for all Americans. Young's plan demanded preferential hiring for qualified blacks to compensate for the "three hundred years of preferential treatment such as white citizens have had."[17]

Civil rights leaders regularly argued that efforts to advance African American economic progress should target black men, thus creating more male-headed families. For example, arguing for his Domestic Marshall Plan, Young cited concerns about "the lack of stability in the Negro family, the absence of a strong father figure, and the presence of the matriarchal pattern."[18] Often, black leaders expressed frankly patriarchal views. As late as 1969, well after the emergence of second-wave feminism, NAACP director Roy Wilkins commented, "Biologically, [women] ought to have children and stay at home. I can't help it if God made them that way, and not to run General Motors."[19] Many ordinary African Americans hoped civil rights gains would enable more black men to support their wives, allowing black women to care full time for their own children rather than working at low-wage jobs, often as domestic servants caring for affluent white families. This desire appeared in African American popular music of the early 1960s, epitomized by Motown Records and such performers as The Shirelles and Marvin Gaye, whose songs about the joys of monogamous heterosexual relationships broke with rhythm-and-blues tradition.[20]

African American leaders often stressed racial self-help as a complement to political action. They drew on a long tradition that suggested the duty of middle-class African Americans to "uplift" lower-class African Americans.[21] King urged African Americans to improve their moral "character" and take individual responsibility for their lives. Whitney Young, in particular, exhorted blacks to uplift themselves. Describing his Domestic Marshall Plan, Young stressed that it was "not a plea to exempt him [the Negro] from the independence and initiative demanded by our free, competitive society . . . [but] to transform the dependent man into the independent man."[22] Young acknowledged "the responsibility of the Negro to do a lot of different types of marching—in front of city halls and five-and-ten-cent stores—to get elementary rights, but at the same time we must march our children to libraries and the parents must march to adult education centers and to PTA meetings and to other places."[23] The importance Young placed on racial self-help was hardly surprising given the Urban League's long embrace of racial uplift, by which educated African Americans such as the league's leaders would aid poorer blacks. His rhetoric played well with white liberals: Young suggested that if the nation did its part, African Americans would do theirs. Conser-

vatives frequently charged that civil rights leaders focused on political mobilization at the expense of racial self-help. But to Young, King, and other civil
rights leaders, massive social investment in African Americans was a just and
necessary measure to ensure racial uplift. Young believed that African American leaders should frankly discuss African American social problems to em-
phasize the need for programs like his Marshall Plan: "Why in the hell should
we sit back and let reactionary magazines and newspapers expose the sad truth
about the Negro crime rate and other social breakdowns? . . . Let's research
and expose these things ourselves. That puts us in the driver's seat; we can
say 'Here's what has happened, here's why it has happened, let's all pull
together to do something about it.'"[24]

Moynihan registered the economic demands of civil rights leaders and
often echoed their rhetoric. In a 1964 speech, Moynihan worried, "We could
develop a dangerous division where a man judged fit to vote was judged not
fit to work." He concluded, "The elimination of discrimination is therefore
only the first step in achieving genuine equality."[25] At times, Moynihan even
supported racial preferences to redress the history of discrimination against
African Americans. In a 1963 memo to Wirtz, he wrote, "I believe in quotas
and a lot of other un-American devices. We have four centuries of exploitation to overcome and we will not do so by giving Negroes an equal opportunity with whites who are by now miles ahead."[26] In a 1964 memo to Wirtz,
Moynihan responded specifically to Young's Domestic Marshall Plan. He
asked, "Has the time come to organize an inquiry into the subject of unequal
treatment for the Negro?" Moynihan declared, "The Negroes are asking for
unequal treatment . . . it may be that without unequal treatment in the immediate future there is no way for them to achieve anything like equal status
in the long term."[27] By the time Moynihan wrote his report, then, he saw
African American inequality not only as a subset of the broader problem
of American poverty, but also as a special problem with its own historical
roots. In this view, he was strongly influenced by white liberals whose thinking was taking a socioeconomic turn by examining how economic inequality damaged black social life.

The Socioeconomic Turn

The growing power of the civil rights movement prompted the development
of Moynihan's interest in African American equality. Once Moynihan

began to pay attention, he immersed himself in a well-developed body of liberal thought about race, drawing particularly on American social scientists. By the early 1960s, white liberal intellectuals, like African American leaders, increasingly stressed that civil rights alone would not be sufficient as African Americans neared the goal of formal equality. However, their conceptions of "equality" differed from those of civil rights leaders in ways that influenced the Moynihan Report.

The most influential liberal book about African Americans was published two decades earlier: *An American Dilemma* (1944), a massive two-volume study written by Swedish economist Gunnar Myrdal and funded by the Carnegie Corporation. *An American Dilemma* was best known for arguing that racism could not be reconciled with the "American Creed" of individual rights. Myrdal optimistically predicted that over time this "dilemma" would be resolved by bringing the status of African Americans into line with American ideals. He articulated key assumptions adopted by Moynihan and other postwar liberals: the main racial divide in the United States existed between whites and blacks; racism was a historical anomaly inconsistent with American democratic norms; racial policy should integrate African Americans into American society; integration could be achieved within the established post-New Deal political and social order; and social-scientific knowledge could enlighten the public and guide policy-makers.

Myrdal famously charged that the "Negro problem," as whites had commonly called it, was in fact a "white man's problem."[28] The low status and position of African Americans resulted not from biological inferiority but from institutionalized racial discrimination and racial prejudice. Myrdal's suggested remedy relied on what he termed the "principle of cumulation": mutually reinforcing efforts to combat white prejudice and improve African American civil rights and social conditions.[29] An economist by training and an architect of the Swedish welfare state, Myrdal was well aware of the low economic position of most African Americans. However, the main effect of *An American Dilemma* was to divert focus from the social and economic dimensions of anti-black racism, common in 1930s scholarship, and toward racism's moral and psychological elements. Its thesis that racism was a white problem suggested that researchers should focus on explaining white bigotry. Thus, in the 1950s, the most influential works on race explained the psychology of prejudice. Religious and educational organizations applied the insights of the new psychology of prejudice to promote racial tolerance by whites through intercultural education.[30]

By the early 1960s, however, liberal intellectuals were emphasizing the socioeconomic dimensions of racism. They increasingly recognized that African American inequality was not simply a Southern issue. Since Myrdal published *An American Dilemma*, millions of African Americans had migrated from the South, moving largely to cities in the Northeast and Midwest. The racial geography of the United States shifted dramatically. In 1962, African American writer James Baldwin shocked educated white readers of the *New Yorker* with his account of oppression, deprivation, and hatred in Harlem. He published an expanded version of his essay as *The Fire Next Time* in 1963. Baldwin alerted readers to the explosive conditions in Northern urban areas as well as to their ignorance of America's racial history and its consequences.[31]

Myrdal contributed to this socioeconomic turn with his 1962 book, *Challenge to Affluence*, which coined the term "underclass," his translation of a Swedish word. Myrdal defined the underclass as the "unemployed, unemployables, and underemployed, more and more hopelessly divorced from the nation at large and without a share in its life, its ambitions and its achievements."[32] Myrdal explicitly related poverty to race, and his fame as the author of *An American Dilemma* ensured that *Challenge to Affluence* would be understood as a contribution to broader discussions of African American inequality.

By 1964, the year Moynihan decided to write *The Negro Family*, most American liberals accepted that racial equality required significant measures to close the economic gap between blacks and whites. This premise prompted an ambitious academic project on "The Negro American" sponsored by the American Academy of Arts and Sciences, an honorary society based in Boston. The project connected academic scholarship and policy-making. Invited to participate, Moynihan served as a conduit between the worlds of intellectual and political elites. Noting that research on African Americans had stagnated since the publication of *An American Dilemma*, the Academy hoped to have an impact similar to that of Myrdal's 1944 book. The project assembled many leading intellectuals. Along with Moynihan, it included historians Oscar Handlin and C. Vann Woodward; sociologists Daniel Bell, Robert Merton, Talcott Parsons, and Lee Rainwater; psychologists Erik Erikson, Robert Coles, and Kenneth Clark; economists Carl Kaysen and James Tobin; anthropologists St. Clair Drake and Clifford Geertz; Urban League leaders Whitney Young, Edwin C. Berry, and John B. Turner; and writer Ralph Ellison. Conference papers resulted in two special issues of the Academy journal, *Daedalus*, published in 1965 and 1966, and collected in a book in 1967. Though a few notable African American intellectuals participated, the project largely reflected a new interest in African American inequality among Northern white liberal intellectuals, who found little strange about white scholars dominating a project on the "Negro American." Like Moynihan, many white participants lacked longstanding expertise on African American issues. *Daedalus* editor Stephen Graubard remembers the 1965 conference as a "learning experience for middle-aged white men" who had few previous encounters with African Americans.[33]

Moynihan's contribution, "Employment, Income, and the Ordeal of the Negro Family" was written at the same time as *The Negro Family*, made the same arguments, and drew on the same evidence. Moynihan attended a planning conference at the Academy held in May 1964 and presented his paper at its April 1965 conference. At the *Daedalus* conferences, he discovered an emerging social-scientific consensus on the need for a socioeconomic turn. Graubard summed up the 1964 conference by noting that "the problem of jobs emerge[d] as primary." The Academy, Graubard concluded, should promote scholarship in the "study of indirect victimization [of African Americans], not simply the exercise of prejudice or discrimination, but the institutional processes, the changing social and economic structures which militate against equal treatment."[34] Talcott Parsons, the leading sociologist of the day, declared at the conference, "a really radical solution of the race problem is not likely to occur until we can virtually eliminate . . . a lower class from our society, regardless of color."[35] Economists and sociologists predominated in the project, indicating the growing perception of the need to supplement the legal, moral, and psychological approaches social scientists had adopted since World War II. At the 1965 conference, Thomas Pettigrew, himself a psychologist, expressed dissatisfaction with the disproportionate influence of psychological approaches to the study of African Americans: "one of the greatest fallacies we have had in the field of race relations for many, many decades has been to worry about attitudes rather than conditions."[36]

Moynihan's participation in the *Daedalus* project enhanced his sense that only special measures could ensure equality for African Americans. At the 1964 conference, he suggested, "if you are ever going to have anything like an equal Negro community, you are for the next 30 years going to have to give them unequal treatment."[37] He stated at the 1965 conference he attended shortly after completing his report, "the problem of the Negro American *is* now a special one, and is not just an intense case of the problem of all poor people." Moynihan argued that while African American inequality was a distinct problem, "in order to do anything about Negro Americans on the scale that our data would indicate, we have to declare that we are doing it for *everybody.*" Whereas Moynihan had told Wirtz in his November 1964 memo that focusing on racial equality could win presidential support for stronger antipoverty measures, he now presented universal social programs as a covert means to combat African American inequality.

The liberal social scientists involved in the *Daedalus* project discussed black family structure as part of their new focus on socioeconomic inequality. All but one of the project participants were men and their interest in the "Negro American" focused almost entirely on the problems of African American men. That so many black families deviated from the two-parent, male-breadwinner ideal indicated the pernicious effects of racism on black social life. Summarizing the 1964 Academy planning session, Graubard observed, "of first importance [is] a study of the family structure of the Negro, of what happens to urbanizing families, the peculiar nature of Negro family and kinship patterns, the sexual roles resulting from Negro matriarchalism, the psychological effects of father-absence, etc., etc."[38] White and black participants in the project shared this concern with family structure. When Moynihan returned to the White House following the 1965 conference, he wrote Bill Moyers, "I was impressed to find out how much my conviction of the importance of family structure and the relation of unemployment to that problem was shared by the Negro participants. They did not have the data, but they knew all about the problem."[39] Indeed, one of the strongest proponents of Moynihan's paper on employment and black families at the 1965 conference was Edwin Berry of the Chicago Urban League: "there is no way to strengthen family life among Negroes . . . until we find a way to give the father his rightful role as breadwinner and protector of his family. . . . We have a very strong matriarchal situation in the Negro community."[40]

Participants in the *Daedalus* project expressed a then-dominant social-scientific view about the negative effects suffered by children of single mothers. Thomas Pettigrew's *Profile of the Negro American* (1964) summarized the prevailing wisdom. He worried that too many black families deviated from the ideal model: "a stable unit with the husband providing a steady income for his family."[41] Citing recent studies, he concluded that children experienced serious psychological problems when raised "in a disorganized home without a father."[42] Pettigrew noted with alarm that many black children from one-parent families had difficulty conforming to conventional gender roles. For example, "Negro girls revealed interests generally associated with males" such as "theoretical and political concerns." Meanwhile, black boys without father figures were insufficiently masculine: "markedly more immature, submissive, dependent, and effeminate than other boys both in their overt behavior and fantasies." As they matured, however, many such boys compensated for gender insecurity through aggressive postures of "exaggerated masculinity."[43]

Like other liberals, Pettigrew advocated bolstering the economic positions of black men so that African Americans could fulfill conventional gender roles. *Profile of the Negro American* called for programs going beyond the War on Poverty: a "massive occupational upgrading of Negroes" that would "require major societal surgery, not the aspirin-type palliatives so far considered by the United States Congress."[44] Similarly, in an influential 1964 book, *Crisis in Black and White*, journalist Charles Silberman concluded, "The difficulty Negro men experience in finding decent jobs—jobs that would accord them a measure of dignity and self-respect and permit them to play the male role of breadwinner—is central to the perpetuation of the matriarchy and of the weakness of family relationships."[45]

This liberal argument about weakened African American families figured in a longer tradition of postwar social thought. As historian Daryl Scott explains, liberals employed the "damage thesis," the notion that white racism injured black psyches and distorted black social life, in order to highlight the injustice of white racism.[46] Black psychological problems appeared literally as the "mark of oppression" in the title of a prominent 1951 study by psychoanalysts Abram Kardiner and Lionel Ovesey.[47] In the *Brown v. Board of Education* decision of 1954, the NAACP argued that segregated schools had negative psychological repercussions for black students. The court agreed, finding that segregated schools created a "feeling of inferiority" among black students. In that case, the portrayal of psychologically damaged African Americans was used to discredit the legal segregation of Jim Crow. By the early 1960s, liberals increasingly argued that racism damaged black social life (not only individual psyches). Pinpointing the lack of male family breadwinners, they advocated reforms to improve the material position of black men throughout the nation, not only in the South.

White liberals were not solely concerned with injustice. They also worried about a threat to social order. In his 1961 book, *Slums and Suburbs*, former Harvard University president James B. Conant described large numbers of unemployed urban black men as "social dynamite" whose potential for crime and delinquency threatened social peace.[48] Similarly, Silberman shifted attention to racial conflict in the North, expressing alarm that if poor economic conditions and black alienation in urban areas were left unaddressed then the "Negro district of every city could come to constitute an American Casbah, with its own values and controls and an implacable hatred of everything white that would poison American life."[49] In *Beyond the Melting Pot*, Glazer voiced anxiety about the threat to social order posed by black men in urban slums: "what . . . are we to do with the large numbers of people emerging in modern society who are irresponsible and depraved?"[50] Liberals were alarmed by the 1964 Harlem riots, a six-night clash between African Americans and police in New York City. Moynihan recalled his alarm that "Harlem, the Negro community I knew best . . . exploded in violence, reminding me very much of the 1943 riot, at which time I had been a high school student in East Harlem."[51] Liberals also worried about the growing appeal of black nationalism, evident in the increasing numbers joining the Nation of Islam and attracted to its charismatic spokesperson, Malcolm X. And they feared that racial inequality hampered American efforts to win support in the Cold War. Silberman hyperbolically claimed that antiblack racism in the United States bolstered the agenda of "Red China" in "its evident desire to unite all the colored peoples of the world in a holy war against the white race."[52] Moynihan alluded to all these concerns—the threat to social order, the growth of black nationalism, and Cold War imperatives—in *The Negro Family*.

The increasing attention that white liberals in the early 1960s paid to socioeconomic roots of racism was accompanied by an emphasis on African American responsibilities. It was insufficient, many liberals now argued, to regard the position of African Americans as solely a problem of white racism as Myrdal once had. Harvard political scientist James Q. Wilson, a friend of Moynihan and later a leading neoconservative, declared in 1960 that, "in addition to the 'white man's problem,' there is also a 'Negro problem,'" explaining that "the ghetto has a life and a logic of its own, apart from whatever whites might do to create and maintain the outer walls of it."[53] Though Wilson advocated civil rights and redistributionist government programs, he also pinpointed the need for African American leaders to change the "culture of the Northern ghetto."[54]

Charles Silberman similarly contended, "only the Negro can solve the Negro problem." A staff writer for the business journal *Fortune*, Silberman stressed African Americans' duty to compete. "The Negro advance," he argued, "depends on changes within the Negro community as well as within the white community. . . . The unpleasant fact is that too many Negroes are unable—and unwilling—to compete in an integrated society." Silberman pinpointed family structure as a source of this problem: "The disorganization of the family is reflected in a disorganization of Negro life itself—an absence, in all too many individuals, of the inner strength and self-discipline necessary if one is to be the master rather than the servant of his environment in a competitive society."[55] Even liberals who favored redistributive government efforts saw forming stable male-headed families as virtually a civic duty for African Americans.

Other liberals who favored racial equality similarly stressed the need to prepare African Americans for economic competition. The Southern writer Robert Penn Warren, who had become a strong supporter of black civil rights, wrote of the " 'Negro's Negro problem'—the problem of taking responsibility to raise standards and enter competitively into general society."[56] The majority of liberals who endorsed special government efforts to rectify economic inequalities also stressed the responsibilities of blacks themselves to ensure they would be prepared for economic competition. They saw no contradiction between supporting government programs to close the socioeconomic gap between whites and blacks and suggesting that blacks needed to take on greater responsibilities for their advancement.

Civil rights leaders and liberal commentators commonly used the metaphor of a footrace in which African Americans could not be expected to compete fairly with others. In his 1965 Howard address, Lyndon Johnson famously declared, "You do not take a person who, for years, has been hobbled by chains and liberate him, bring him up to the starting line of a race and then say, 'you are free to compete with all the others' and then still justly believe that you have been fair."[57] By focusing on upgrading the runners, liberals risked neglecting the need to change the rules of the race. Liberal emphasis on African American weaknesses reflected assumptions that passing civil rights legislation would remove all institutional barriers to African American progress. They understood the damaging historical effects of racism primarily as affecting characteristics such as family structure that hindered African Americans' ability to compete in the marketplace. Liberals' focus on African Americans' need to compete in the race reflected a meritocratic ideal of

American society that limited their acceptance of the extensive measures demanded by civil rights leaders.

Statistics, Sociology, and Social Pathology

Moynihan's engagement with civil rights leaders' economic demands and liberal intellectuals' ideas convinced him he had a perspective on African American inequality that could capture the president's attention. In late 1964, he resolved to write his famous report after talking informally with senior White House staff members including Bill Moyers and Douglass Cater, both special assistants to the president, and Harry McPherson, an assistant secretary of state but with access to the president's ear. Moynihan decided these men were too confident that desegregation would lead to racial equality: since they were Southerners like the man they served, they were unaware of the problems facing blacks in Northern urban areas. Moynihan believed examining the black family would convince the president's advisers to see things in socioeconomic terms as he and other Northern liberals did. Johnson had just won reelection in a landslide that brought new majorities to Democrats in Congress, and Moynihan calculated that the administration might consider new approaches to civil rights and antipoverty policy. Awaking one December night, he decided to write a paper "to explain to the fellows [in the White House] how there was a problem more difficult than they knew and also to explain some of the issues of unemployment and housing in terms that would be new enough and shocking enough that they would say 'Well, we can't let this sort of thing go on.'"[58] On New Year's Eve 1964, Moynihan assembled staff to announce they would write a report on the black family.

Moynihan recalled a dramatic midnight revelation, but he had contemplated writing the report for several months. His interest in black family structure grew throughout 1964. He discussed the issue at length at the American Academy conference in April and was invited by *Daedalus* later that year to write an essay on the effects of unemployment on the black family.[59] In May, he collected data later used in the report. Moynihan's position as head of the policy planning unit allowed him unusual leeway to generate a report of this kind, but he still had to secure the support of his boss, Willard Wirtz. Moynihan's previously strong relationship with Wirtz had soured by late 1964. Wirtz was angry that Moynihan had insufficiently protected the department's administrative turf when planning the War on Poverty.

Nevertheless, Wirtz wanted Moynihan to stay for Johnson's second term. That Moynihan remained on condition that he could write a report on the black family indicates that he felt he had stumbled upon a subject that could earn him the attention of top policy-makers.[60]

In compiling research, Moynihan relied heavily on staff whom he expected to work almost as hard as he did. His unit had three members: Philip Arnow, Paul Barton, and Ellen Broderick. Barton, a staff researcher, and Broderick, Moynihan's personal secretary, updated Moynihan daily on their work on the report. Barton assisted Moynihan with *One-Third of a Nation* and played such a pivotal role in researching *The Negro Family* that some later referred to it as the Moynihan-Barton report. Born in 1931, Barton grew up in the hills of Kentucky; like Moynihan, his father had deserted him. Also like Moynihan, Barton benefited from new opportunities for white men in the years after World War II. He graduated from Hiram College in Ohio on a scholarship, where he studied social science. After two years in the army, he attended Princeton's Woodrow Wilson School of Public and International Affairs. Barton had an academic background in American race relations. He read the sociological classics of Myrdal and John Dollard as an undergraduate and assisted a Princeton professor in a study of educational desegregation in North Carolina. After graduating from Princeton, Barton went to work for the federal government. When Moynihan was promoted in 1963, Barton was part of the staff he inherited. Barton's main role in researching *The Negro Family* was analyzing statistics and assembling the report's numerous charts.[61]

Moynihan used his position and personal connections to secure data on female-headed families, out-of-wedlock births, welfare cases, and unemployment. As head of Policy Planning, Moynihan supervised the Bureau of Labor Statistics, among the most advanced statistical organs of the federal government. Already in May 1964, he instructed the Bureau to prepare charts on the relationship between unemployment and "family disruption" among African Americans. The data indicated that the proportion of "broken families" correlated strongly to male unemployment rates.[62] Moynihan also contacted others throughout the federal government. For example, he wrote the National Institutes of Health in September 1964 to ask if they had any data that could answer his question: "Is unemployment wrecking the Negro family?"[63]

The breadth and volume of statistics in *The Negro Family* were crucial to its claims to authority. Numbers offered the appearance of objectivity.[64]

Moynihan agreed with social scientists who thought statistics offered a form of democratic representation to those they identified, as in public opinion polling. He thought statistics could capture the experiences of Americans who were otherwise unrepresented. Comparing lower-class Americans to the "thoroughly tabled and tabulated" middle class, Moynihan remarked, "When a youngster drops out of school he also drops out of sight. Our statistics are based on small samples and there are no lists of the names of those who need help."[65] His faith in statistics contributed to Moynihan's discounting his lack of personal experience of African Americans as an impediment to objectively and compassionately representing African American families.

As Moynihan gathered data for his report, Bureau of Labor Statistics staff questioned his use of statistics. They warned, "social statistics need to be treated with considerable caution because of the difficulty of obtaining accurate information." In particular, they raised concerns about reported illegitimacy rates. Different cultural standards, they told Moynihan, meant that many white middle-class families hid illegitimate births while many lower-class blacks formed stable unions even when not legally married.[66] Moynihan cited but dismissed this concern in *The Negro Family*. Some of the report's earliest critics were government officials skeptical that its cross-racial comparisons failed to control for income and that its alarmist conclusions lacked support. During the controversy's early stage, critics within government shared these concerns with contacts outside government who could articulate them publicly.[67] The report's most significant statistical error was confusing correlation and causation. While Moynihan showed that black male unemployment and black family structure were related, he had little definitive proof for his more sweeping claims regarding whether one caused the other.[68]

When interpreting statistics and offering a broader historical and sociological perspective, Moynihan turned to the work of two African American scholars: E. Franklin Frazier and Kenneth Clark. Both Frazier and Clark tied problems of black families to African Americans' broader economic position and called for drastic reforms. Reliance on their scholarship prominently figured in the controversy over the report. Moynihan's supporters cited these black scholars' authority to prove his social scientific objectivity. Critics charged Moynihan with intellectual tokenism that provided a false impression that Moynihan appreciated African American perspectives. Neither view fully captured Moynihan's use of Frazier and Clark. Much of Moynihan's portrait of black families and black urban communities derived from Frazier and Clark, but he put their findings to his own purposes.

Early on Moynihan assigned Barton to read and take notes on Frazier's classic work tracing the development of black families from slavery to urban migration, *The Negro Family in the United States*.[69] Over twenty-five years after its 1939 publication, Frazier's book remained the definitive scholarly work on African American families. Frazier proved the most influential scholarly source for the Moynihan Report. Moynihan titled his report *The Negro Family* as a tribute to Frazier, though most probably missed the reference since the title was so ordinary.[70] Moynihan imagined himself updating Frazier. He later explained that Frazier "reported trouble," but he showed that "trouble had come to pass."[71] Though Frazier died in 1962, his unsought connection with the report forever changed his reputation. When Frazier's *The Negro Family* was republished in 1966 with an introduction by Moynihan's scholarly collaborator Nathan Glazer, it had become indelibly associated with Moynihan's report of the same name.[72]

Frazier ranks among the greatest American sociologists. Born in 1894 to a working-class Baltimore family, he attended Howard University as a scholarship student. He received his Ph.D. from the University of Chicago in 1933, then the most influential center for developing sociological ideas about race, ethnicity, and the city. In 1933, Frazier was hired at his undergraduate alma mater, Howard, where he taught until his death. Frazier's intellectual personality had two sides. As an academic, he was a cautious professional and a meticulous scholar. His efforts saw him elected president of the American Sociological Society in 1948, making him one of the first African Americans to head an interracial professional organization. Yet Frazier was also a dedicated socialist, a militant activist for civil rights, and an acerbic critic. After the *Brown* decision of 1954, he sarcastically remarked, "The white man is scared down to his bowels, so it's be-kind-to-the-Negroes decade at last."[73] Frazier's *Black Bourgeoisie*, first published in 1955, sharply attacked what he saw as an overly complacent and status-conscious black middle class. Frazier defended W. E. B. Du Bois when others deserted him in the early 1950s as Du Bois moved closer to Communism and became a target of McCarthyism. When Frazier died, he donated his library to Ghana, the newly independent African socialist state.[74]

Moynihan ignored Frazier's radical side, if he even knew it existed. Moynihan occupied a very different space in American intellectual and political life than did Frazier. Nevertheless, Moynihan found that Frazier's landmark study confirmed many of his assumptions. Frazier stressed that family structure could only be discussed in a broader socioeconomic context: "The poverty and disorganization of Negro family life in the urban environment only becomes intelligible when they are studied in relation to the organization of Negro communities and the social and economic forces which determine their development."[75] Moynihan and other 1960s liberals were indebted to Frazier when they linked black family structure to economic developments. Frazier also valued the family as a socializing institution and favored the male-breadwinner model as best adapted to the modern urban context. Frazier insisted on financially supporting his college-educated wife; in her words, he was "obsessed" with providing her economic security.[76]

Frazier applied the European immigrant analogy to explain black urban migration, an analytical staple of the Chicago School of Sociology that Moynihan adopted by way of Glazer. To Frazier, African Americans resembled European peasants who moved to American cities. Black migration from the rural South to the urban North, he claimed, was a move "from medieval to modern America."[77] Frazier also insisted that slavery had decimated the African cultural heritage of African Americans. On this point Frazier engaged in a significant scholarly controversy with his contemporary, Jewish anthropologist Melville Herskovits. Herskovits's 1941 book, *The Myth of the Negro Past*, emphasized African roots of African American culture, including its family structure.[78] Frazier worried that stressing African roots supported racist views that African Americans differed fundamentally from other American groups. He asserted that slavery nearly erased the African cultural heritage. "Probably never before in history," he wrote, "has a people been so nearly completely stripped of its social heritage as the Negroes who were brought to America."[79] Modern African American culture, Frazier claimed, differed from African culture "as the culture of the Germans of Tacitus' day was unlike the culture of German-Americans."[80] In the mid-twentieth-century, Frazier largely won the debate with Herskovits. Moynihan echoed Frazier's view that deviation from nuclear family norms resulted from low economic position, not from cultural difference. Later in the 1960s, Herskovits's anthropological view of the black family would be rediscovered and figure prominently in critiques of the Moynihan Report.

Moynihan adapted Frazier's ideas for his own ends. For example, their notions of what constituted a "disorganized" family differed. To Moynihan, father absence, illegitimacy, and matriarchy signaled "disorganization." Frazier, however, used the term in the Chicago School tradition, in which a group's *own* standards, not the external measuring stick of the sociologist, defined "disorganization."[81] Frazier claimed that female-headed families were positive adaptations among rural Southern African Americans in the post-Civil War era. "Illegitimacy" in the rural postbellum South, he argued, was "generally a harmless affair since it does not disrupt the family organization and involves no violation of the mores."[82] Frazier thought family stability required male breadwinners only in the modern urban context. Because Moynihan assumed that contemporary African Americans favored the male-breadwinner family, he too could be interpreted as treating urban female-headed families as "disorganized" in the Chicago School sense because of their failure to conform to the black community's own standards. But unlike Frazier, Moynihan conducted no research on what kinds of families African Americans desired. He thus opened himself to criticism that he unthinkingly applied an external, white middle-class standard of family structure.

Moynihan, as a white man who lacked personal experience of racial prejudice, was blind to how his work could play into racist stereotypes in a way Frazier never was. Frazier's case history method humanized his subjects in a way Moynihan's statistics did not. Frazier also emphasized the heterogeneity of black family models based on time, place, and social class. His University of Chicago dissertation, published as *The Negro Family in Chicago*, argued that blacks "exhibited variations in family life that were obscured when the Negro population was treated as an undifferentiated mass."[83] Both Frazier and Moynihan wrote works titled *The Negro Family*. But since Moynihan's lacked Frazier's attentiveness to heterogeneity, he could more easily be read as saying that "disorganized" Negro families were *the* Negro family.

Moynihan was more pessimistic about black urbanization than Frazier. Citing Frazier, Moynihan referred to the Northern black ghetto as the "city of destruction": a place where family disorganization mixed with a host of social problems. Unlike Moynihan, Frazier saw Northern cities as places of "rebirth" as well as "destruction" for African American migrants.[84] Urbanization destroyed earlier values, but also opened new possibilities: "In the new environment new hopes and ambitions are kindled, and the Negro acquires a new sense of his personal worth and rights."[85] Where Moynihan perceived ever-increasing urban disorganization, Frazier had a more cyclical view that owed partly to his Chicago School training, which held that following "disorganization" immigrant groups experienced a phase of "reorganization" that established new norms better adapted to the urban environment.

Frazier's more hopeful outlook on African American urbanization also resulted from his left-wing politics. When he wrote *The Negro Family* in the 1930s, he belonged to a group of younger militants within the NAACP who advocated a strong interracial labor movement. Frazier thought urban African American families would reorganize through industrial employment and labor organization. He placed hopes in "liberal and radical labor organizations . . . attempting to create a solidarity between white and black workers."[86] The fight for the family wage would be the basis of interracial cooperation: "As the Negro has become an industrial worker and received adequate compensation, the father has become the chief breadwinner and assumed a responsible place in his family."[87] Whereas Frazier advocated a mass movement to extend the family wage to African Americans, Moynihan placed his faith in technocratic social engineering. Thus, even though Moynihan and other white liberals of the 1960s recaptured the economic concerns that drove scholarship on African Americans during the 1930s and 1940s, their mechanisms for redressing black economic inequality differed. Frazier favored the mass political empowerment of African Americans, not simply their economic advancement and assimilation to the nuclear family norm.

After Frazier and Nathan Glazer, Kenneth Clark was the most important influence on the Moynihan Report. Initially one of *The Negro Family*'s staunchest defenders, Clark became a vociferous critic of Moynihan after his 1970 "benign neglect" memo to Nixon. Born in 1914 in the Panama Canal Zone, Clark grew up in Harlem. Like Moynihan, Clark came from what he referred to as his "broken home," since his father did not move with the family to New York. After completing an undergraduate degree at Howard, in 1940 Clark became the first African American to receive a Ph.D. in psychology at Columbia University. He landed a faculty position at the City College of New York. With his wife, Mamie Phipps Clark, he conducted famous psychological studies with black schoolchildren using black and white dolls. The doll studies claimed to prove that segregated schools damaged African American children psychologically. The NAACP cited them in legal battles against Jim Crow education, and the Supreme Court's 1954 decision referred to them. By 1964, Clark was a prominent media expert on the problems of black urban areas.[88] Clark published his classic study, *Dark Ghetto*, in the same year as *The Negro Family*. While the manuscript of *Dark Ghetto* was not available to Moynihan, it was based largely on *Youth in the Ghetto*, a 1964 report of Harlem Youth Opportunities Unlimited (HARYOU), a community agency founded by Clark. Moynihan cited *Youth in the Ghetto* in his report and also consulted Clark personally.[89]

Clark provided Moynihan one of the report's key terms: "pathology." Clark represented a prevalent social-scientific school known as "pathologism" that stressed how racism damaged African American social life. Using a medical analogy, sociologists applied the term "pathology" to the study of urban areas to describe the social ills affecting a community. As used by liberal social scientists including Clark, "pathology" denoted social health and did not imply a moral judgment about individual behavior. He wrote about *social* pathology, meaning that individual pathologies were caused by the sickness of society as a whole. By showing how American society victimized blacks, Clark invited the compassion of sympathetic whites.

Moynihan lifted *The Negro Family*'s most controversial phrase, "tangle of pathology," from Clark's *Youth in the Ghetto*, which cited seven kinds of pathology in Harlem: juvenile delinquency, narcotics addiction, venereal disease, infant mortality, high welfare rates, suicide, and homicide. The phrase "tangle of pathology" indicated that these issues were interrelated and symptomatic of the underlying causes of "education, employment, and family life."[90] Moynihan used it in this sense to refer to the interrelated social problems of urban African Americans. He did not, as some commentators alleged, refer to the African American family *itself* as a "tangle of pathology." However, Moynihan did draw on Clark to analyze black family "pathology." Clark highlighted "matriarchy" and the "distorted masculine image" as aspects of social pathology in Harlem.[91] For him, family structures that deviated from the male-breadwinner norm indicated how racism distorted black social life; they were another instance of how blacks were "forced to be different."[92] Unlike Moynihan, however, Clark never suggested that family structure was the central cause of the "tangle of pathology."

Clark's analysis of social pathology had a noticeably more radical dimension than Moynihan's. In fact, pathologism was more diverse than historians have acknowledged. Clark recognized the risk that "pathology" discourse would dehumanize poor urban blacks. Like Frazier and unlike Moynihan, Clark personalized his subjects. *Dark Ghetto* quoted Harlem residents extensively, allowing them to describe in their own terms the problems of their neighborhood. As one who had grown up in Harlem and remained connected to the community, Clark claimed *Dark Ghetto* was "in a sense, no report at all, but rather the anguished cry of its author."[93] In *Dark Ghetto*, Clark traced Harlem's social ills to its residents' political "powerlessness." "The dark ghettos," he wrote, "are social, political, educational, and—above all—economic colonies. Their inhabitants are subject peoples, victims of the greed, cruelty, insensitivity, guilt, and fear of their masters."[94] Presenting black ghettos as colonies that benefited outside white interests offered a very different explanation for African American inequality than the one favored by Moynihan and other white liberals—the inability of black men to compete in the marketplace. In fact, in addition to influencing the Moynihan Report, Clark influenced a key text of black radicalism, Stokely Carmichael and Charles Hamilton's *Black Power* (1967), which coined the phrase "institutional racism."[95]

Clark and Moynihan saw largely the same pathologies, but Clark viewed them as direct effects of a hierarchical and racist urban structure while Moynihan saw them as indirect effects of racism's legacy. Though Clark favored liberal social engineering, he also advocated democratic mobilization of dark ghettos' residents to restore their communities to social health. He viewed rebellion against injustice in positive terms, even when it took destructive and ineffective forms as in the 1964 Harlem riots.[96] Versus Moynihan, Clark related the pathology of the ghetto more clearly to the racist pathology of American society as a whole and thereby better avoided the danger that pathologism might stigmatize the victims of social illness.

The Master Problem

Moynihan finished *The Negro Family* on March 19, 1965, and took the unusual step of printing it. The hundred published copies were kept under lock and key to generate an impression of the document's significance.[97] Stylistically, *The Negro Family* blended a bureaucratic report, an academic article, and a muckraking magazine feature. Marked "official use only," the plain black cover bore the title in white lettering. Befitting a bureaucratic document, Moynihan's name appeared nowhere. The report contained 78 pages, 48 of which were text. Footnotes, an appendix, and 45 charts and tables littered the entire document. Moynihan frequently adopted the tone of an academic expert or government bureaucrat. Reading the report's drier passages today, it is hard to imagine it ever became an object of public fascination. At other points, however, Moynihan employed passionate, emotional language and clever turns of phrase. An experienced popular writer, Moynihan sought to grab the attention of White House officials. His more arresting language made excellent fodder for media articles after the report became public.

Introduced with a one-page preface, *The Negro Family* contained five chapters. The first, "The Negro American Revolution," laid out the broader social and political context. The next, "The Negro American Family," introduced what Moynihan saw as the deficiencies of black family structure. "The Roots of the Problem" relied heavily on Frazier and traced black families from slavery to the Great Migration. Moynihan discussed black family instability in connection with broader social problems in "The Tangle of Pathology." Finally, "The Case for National Action" considered policy implications.

Moynihan began by reminding his primary audience, White House officials, of the broader stakes of racial equality. He recounted the international importance of the African American struggle in the Cold War context. In a world where nations might "divide along color lines," Moynihan claimed, "the course of world events will be profoundly affected by the success or failure of the Negro American revolution in seeking the peaceful assimilation of the races in the United States."[98] He also alluded to social disorder that would result from racial conflict. If African American inequality was not addressed, he warned, "there will be no social peace in the United States for generations." He noted the development of black radicalism among adherents of "Black Muslim doctrines" as well as "the attractions of Chinese Communism" to the "far left."[99]

Moynihan argued for a second stage of the civil rights movement that surpassed political "liberty" to encompass economic "equality." Moynihan advocacy of "equality of results" rather than "equality of opportunity" at once registered the civil rights movement's egalitarian impulse while blunting its calls for economic transformation. Moynihan defined "equality of results" as that "the distributions of success and failure within one group be roughly comparable to that within other groups."[100] He lifted the phrase, which his report helped popularize, from a 1964 article by Glazer that expressed alarm that African Americans were demanding economic parity with other ethnic groups such as Jews.[101] Unlike Glazer, Moynihan felt this was a legitimate demand. Moynihan approvingly quoted Bayard Rustin's statement that the civil rights movement was "now concerned not merely with removing the barriers to full *opportunity* but with achieving the fact of *equality*."[102] However, he mischaracterized Rustin as demanding a "distribution of achievements among Negroes roughly comparable to that among whites."[103] Rustin in fact advocated an extensive social transformation of American society that would redress its "failure to meet not only the Negro's needs, but human needs generally."[104]

In adopting Glazer's understanding of American society as a competition between ethnic groups rather than between social classes, Moynihan undercut his sense of economic security as a basic right. His definition of "equality of results" did not treat material deprivation as injustice, only the uneven distribution of economic success among various ethnic groups. Thus, Moynihan, who had set out to write about African American families to highlight the general problem of economic inequality in American society, slipped into defining that inequality primarily in racial terms. As critics noted, the report's statistics on African American families did not control for income, suggesting that race, not class, was determinative.

However "equality" was defined, confronting the vast economic disparities between whites and African Americans was a momentous goal that required state intervention. However, Moynihan assumed that "equality of results" would ultimately be achieved through marketplace competition. Hence, *The Negro Family* focused on characteristics of African Americans that hindered their advancement. The damaged family structures of African Americans, Moynihan argued, reflected historical injustice that would need to be redressed if African Americans were to achieve results equal to those of other ethnic groups. Thus, even the jobs and income programs advocated by Moynihan were presented as means to strengthen black families to solve the underlying problem: "In terms of ability to win out in the competitions of American life, they [African Americans] are not equal to most of those groups with which they will be competing."[105]

In Chapter 2, Moynihan moved to his main subject, the family, to explain African Americans' lack of competitiveness. Family structure, he argued, was "the fundamental source of the weakness of the Negro community."[106] African American families were "increasingly disorganized," "highly unstable," and "approaching complete breakdown."[107] Moynihan supported these explosive statements with a ream of statistics. Of urban nonwhite marriages, 23 percent dissolved through divorce or separation versus only 8 percent of white urban marriages; 24 percent of nonwhite babies were born out of wedlock versus 3 percent of white babies. Almost one-fourth of all black families were headed by women. Finally, the "steady disintegration of Negro family structure" created "welfare dependency"—long-term reliance on public relief.[108] Moynihan took for granted that his readers would interpret high rates of marital separation, illegitimate births, female-headed families, and reliance on welfare as alarming signs of increasing family instability and community weakness among blacks.

Statistics burdened Chapter 2; Chapter 3 offered interpretation. The roots of the problem, Moynihan argued, lay in slavery. Along with Frazier, Moynihan's primary historical source was Stanley Elkins's *Slavery* (1959). Elkins compared American slavery to Nazi concentration camps and dwelled on its devastating psychological effects. To Elkins, "Sambo" was not simply a racial stereotype of the submissive slave, but an accurate description of slavery's psychological effects on African Americans. Elkins's history fit with the broader postwar liberal focus on how racism victimized African Americans and damaged their social life. Moynihan's use of *Slavery* helped fuel a sharp historiographical conflict over Elkins's interpretation of slavery starting in the late 1960s.[109] While Elkins did not speculate on slavery's lasting effects on contemporary African Americans, Nathan Glazer concluded in his influential 1960 review of *Slavery* that the peculiarly harsh nature of slavery in the United States explained why African Americans lacked the "self-confidence and energy" of blacks in the West Indies.[110] In fact, the Moynihan Report did not cite Elkins directly, but rather Glazer's commentary.

Moynihan focused on long-term effects of slavery and its aftermath on African American families. He claimed slavery destroyed family life, most of all by separating family members through the slave trade. Reconstruction, Moynihan argued, failed because former slaves gained "liberty" but not "equality," a warning of what might happen if the same course were followed in the civil rights era.[111] The imposition of Jim Crow discrimination following Reconstruction, Moynihan argued, "worked against the emergence of a strong father figure" in black families.[112] Moynihan saw black men as the primary victims of segregation: "Keeping the Negro 'in his place' can be translated as keeping the Negro male in his place: the female was not a threat to anyone." Moynihan's brief history of how slavery and segregation damaged black men implied national responsibility for black family structures that deviated from the male-breadwinner model. However, he also suggested the historical roots of racial inequality were distant not proximate.

Like Frazier and others, Moynihan highlighted the disorganizing effects of urbanization on African Americans. Using the European immigrant analogy, Moynihan likened black ghettos to "the wild Irish slums of the 19th Century Northeast" he discussed in *Beyond the Melting Pot*.[113] Moynihan presented statistics that showed "family pathology" rates among African Americans were highest in urban areas. Here, Moynihan pointed to the crucial effects of black unemployment, which typically ran twice as high as white unemployment. With the exceptions of World War II and the Korean War, Moynihan emphasized, African American unemployment "*has continued at disaster levels for 35 years.*"[114] When employment was more readily available to black men, "the Negro family became stronger and more stable."[115] Finally, Moynihan pointed to high birth rates among nonwhite mothers that would soon lead to "an unconcealable crisis in Negro unemployment," with more young black men competing for already scarce jobs.[116]

The fourth chapter, "The Tangle of Pathology," was the report's most pivotal. It sought to demonstrate the effects of the "weakness of family structure" on the broader "tangle of pathology." "Once or twice removed," Moynihan wrote, family structure "will be found to be the principal source of the aberrant, inadequate, or anti-social behavior that . . . now serves to perpetuate the cycle of poverty and deprivation." The lack of male-breadwinner-headed families, Moynihan argued, was partly responsible for crime, juvenile delinquency, poor educational achievement, drug addiction, and psychological alienation. Moynihan estimated that while half the black population was "middle-class," the other half was "in desperate and deteriorating circumstances." Because of housing segregation, however, even the black middle class was "constantly exposed to the pathology of the disturbed group."[117]

Moynihan feared not only one-parent families headed by women, but also what he took to be the skewed balance of power between black men and black women in intact marriages. Female-headed families, he wrote in an earlier draft of the report, were only the "visible portion of the matriarchy iceberg."[118] Even in two-parent homes, Moynihan claimed, black family life suffered from the "often reversed roles of husband and wife."[119] Moynihan's evidence for this claim was weak. He relied on Robert Blood and Donald Wolfe's 1960 study, *Husbands and Wives*, which found that 44 percent of African American families were "wife dominant." However, this conclusion was deeply flawed by the authors' open presumption of male dominance that stated, "the husband's work is his chief role in life," while the wife's' "work is seldom her major preoccupation."[120] Even if most African American wives took leading roles in decisions such as where to vacation or whether to work, as Blood and Wolfe found, it hardly made them dominant family figures. Moynihan used the term "matriarchy" to underscore African American men's lack of authority and position, but could not support its literal definition of a family or society in which power lay primarily in women's hands.

Black men, Moynihan argued, lacked the educational and economic advantages over black women that white men had over white women. Some statistics Moynihan cited suggested relative parity, such as the fact that slightly more black men than black women attended university. However, twice as many white men than white women went to college, a ratio that he implied was more desirable. Moynihan also thought black families' dependence on mothers' incomes damaged child development. Black women working outside the home not only undermined "the position of the father" but also deprived "children of the kind of attention, particularly in school matters, which is now a standard feature of middle-class upbringing."[121] Moynihan assumed that these negative effects of matriarchy were "hardly to be doubted."[122] Indeed, the report contained a page of testimony, including quotes from psychologist Thomas Pettigrew and civil rights leaders Whitney Young.

Moynihan's analysis of matriarchy, largely shared by liberal intellectuals and civil rights leaders, asserted that black women emasculated black men. His report bolstered widespread and long-standing stereotypes of black women as sexually promiscuous "Jezebels" or domineering "Sapphires." As historian Ruth Feldstein shows, it also reinforced mid-twentieth-century concerns with "momism": fears of the allegedly excessive, smothering power of wives and mothers that emasculated their husbands and sons. However, Feldstein's description of Moynihan's analysis as "mother-blaming" is misleading because it suggests that Moynihan stressed the causal agency of African American women.[123] In fact, Moynihan pointed to historical and sociological factors that he believed skewed black family life. "The Negro community," he asserted, "has been *forced* into a matriarchal structure."[124] Moynihan assumed that families headed by responsible males would be better for everyone, women included, and that blacks would choose male-headed families if given the opportunity. He supported his position with a quote from Dorothy Height, head of the leading organization advocating for African American women, the National Council of Negro Women: "If the Negro woman has a major underlying concern, it is the status of the Negro man and his position in the community and his need for feeling himself an important person . . . in order that he may strengthen his home."[125] Moynihan viewed "matriarchy" as a symptom of how black social life had been distorted by slavery, Jim Crow, and unemployment. Like most other liberals, he subsumed the problems of black women to those of black men, whom he viewed as the primary victims of American racism. "By contrast," he thought, "Negro women have always done and continue to do relatively well."[126] He ignored the difficult burdens of black women, who faced a brutal mix of racial and gender discrimination.

Though Moynihan did not fault individual African American women for what he perceived as their dominant roles in black family life, he believed their power should be reduced relative to that of African American men. Moynihan's belief that black men's advancement should come at the expense of black women differentiated him from other advocates of the black male breadwinner model such as Height. In a January, 1965 memo to Bill Moyers, one of the White House officials for whom Moynihan wrote *The Negro Family*, he reported: "I asked a distinguished Negro sociologist recently what could be done for the Negro man. He replied that he did not know what, if anything, could be done but that he was sure of one thing. Anything that could be done to hurt the Negro woman would help. He was not smiling."[127] Moynihan advised Lyndon Johnson in a memorandum summarizing the report's findings: "We must not rest until every able-bodied Negro male is working. Even if we have to displace some females."[128] *The Negro Family* cited a program to hire African Americans at his own agency, the Department of Labor, that Moynihan worried "redounded to the benefit of Negro women, and may even have accentuated the comparative disadvantage of Negro men."[129] At the 1965 American Academy conference, Moynihan imagined how his department's hiring of black women skewed power relationships in their families: "You can stand in front of the Department of Labor any morning at eight-thirty, and it is a sight: spectacularly well-dressed, competent, beautiful [black] young women . . . spending the day on the phone with the Attorney General and seeing ambassadors, then coming home and asking the old man, what did you do today?"[130]

Moynihan offered conflicting explanations for the superiority of the male-headed family model. At one point he asserted, "There is . . . no special reason why a society in which males are dominant in family relationships is to be preferred to a matriarchal arrangement." However, he maintained matriarchal families were poorly adapted for African American advancement. When black family structure was "so out of line with the rest of American society," he claimed, it "seriously retards the progress of the group as a whole." As a minority group, African Americans needed to conform to American society that "presumes male leadership in private and public affairs."[131] At other times, however, Moynihan suggested that men were biologically best suited to head families. Citing anthropologist Margaret Mead, Moynihan asserted that the primary male role in all human societies is family provider. Here, he suggested that men had a natural need to be in charge. In a much-quoted passage, he wrote, "The essence of the male animal, from the bantam rooster to the four-star general, is to strut."[132]

The report's central inconsistency related to the significance of family structure as an explanation for black inequality. Did Moynihan view family structure as only one of a series of interrelated difficulties facing African Americans? Or was it the central problem? One line of argument from the report suggested that family structure was just one measure of "social health or social pathology."[133] Moynihan later explained that highlighting family structure to dramatize the broader issue of race-based social and economic inequalities could best convince policy-makers and the public of the need for action on multiple fronts including employment, education, and housing. Moynihan believed that unemployment statistics were dry and bloodless, but that people could more easily relate to the tragedy of family break-up. He later explained his "strategy" of appealing to family to win support from white Americans for programs targeted at achieving racial equality: "by couching the issue in terms of family . . . white America could be brought to see the tired old issues of employment, housing, discrimination and such in terms of much greater urgency than they evoke on their own." Moynihan even thought "family as an issue raised the possibility of enlisting the support of conservative groups for quite radical social programs" especially by appealing to "the intense moralisms of conservative Catholic and Protestant religion."[134]

When Moynihan began writing the report, he seemed convinced that unemployment principally caused black family instability, an idea that flowed from his liberal belief in the family wage and his heavy reliance on Frazier's work. One of the first charts he assembled for the report suggested that lack of jobs for black men broke up black families. It indicated that the percentage of nonwhite women separated from their husbands lagged a year behind the unemployment rate for nonwhite males. In an early draft of the report as well as in his concurrently written *Daedalus* article, Moynihan described unemployment as "the master problem" affecting African Americans. Unemployment, he explained in his draft, "destroys men, wrecks families, and is ruining the lives of millions of American children."[135] As Moynihan wrote *The Negro Family*, however, his views underwent a subtle but significant shift. He began to interpret black social problems rooted in the family not as *effects* of economic inequality but as *causes* of the inability of African Americans to compete with other groups. In the final draft of *The Negro Family*, Moynihan asserted that family structure was the "*fundamental* source of the weakness of the Negro community."[136] In a memo summarizing the report for Lyndon Johnson, Moynihan went even further, declaring, "*the master problem is that the Negro family structure is crumbling*."[137] When Moynihan argued that family structure was the essential problem facing African Americans, he diverged from the sources on black families upon which he had relied. Frazier, Clark, and others had identified similar problems in black family structure, but they never argued that family structure was the main problem. Moynihan's decision to compare African Americans *as a group* to whites *as a group* without regard for class distinctions suggested that racially different family structures produced economic inequality, not *vice versa*.

Seeing family structure as the central cause of African American inequality suggested it might be an intractable problem immune to government intervention. The report's most controversial chart showed rising numbers of AFDC cases in recent years *despite* decreases in the unemployment rate for black men. Taking the number of women on welfare as an indicator of dissolved marriages, Moynihan implied that creating more jobs for black men would not necessarily lead to more two-parent families. This finding was later celebrated by neoconservatives such as James Q. Wilson, who dubbed the chart "Moynihan's scissors," referring to the shape on the graph made by the rising number of AFDC cases and falling rate of black male unemployment.[138] As Moynihan's critics later pointed out, the finding was faulty because AFDC cases inadequately measured whether families remained intact. Cases rose in the early 1960s for many reasons, including legal changes to the program and greater knowledge of benefits among qualified recipients. Regardless, Moynihan used this chart to suggest that male unemployment might no longer be the primary cause of black family instability. If so, he speculated, then "the situation may indeed have begun to feed on itself."[139] If black family problems perpetuated themselves, then the traditional employment, education, and housing policies advocated by liberals seeking black advancement could prove ineffective. Interestingly, Moynihan's primary collaborator, Paul Barton, expressed doubts about this chart. Barton believed that the statistics for black male unemployment were unreliable, and he worried that the finding weakened the report's call for job creation. "I just prefer to believe that a real improvement in the employment situation in the slum will be of some real help in reversing the situation," Barton wrote in a 1967 letter to Moynihan.[140]

The Negro Family could still be interpreted as using the family to dramatize the need for jobs for black men. It emphasized that damaged families were one of the "social and personal consequences" of unemployment.[141] Moynihan continued to support full employment, the family wage, and family allowances as solutions to racial inequality. His boss Willard Wirtz, who strongly backed the report, interpreted it as offering support for the expanded employment and training programs that he advocated as secretary of labor. Nevertheless, the report's suggestion that family structure might in fact be the central problem crucially affected its later reception. It alarmed many liberal opponents, but appealed to some conservatives and provided the germ of Moynihan's own later turn toward neoconservatism. Most important, the report's ambiguity over "the master problem" explains how it could be interpreted in such widely varying ways, particularly with regard to policy implications.

The Limits of National Action

Given that *The Negro Family*'s final chapter was entitled "The Case for National Action," it strangely lacked policy proposals. Moynihan explained that he designed *The Negro Family* to convince policy-makers that "a national effort towards the problems of Negro Americans must be directed towards the question of family structure," but left particular solutions to future discussion.[142] Indeed, he originally subtitled the report, "A strategy for national action," substituting "case" only at Wirtz's insistence.[143]

At a deeper level, however, the report's lack of policy proposals resulted from its ambivalent analysis. The concluding chapter wondered whether the federal government could do anything to address African American inequality: "it is necessary to acknowledge the view, held by a number of responsible persons, that this problem may in fact be out of control." In a tortured passage reflecting his internal confusion, Moynihan asserted that this viewpoint "must be acknowledged" even though he "emphatically and totally disagree[d]."[144] If Moynihan really wanted to disassociate himself from this position, he would not have given it any credence. In fact, the notion that African American family instability was an "out of control" self-perpetuating pathology followed from the report's line of argument that family structure primarily caused African American inequality. The damage to black social and family life could not be easily repaired, even if white racism ceased: "the present tangle of pathology is capable of perpetuating itself without assistance from the white world." Here, Moynihan argued that his scissor-shaped data on black male unemployment rates and the rates of black women on welfare "should be understood before program proposals are made."[145] This line of argument sounded more nearly a case for *in*action. It questioned whether social-scientific knowledge could effectively guide political action, raised doubts about using liberal social engineering to redress racial inequality, and implied that the problem of black economic inequality was either insoluble or could be addressed only by African Americans themselves. Moynihan undermined his call for action and sowed the seed of a neoconservative challenge emerging from within postwar liberalism.

Alternatively, Moynihan's dire warnings could be taken as an urgent call for government action. His assertion that "Measures that may have worked in the past . . . will not work here" could be read as endorsing a new "national effort" to stabilize black families. In his *Daedalus* article, for example, Moynihan declared, "The crisis of commitment is at hand."[146] Despite Moynihan's doubts, *The Negro Family* mainly urged the government to reorient programs toward strengthening the black family.

Though its final section, "A Case for National Action," contained no policy proposals, a careful reader could detect clues. It hinted at policies that would move the American welfare state toward a more extensive Northern European model. Moynihan complained that unlike in similar industrialized nations, U.S. wages were "rarely adjusted to insure that family, as well as individual needs are met."[147] Here, he implied that the U.S. should adopt a system of family allowances to provide a minimum income to all American families. Given the report's emphasis on unemployment, *The Negro Family* also clearly indicated the need to create jobs for African Americans. Its most concrete proposal was to recruit more black men into the army. If the military hired African Americans proportionately to their percentage of the population, Moynihan estimated, the unemployment rate for black men would fall over two percentage points. *The Negro Family* emphasized retraining those who failed the armed forces entrance exam, something Moynihan already promoted in *One-Third of a Nation*. As White House readers may have grasped, recruiting more black soldiers would require no legislative fight and help meet the need for more soldiers created by the escalating war in Vietnam.

Moynihan believed the army could provide black men with jobs and training and deliver an antidote to damage suffered growing up in a matriarchal culture. Sounding like a military recruiter, Moynihan even quoted the slogan, "In the U.S. Army you get to know what it means to feel like a man."[148] The army, he stated, was a place where "discipline, if harsh, is nonetheless orderly and predictable."[149] To Moynihan, the military offered black men the means to support their families and trained them to become responsible heads of household. Tellingly, though, men in military service might have to spend significant time away from their families. Thus, for Moynihan, the true mark of fatherhood was providing for one's family, not continuous physical presence.

Moynihan also claimed that black men would benefit from what he asserted was the meritocratic nature of the armed services. Military service was "the *only* experience open to the Negro American in which he is truly treated as an equal: not as a Negro equal to a white, but as one man equal to any other man in a world where the category 'Negro' and 'white' do not exist." However, one of Moynihan's charts belied this assertion by indicating the paltry percentages of black officers in the armed forces (ranging from 0.2 percent in the navy and marines to 3.2 percent in the army). Black soldiers were virtually certain to be subjected to white authority. Moynihan appreciated the role of military service for his own advancement, but he falsely equated his experience as a naval officer with that awaiting most African American soldiers.

While Moynihan's policy preferences in *The Negro Family* remained vague, he fleshed them out in a memo to the president after he won the attention of top White House officials. Soon after the report was ready, Wirtz called Bill Moyers and forwarded a copy, suggesting that it deserved "*very serious* consideration." Wirtz became the first to refer to *The Negro Family* as the "Moynihan report."[150] Meanwhile, Moynihan took a copy along with a bottle of whiskey to his friend, White House aide Harry McPherson, then in the hospital. The two drank and discussed, and McPherson was impressed. Moyers must have been impressed too, for a few weeks later he asked Moynihan to put his ideas in a memo to the president.[151]

Wirtz forwarded Moynihan's memorandum summarizing *The Negro Family* to Johnson on May 4, 1965, declaring it "nine pages of dynamite about the Negro situation." Wirtz strongly endorsed Moynihan's conclusions: "Federal policy should be built around the necessity to restore the structure of the Negro family." In his memo, Moynihan appealed personally to Johnson: "You were born poor. You were brought up poor. Yet, you came of age full of ambition, energy, and ability. Because your mother and father gave it to you. The richest inheritance any child can have is a stable, loving, disciplined family life." Moynihan also played to Johnson's concern for social disorder, warning that the break-up of black families was "the problem that is making our cities ungovernable."[152]

At Wirtz's insistence, Moynihan listed specific policy proposals in his memo. He still stressed that he proposed more of a shift in overall government "strategy" than any particular policy. Statistics about family stability, he argued, were useful indicators of overall black progress, an "absolute measure of whether or not our efforts are producing any results." Moynihan urged Johnson to appoint a working group to reexamine federal policies to ensure that they strengthened black families. Moynihan called for creating more jobs, but made few specific proposals other than that more black men be recruited for the armed forces and reserving some jobs held by black women for black men. He did not propose public works projects that he had previously favored, likely because he knew of Johnson's opposition. He advocated housing reform to help middle-class black families escape urban ghettos: "We must find ways to get emerging middle class Negro families into the suburbs, where the surroundings tend to reinforce the integrity of the family."[153]

White House officials were receptive to *The Negro Family* because they worried about always reacting to the civil rights movement's demands rather than setting the agenda themselves. "We could never catch those guys," one official explained, "the only thing to do is to get ahead of them."[154] As Moynihan later detailed, the strategy was "to deliberately leap frog the civil rights movement—to get out in front so far that you would avoid the impossible task of chasing it."[155] Moynihan's focus on family structure could redirect the conversation about black civil rights. Administration officials were attracted to Moynihan's proposal that the government could lead the way toward a new stage of the movement. In viewing Moynihan's focus as new, however, officials demonstrated ignorance of long-standing economic programs of civil rights organizations. To the extent that the Johnson administration recognized the broader social and economic aspects of racial inequality, they were still catching up.

Moynihan was canny in capturing White House attention by addressing a perceived political need, but his attempt to use the issue of African American families to get Johnson to commit to expanded jobs and income transfer programs largely failed. *The Negro Family*'s significant effect was not on the administration's policy but on its rhetoric. It inspired a major address Johnson made at Howard University on June 4, 1965. The strategy of leap-frogging the civil rights movement motivated Johnson's address, which drew heavily on the Moynihan Report. As Moynihan recalled, Moyers talked to Johnson about making the "Negro family thesis" the basis of a speech that would be "an effort to go beyond the current demands of any civil rights group."[156] Moynihan helped presidential speechwriter Richard Goodwin prepare the address. The two worked until the early morning before the address.[157] The speech was almost entirely Goodwin's work, but the Moynihan Report's influence was clear.[158] Goodwin distilled Moynihan's ideas into clear and graceful prose that became one of the most powerful speeches of the Johnson presidency.

In the speech's most famous line, Johnson declared, "Freedom is not enough." Legal and political rights for African Americans alone would not

ensure true equality. Johnson declared his support for "the next and most profound stage of the battle for civil rights." Adapting Moynihan's call for "equality of results," Johnson proclaimed, "We seek not just freedom but opportunity,
not just legal equality but human ability—not just equality as a right and a
theory but equality as a fact and as a result." Johnson tied black civil rights
to his existing anti-poverty campaign. However, he also asserted a *national*
responsibility to ensure African American economic progress because of the
"special nature of Negro poverty" rooted in the American history of racial
oppression. Johnson endorsed the need for racial self-help: "The Negro . . .
will have to rely mostly on his own efforts." Yet, he also advocated special
programs based on liberal arguments about blacks' inability to compete in
the marketplace. Unlike other groups, Johnson claimed, African Americans
"just cannot do it alone. For they [other minorities] did not have a cultural
tradition which had been twisted and battered by endless years of hatred and
hopelessness."[159]

Though Johnson's address emphasized family less than Moynihan's report, it did contain five paragraphs on "family breakdown." Drawing on
Moynihan, Johnson described family structure as the key to explaining blacks'
difficulties in competing on equal terms with other Americans. Citing family structure as an explanation for black poverty, Johnson commented, "Perhaps most important—its influence radiating to every part of life—is the
breakdown of the Negro family structure. For that, most of all, white America must accept responsibility. It flows from centuries of oppression and per-
secution of the Negro man." Endorsing the family's centrality, Johnson
declared, "When the family collapses it is the children that are usually damaged. When it happens on a massive scale the community itself is crippled."

Johnson's speech won wild applause from an audience gathered for grad-
uation at the nation's most prominent black university, once the home of
E. Franklin Frazier. Civil rights leaders hailed the speech. It was read to Martin Luther King, Roy Wilkins, and Whitney Young before it was delivered.
All were enthusiastic because Johnson articulated ideas they had long voiced
themselves.[160] For the first time, an American president accepted white responsibility for black social advancement. In declaring that freedom was not
enough, Johnson said no more than civil rights activists had for decades. But
when he said it, it promised government action.

Later that summer, the escalation of the Vietnam War distracted the administration from its domestic programs and the Watts riots changed the national discussion about African Americans. In retrospect, many liberals looked

at the Howard speech as a halcyon moment. It promised an alternative path that never materialized—a national commitment to racial equality in all its facets. Both speechwriters came to view the speech in these terms. For Goodwin, Vietnam spoiled liberal hopes; for Moynihan, the reaction to his own report did.[161]

The Howard speech hardly represented a lost opportunity. Its most important contribution was rhetorical. Johnson boldly committed to pursuing racial equality, declaring it would be a "chief goal of my administration." When it came to precise policies, however, his speech was even more vague than the Moynihan Report. "Jobs," were part of answer, Johnson claimed, as were "decent homes," "welfare and social programs," "care of the sick," and "an understanding heart." But Johnson did not explain how these goals might be reached, nor did he promise any new programs. Instead, he called for a White House conference on the theme, "To Fulfill These Rights," at which scholars, experts, and black leaders would deliberate the next steps. Interestingly, Moynihan's draft of the speech detailed more specific objectives. But Johnson rejected his language that would have committed his administration to "full employment for everyone" and a "family wage for all workers," precisely the goals for which Moynihan had long fought.[162] Little evidence suggests that Johnson planned to follow up his Howard pronouncements with equally ambitious programs. Moreover, the administration's leap frogging strategy indicated its desire to co-opt the civil rights movement's independent voice and tame its demands.

Even the policies Moynihan advocated fell short of the economic programs advocated by civil rights leaders and would have failed to bring blacks to economic parity with whites. Trying to achieve more than just legal equality for African Americans revealed how far the Johnson administration and its liberal allies were willing to go to achieve "equality as a fact and as a result." Moynihan himself recalled that the list of policy recommendations he drew up alongside the report "didn't add up to much in terms of . . . how serious our situation was."[163] Harry McPherson, the Johnson aide who championed the Moynihan Report, recalled being dismayed by the Howard speech because it highlighted how significant a problem African American inequality was: "It just seemed like there wasn't enough time, there wasn't enough money, there wasn't enough understanding—we'd never do it. . . . It was like converting a crippled person into a four-minute miler. You just couldn't do it."[164] In confronting the problem of African American inequality, postwar liberalism reached its limits.

The Howard address, like the Moynihan Report, rested on assumptions liberals presumed consensual but would soon be contested. By calling for a conference of experts to determine future action, Johnson indicated reliance on social engineering. The speech clearly endorsed the male-breadwinner family model as ideal as well as the long-standing liberal sentiment that blacks could best advance in American society by adopting white middle-class norms.

All these liberal assumptions would be challenged through the controversy that soon engulfed the Moynihan Report. Moreover, by shifting discussion to the next stage of the civil rights movement and by highlighting the presumed weaknesses in black social life without endorsing any specific policies, the Howard address contained the same political ambiguities as the report on which it was based. Johnson, not Moynihan, called African American culture "twisted." But the Moynihan Report, not the Howard address, became the lightning rod for critics who challenged the depiction of black social life as pathological. When the Moynihan Report went public in late summer 1965, the surrounding controversy centered on whether it called for bold new measures to rectify black inequality or signaled a white liberal retreat by implying that African Americans had to help themselves.

CHAPTER 3

The New Racism

"You must have written the Report in disappearing ink," White House aide Harry McPherson mused in a 1966 letter to Moynihan, "making it possible for people to write into it whatever they choose."[1] When *The Negro Family* became public in late summer 1965, it invited divergent reactions. Liberals hailed it as promising new initiatives to alleviate economic inequality, while conservatives thought it proved African Americans should rely on their own efforts. Some segregationists took it as support for their worldview, while others wrote Moynihan hate mail accusing him of racial treason. Early critics worried that the Moynihan Report fostered a new racism that blamed the victims of institutionalized discrimination rather than the system that victimized them. Michele Wallace's recollection that African Americans "wanted to cut Daniel Moynihan's heart out and feed it to the dogs" was incorrect. Some civil rights leaders and ordinary African Americans cheered the report for drawing attention to problems previously ignored by white elites, though others were appalled that it promoted negative stereotypes of African Americans.[2]

With different groups reacting to the report so variously, the controversy was never the simple debate between Moynihan and his critics on the left that historians often portray. The most influential historical accounts of the debate have accepted Moynihan's own assessment that the controversy was "a nightmare of misunderstanding, and misinterpretation, and misstatement."[3] In fact, the report was bound to produce conflicting reactions because of its ambiguities and because it redirected public attention to African American families at a time of volatile political and intellectual change.

The controversy peaked in the months following the document's release in August 1965. *The Negro Family* initially influenced organizers of the November White House Conference on Civil Rights to structure the meeting around the topic of the family. But the report's direct influence on government policy was short-lived. In October, after discontent emerged from civil rights circles, conference organizers quickly abandoned their original agenda, and the Johnson administration soon disowned the report. However, many Americans continued to see *The Negro Family* as politically significant. From fall 1965 to spring 1966, the press reported Moynihan's ideas widely. Discussion filtered beyond elites. Heated arguments broke out in letters to the editors of magazines and newspapers, and hundreds of ordinary Americans wrote directly to Moynihan to share their views.

The dispute catalyzed new conceptions of racism. Critics challenged Moynihan's understanding of racism, which stressed the "virus" of individual racial prejudice and the effects of historical oppression on African American social structure. Moynihan's two most influential critics, William Ryan and Benjamin Payton, were activists in Northern cities attuned to how metropolitan politics reinforced racial inequality. They viewed African American inequality as the result of ongoing racism embedded in American institutions. Ryan famously accused Moynihan of "blaming the victim" by focusing attention on African American families rather than the system that oppressed them. Citing lurid press accounts of "biological anarchy" among African Americans, Ryan also argued that the report's focus on statistics such as out-of-wedlock births perpetuated long-standing racial stereotypes. Though Ryan and his followers did not attack Moynihan personally as a "racist," they argued that his report fueled a new racism.

From Watts to the White House Conference

Though only a few months passed between Moynihan's completion of the report in March 1965 and its publication by the Government Printing Office (GPO), the political context had altered. On August 6, Johnson signed the Voting Rights Act, which provided federal enforcement of African Americans' constitutional right to vote, sounding the legislative death knell for Jim Crow. Just five days later, an incident of police brutality touched off a week of conflict that began in Watts and spread throughout south Los Angeles. Thirty-four people died, 1,000 were injured, 4,000 were arrested, and estimated property damage was $200 million. Given that the "riots" expressed long-simmering discontent with police mistreatment and economic and political marginalization, they are better understood as an "uprising." The violence was spontaneous but not random, as rioters targeted the police and white-owned businesses. Police forces exercised the most deadly violence. Watts gathered significantly more public attention than the Harlem riots the previous summer and served as the reference point for future 1960s uprisings, including those of the "long hot summer" of 1967, when the most destructive incidents occurred in Detroit and Newark.[4]

Watts directed public discussion of African American inequality away from the Jim Crow South. Moynihan and others already focused on the urban North saw their ideas suddenly in demand. Moynihan's report now seemed prescient in arguing that the U.S. would have "no social peace" unless it addressed persistent social and economic inequalities. The week of the Watts rebellion, *Newsweek* readers flipped their pages to the first long media article on the Moynihan Report. The post-Watts context exacerbated the central ambiguity of *The Negro Family* in a manner that foreshadowed competing responses to urban rebellions of the late 1960s. Pointing to deep inequalities suffered by African Americans, *The Negro Family* suggested that staving off further unrest would require the redistribution of economic resources. That strand of Moynihan's argument anticipated the conclusions of the Kerner Commission, appointed by Johnson in 1967 to investigate urban riots, which indicted "white racism" as the ultimate source of rioting and proposed expanded jobs and housing programs.[5] Yet highlighting family structure also encouraged explanations that ignored underlying racism and economic inequality and stressed flaws in African American social structure.

The report had influenced Johnson to call a White House Conference on Civil Rights. Initially, conference planners intended to make black family structure the focus around which participants could discuss broader aspects of African American inequality. But organizing the conference around the theme of family precipitated criticism of the Moynihan Report by civil rights activists. Johnson officials quickly realized that a conference on the family would prove too divisive, and they eventually settled for an agenda listing family as only one of several items. Partly due to controversy over the Moynihan Report, organizers delayed the main conference until 1966, and instead convened a large planning session in November 1965. As Johnson officials weathered criticisms of *The Negro Family* in the run-up to the conference, Moynihan's stock with the administration quickly fell. He was invited only at the last minute to attend the meeting.[6] Following the conference debacle, Johnson reprimanded his staff: "You boys have gotten me in this controversy

over Moynihan."[7] The Moynihan Report would remain a touchstone for political and intellectual debate, but after November it was effectively dead as a
source for White House policy.

The November planning conference failed not only because of discontent
with the Moynihan Report, but also because of the administration's disorganized civil rights policy and its escalation of the Vietnam War, two factors that
crucially affected the reception of *The Negro Family*. Even those who planned
the conference were unclear about its goals. Participants were divided into
panels on different issues, but it was never apparent how their reports would
feed into administration policy. The fundamental problem was Johnson's unwillingness to enact the programs endorsed at the conference. Honorary chair-
man A. Philip Randolph, instrumental in organizing the March on Washington
two years before, proposed a $100 billion "Freedom Budget" to provide the re-
sources needed for a real war on poverty, including New Deal-style public
works programs and a massive upgrading of housing, health, and educational
infrastructures serving lower-class Americans. Johnson's aides, however, envisioned only "stronger training and education programs" as the conference's
result.[8] For many participants, the conference revealed Johnson's failure to live
up to the lofty rhetoric of his Howard speech. According to a confidential government memo, rather than coalescing support around a new set of policies,
the conference's main accomplishment was to "consolidate and intensify the
dissatisfaction, frustrations, and militancy of the Negro leadership."[9]

The tensions surrounding the White House conference provided a crucial subtext for the reception of the Moynihan Report, which to some became
a symbol for Johnson's lack of commitment to racial equality. Johnson's escalation of the Vietnam War in summer 1965 also alarmed many conference
participants. Some activists opposed the war, but all were concerned that it
would distract from Johnson's domestic agenda. Indeed, that summer Johnson turned civil rights strategy over to his aides in order to concentrate on
Vietnam. The civil rights movement began to split; its more radical wing became increasingly outspoken in criticizing the administration and white liberals in general. The Student Nonviolent Coordinating Committee (SNCC)
boycotted the spring 1966 conference, dismissing it as an effort to "rubber
stamp the administration's 'do practically nothing and make the nation think
it cares' policy."[10] Leaders of the Congress of Racial Equality (CORE) participated in the 1966 conference, but sponsored an antiwar resolution. In the end,
the 1966 meeting proved less divisive than the 1965 planning session, but only
because Johnson packed the conference with supporters.[11] Johnson's reticence

to endorse significant antipoverty programs benefiting African Americans convinced many activists that the Moynihan Report was a rationalization for his inaction.

Going Public

Who "leaked" the Moynihan Report to the press has long been a mystery. One account hypothesizes that Moynihan leaked it himself to enhance his personal stature.[12] Another speculates that a "jealous government official" or a "racist civil servant" released it to poison the report's reception.[13] In fact, in an unpublished document, Moynihan confessed that he provided *The Negro Family* to *New York Times* journalist John Pomfret, who published the first story on the report: his July 19 front-page article quoted the document extensively. Moynihan, who had left the Johnson administration earlier that month to run for New York City Council president, claimed that he had White House permission.[14] It is unlikely that he acted on his own initiative. Pomfret's article did not even mention Moynihan; instead, it inaccurately attributed the report to a "White House study group."[15]

How Pomfret first learned of the report remains unclear, but his article was apparently not the result of an unauthorized "leak." It was in any case unlikely that the report could have been kept secret, given its political relevance as a source for Johnson's Howard address and the upcoming Civil Rights Conference. That Moynihan and White House officials cooperated in the report's release suggests that they were so unaware of its contradictions and so convinced of the consensual nature of its liberal assumptions that they did not anticipate the firestorm it would spark. If Moynihan hoped to make his name with the report, he succeeded, even if he never anticipated that publicizing the report would open Pandora's Box.

Pomfret's article set off an avalanche of press coverage. Moynihan, whose authorship of the report soon became known, continued to cooperate with the press. He provided copies of *The Negro Family* for the two most important subsequent press articles: an August 9 *Newsweek* feature and an August 18 syndicated column by political pundits Rowland Evans and Richard Novak.[16] Others with access to the report, including White House press secretary Bill Moyers, also apparently distributed copies to reporters.[17]

Pomfret's story prompted the Johnson administration's decision to make *The Negro Family* publicly available. Two days after the article appeared,

Johnson officials decided to give the report "further circulation" and asked the Labor Department how to do so.[18] Labor Department official John W. Leslie was tasked with analyzing the impact of releasing the document. He advocated publication, concluding that despite its possible misuses, publication would "serve a very useful purpose by calling attention to a problem, with many complex facets, which needs national attention."[19] Johnson aide Lee White concurred, reasoning that the report would become public no matter what the administration did.[20] From the end of August, anyone could purchase *The Negro Family* for 45 cents from the GPO.[21]

Some officials recognized possible dangers in releasing the report. One warned, "parts of it will be picked up by the segregationists and used against the Negro." Despite advocating publication, Leslie feared that Moynihan's findings could be used to "job the Negro." He recognized that the report would be interpreted in multiple ways and "used out of context to prove this point or that point."[22] Though officials correctly predicted segregationists' use of the report, they failed to anticipate that conservatives would use it to argue for racial self-help rather than national action, press reporting would use it to bolster racial stereotypes, and civil rights activists would attack it.

The Negro Family was publicized in a haphazard manner that crucially affected its reception, leading to a widespread misimpression that the report was classified or had been suppressed. Before the first GPO printing, only 100 copies existed and obtaining a copy was nearly impossible. In August, the Department of Labor was unable to provide copies even to Congress members, who read about it in the nation's leading periodicals. *New Yorker* political correspondent Richard Rovere paid $40 (roughly $300 in 2015 dollars) to obtain a photocopy.[23] After the first GPO printing, it quickly went out-of-stock due to high demand. Also, many Americans did not know how to obtain a publication from the GPO. Confusion about the report's status was widespread. In January 1966, over four months after anyone could purchase the report from the GPO, a columnist demanded the government release it.[24]

Conflicting media interpretations of the report resulted primarily from its ambiguities. Some press accounts picked up on the report's stress on unemployment as a cause of family instability, perceiving it as advocating antipoverty programs to benefit urban African Americans. Others, however, concluded that family structure was the fundamental problem African Americans faced and deduced there was little that government could or should do. Regardless how they interpreted the report, journalists frequently offered lurid depictions of African American life that colored the report's statistics on out-of-wedlock births and female-headed families and reinforced existing racial stereotypes.

Newsweek set the template for interpreting the report as presaging new government efforts to redress socioeconomic inequalities among African Americans. Its August 9 feature, "New Crisis: The Negro Family," was the first story to identify Moynihan as the report's author. It quoted extensively from *The Negro Family*, highlighted its call to create more jobs for black men, and portrayed black family instability as resulting from deeper economic problems. The article explicitly rejected racial self-help as an adequate solution and advocated measures "beyond the conventional rights-and-opportunities approach of the past." Whitney Young's Marshall Plan of massive federal investment to improve the economic lot of urban African Americans, *Newsweek* hinted, would be a logical basis for government action.[25] *Newsweek* inflated the extent to which Moynihan initiated a "quiet revolution" in Johnson's civil rights policy. Similarly, *New Yorker* writer Richard Rovere mistakenly predicted that Johnson would press for a "Marshall Plan" of "long-term subsidy for the entire Negro community."[26]

The report appealed to some on the left. Socialist Michael Harrington hailed the report in a newspaper column as proof the U.S. needed the Freedom Budget advocated by civil rights leaders: "As the Moynihan Report makes plain, unemployment and under-employment are fundamental to the problems of the Negro family."[27] Similarly, in January 1966, Victor Navasky praised *The Negro Family* as a "call to action." He saw Moynihan's grim depiction of black family instability as offering a form of "democratic shock treatment" designed to "incite social change."[28]

Unsurprisingly given the influence of Catholic social thought on Moynihan, the Catholic press was the most consistent and vocal source of support for reformulating civil rights policy around the family. Catholic journalists believed the report endorsed family allowances, a policy of federal government payments to all families with dependent children. Moynihan actively sought Catholic support with a September 1965 article in the Jesuit journal *America*. In "Family Policy for the Nation," Moynihan endorsed a system of universal family allowances paid to all Americans with children as an alternative to welfare, claiming it would especially benefit African Americans.[29] An editorial greeted Moynihan's article as evidence of "Growing Support for Family Allowances." "Far from deeming them radical," the editors concluded, "socially literate Catholics accept [family allowances] as a logical application in our times of the Church's insistence on a family living wage."[30] At least one *America* reader saw family allowances as a means to circumvent divisive Catholic debates over birth control by providing families of any size with necessary resources.[31]

Catholic journalists saw family instability as evidence of social injustice and called for measures specifically directed at alleviating African American inequality. *America* editors advocated "swift, uncompromising national action in favor of Negro family structures." They asserted that African American family instability was the moral responsibility of the white community for its "grievous sin" of slavery and concluded that urban riots resulted from a "whirlwind that we prepared."[32] Similarly, a multi-part series in the *St. Louis Review*, published by the St. Louis Archdiocese, saw the report as advocating a domestic Marshall Plan in addition to a universal system of family allowances.[33] The *Catholic Family Leader*, bulletin of the natalist Family Life Bureau, acquired stacks of the report, which it sold for 45 cents to subscribers who were "expected to have a particular interest in it." It concluded that one of the rights owed African American citizens was "the right to a decent, stable family life." It implored whites to accept responsibility for "centuries of degradation" of black families.[34]

Catholic support for *The Negro Family* suggests that Moynihan's professed strategy of gaining support for liberal social programs by highlighting family issues met some success. Yet this strategy backfired among many conservative commentators, who immediately deployed the report's arguments to rationalize African American inequality and set the stage for the widespread conservative appropriation of the report in the 1980s. Conservatives believed the report implied that African Americans must rely on their own efforts to progress. Both Southern segregationists and Northern conservatives seized on Moynihan's depiction of black family instability to argue against a domestic Marshall Plan.

Government officials correctly predicted that segregationists would misuse the Moynihan Report. The leading segregationist organization, the White Citizens' Council, was so impressed by *The Negro Family* that it advertised photocopies for sale in its publication *The Citizen* for $1 (when it could be bought from the GPO for 45 cents). *The Citizen* advertisement rejected what it saw as Moynihan's policy solution, a domestic Marshall Plan, but maintained, "the factual information contained in the report far outweighs the erroneous conclusions drawn by its authors." Titled "'Secret' Government Report 'The Negro Family' Now Available!" the advertisement implied that the government suppressed *The Negro Family* because it undermined liberal racial policies. *The Citizen* suggested that biological inferiority explained why African Americans were "not equal to most of those groups with which they will be competing."[35]

Similarly, Birmingham, Alabama, journalist Albert C. Persons cited the Moynihan Report in a 1965 post-Watts pamphlet, *Riot!*, in which he sought to discredit civil rights gains by painting crude racial stereotypes of blacks as uncivilized and violent. To Persons, Moynihan's statistics demonstrated, "the composite Negro in American society can be identified as an individual who quite possibly was born out of wedlock and grew up wild on the streets of some large city." According to Persons, Moynihan proved that "no phony legislation purporting to guarantee social equality" could address the root cause of rioting: the deterioration of the "Negro-American social fabric."[36] Likewise, a letter to the editor printed in the *Arkansas Democrat* in Little Rock, Arkansas, site of a famous 1957 conflict over school integration, used the report to argue against desegregation: "These statistics—by Northern liberals, not Southern fanatics—prove that the Negro problem is far more complicated and deserves a better solution than mixing the children with whites in the public schools. The change should begin at home, not in the public schools."[37]

Conservative journalists' adoption of the Moynihan Report was more significant than that of Southern segregationists, whose open racism was quickly becoming discredited. An August 1965 front-page article in the nation's leading business newspaper, *Wall Street Journal*, indicated how conservatives exploited the report's emphasis on perceived problems within the African American community. "Behind the Riots: Family Life Sows Seeds of Race Violence" cited the Moynihan Report and interviews with sociologists to explain the Watts uprising as resulting from "family breakdown." Concentrating on how African American families deviated from a middle-class ideal, the article glossed over the event that sparked the uprising as a "routine police incident." (This was almost certainly not a reference to the commonplace nature of police brutality against African Americans.) Citing sociological authorities that "husbandless homes spawn young hoodlums," the article concluded that government could hardly address the problems of Watts residents. Family instability was "a sickness that all the new civil rights legislation is powerless to cure."[38]

Conservatives interpreted *The Negro Family* as advocating racial self-help. A July editorial in the *Wall Street Journal* responded to Johnson's Howard address by dismissing civil rights demonstrations and government poverty programs as useless. Instead, African Americans needed to change their "prevailing culture" marked by "disintegration of family life, lack of good example and negation of such success-oriented values as education, ambition, responsibility, and self-respect." Promoting racial self-help, the editors proclaimed that successful African Americans had to "enlighten even the most downtrodden Negro to the middle-class outlook."[39] Other journalists followed the *Wall Street Journal*'s lead. Syndicated columnist Richard Wilson, commenting on the report, assigned "primary responsibility" for African American advancement to "the complacent, satisfied, well-to-do Negro middle class." Wilson summarized, "the problems which now are faced do not lend themselves to statutory solutions nor constitutional interpretations. It is a question whether or not anything can be done at all."[40]

Ralph de Toledano, a founder of *National Review*, the leading journal of postwar conservatism, turned to the report to explain the Watts uprising. Moynihan, he claimed, "showed clearly that much of what is laid to the 'white power structure' or 'discrimination' was due to ills within the Negro community that could not be cured by civil rights acts, voting rights measures, or increased job opportunities." De Toledano found the report "so convincing" on this point that he accused the Johnson administration of being "afraid" to release it.[41] In a later column, he claimed that government programs targeted at reducing racial inequality would in fact unequally privilege blacks at the expense of other Americans, since Moynihan had shown that African American poverty resulted from a defective culture. Marking a shift toward rhetoric of "reverse racism" among defenders of white privilege, de Toledano claimed liberals would grant black baseball players "four strikes when at bat, to compensate for their socially underprivileged status in our society." That this column by de Toledano, a New York Jew, appeared in the *Huntsville News*, suggested that Northern conservatives and Southern segregationists were converging on their explanations for African American inequality.[42] De Toledano's arguments were a minority strain in initial debates over the Moynihan Report, but would become a dominant one by the 1980s. As overt racism based on notions of biological difference lost potency, the Moynihan Report's focus on family provided conservatives with a new, sociological justification for racial inequality.

Moynihan and his supporters later blamed the press for misreading his report, but those who thought the report advocated racial self-help believed they had interpreted it correctly. For instance, *Washington Star* columnist Mary McGrory, a personal acquaintance of Moynihan and fellow Irish American, saw even the Howard speech as a call for racial self-help, declaring, "the time has come for [Negroes] to come to grips with their own worst problem, 'the breakdown of Negro family life.'"[43] When Moynihan reprimanded Mc-Grory for misrepresenting the report, she sarcastically retorted, "In my severely retarded way, I had thought that the *contents* of the report has something to do with its reception."[44]

Journalists who portrayed the Moynihan Report as a case for racial self-help alarmed civil rights critics, as did media stories that reinforced racial stereotypes. Celebrated journalist Theodore White was the first to use the report, in his bestselling book, *The Making of the Presidency—1964*, published in July 1965. White relied heavily on Moynihan's statistics and analysis for his chapter on the 1964 Harlem riots. In 1964, Moynihan shared with White data on African American families, and he later read drafts of White's chapters. As White was finishing his book in the spring of 1965, he obtained a copy of *The Negro Family* from the White House.[45]

White's explanation for the Harlem riots was simple: "biological anarchy—a decomposition of family life and family discipline which simply cannot be contained in the traditional forms of American democracy or orderly politics." Citing Moynihan's statistics on out-of-wedlock births, White decried "a pattern of mating and breeding which imposes so large and growing a population of illegitimate, yet innocent, children who mature from indifference to violence." Many Harlem residents, he concluded, did not "adhere to the common standards of American culture and Western morality." African Americans, he claimed, were dividing into two groups: "one that is beginning to achieve, and another that is threatened with collapse of all human values, all dignity, all function." White's dehumanizing language of "biological anarchy," "mating and breeding," "junior savages," and "zoological tenements" fitted racist tropes dating back centuries.[46]

White's analysis crucially influenced the reception of *The Negro Family*. For example, a September *U.S. News and World Report* story on the Moynihan Report quoted White's book extensively.[47] White offered conservatives a reason to deny white responsibility for African American poverty. Citing White in his commentary on the report, newspaper columnist Richard Wilson claimed that government action would be ineffective since "biological anarchy may have gone too far."[48] White's explanation for the Harlem riots, which wholly targeted perceived flaws among African American families while ignoring the broader economic and political context, anticipated racist understandings of the Watts uprising that explicitly evoked the stereotype of the "black savage." Los Angeles police chief William Parker compared African

Americans to "monkeys in a zoo," while national columnist George Todt attributed the Watts rebellion to "weak character traits in uncivilized human beings who yielded to their savage emotions in a barbaric display of ill will and hate."[49]

In *The Negro Family*, Moynihan eschewed loaded language of the kind used by White. Nevertheless, the fact that Moynihan aided White in writing his chapter means that Moynihan stood indirectly responsible for the dehumanizing accounts of African American social life offered by White and other journalists. Moynihan should have seen how easily the sociological data presented in *The Negro Family* could be used to support racist tropes of "uncivilized" blacks, but his relative inexperience with racial issues and optimism that the racist "virus" infecting Americans was fast disappearing rendered him unaware of the power of stereotypes.

Mainstream press accounts of the Moynihan Report frequently echoed racist depictions of blacks as uncivilized and violent, even those that endorsed a Marshall Plan remedy to racial inequalities. The August 1965 *Newsweek* article, which Moynihan felt adequately captured his views, ran a photo captioned: "Harlem street scene: a time bomb ticks in the ghetto." The image depicts four unsupervised African American teenagers walking on a rubble-filled street. One appears to throw a rock in the direction of the camera.[50]

Surprisingly, given the report's use in bolstering racist stereotypes, it initially received positive coverage in the African American press. A syndicated October column appearing in major black newspapers including the *Chicago Defender* and *Pittsburgh Courier* remarked that in the report, "we [African Americans] have come to see pretty well verified what we know about ourselves and our conditions." The writer, G. C. Oden, lamented that it was "unpleasant to accept that some 25 percent of our notoriously churched people are illegitimate." Surprisingly, given how many African Americans came to see the Moynihan Report as a slander against their race, Oden interpreted *The Negro Family* as a cause for racial pride. Accepting Moynihan's analysis of how slavery destroyed African culture, he quoted the report that "a lesser people might simply have died out." To Oden, Moynihan underlined African Americans' ability to survive horrendous oppression, and thus provided them a "basis for pride in ourselves."[51]

The African American *Philadelphia Tribune* ran a sympathetic five-part series on the Moynihan Report. Reporter Jacob Sherman thought Moynihan clearly held white Americans responsible for African American family instability; he called *The Negro Family* "one of the most blistering indictments this nation has ever had to face."[52] Sherman's account also indicated that many middle-class African Americans, the newspaper's primary readership, endorsed the report's account of lower-class black pathology. Sherman's account was as lurid as those found in white newspapers:

> Statistics are cold things. They do not describe the misery, dejection, and hopelessness which the ghetto dweller strives against day to day. Nor do they suggest the smell of the filthy hovels he has to live in. The rising and falling line of a graph says nothing of the despair which can only be drowned out in the corner taproom. Neither does it speak of the frustration which finds its release in a woman's body.[53]

This depiction undercut Sherman's effort to hold white Americans accountable for black poverty. Ultimately, he came to the same conclusion as conservatives: black family instability was a "problem to which all the laws in the world are not going to make a dent."

By the end of 1965, some African American newspapers turned against the Moynihan Report. A December 1965 editorial in the *Chicago Defender* warned that the report undermined Johnson's plea in his Howard speech for whites to view blacks with an "understanding heart." The report's "grim" and "exaggerated" statistics created the misimpression that "Negroes tolerate promiscuity, illegitimacy, one-parent families, and welfare dependency."[54] The editorial cited William Ryan, Moynihan's most influential challenger, indicating how critics in the civil rights movement had altered discussion of the report. Nevertheless, the report still received positive coverage from many black journalists, as in a January, 1966 editorial in the middle-class magazine, *Ebony*, which praised *The Negro Family* for offering liberal social measures to help ensure that black families would have, as the article was titled, "A Man Around the House."[55] Like the African American press, civil rights leaders were divided in their responses to the report.

Dangers and Opportunities

Martin Luther King, Jr., claimed that newfound public attention to black family instability sparked by the Moynihan Report contained both "dangers and opportunities." In an October, 1965 speech, he explained, "The opportunity will be to deal fully rather than haphazardly with the problem as a whole—to see it as a social catastrophe and meet it as other disasters are met with an adequacy of resources. The danger will be that the problems will be attributed to innate Negro weaknesses and used to justify neglect and rationalize oppression."[56] King understood that an ideological struggle would define the report's impact. While some civil rights leaders saw it as an opening to expand the discussion of racial equality to social and economic issues, others worried that it denied white responsibility by urging racial self-help.

King largely saw the report as an opportunity. He responded to the report at a time when he was moving toward more direct engagement with African American inequality in Northern cities; in January 1966, his Southern Christian Leadership Conference announced a major campaign in Chicago. Without mentioning the report by name, King quoted statistics from *The Negro Family* on divorce rates and out-of-wedlock births among African Americans and endorsed Moynihan's "alarming conclusion that the Negro family is crumbling and disintegrating." Like Moynihan, King decried the "matriarchal" family structure of many black families and pointed to the history of slavery and urban migration to explain the "shattering blows" they suffered. Recognizing these facts about African American family life, King argued, could focus attention on alleviating "pervasive and persistent economic want," especially that faced by black men who needed decent jobs to enjoy the "authority of fatherhood."[57] King's description of the "Negro family" as "fragile, deprived, and often psychopathic" illustrated how pervasive pathologist language was during the mid-1960s. King did not change his perspective after the report came under heavy criticism, delivering a nearly identical version of his speech in Chicago in January titled "The Negro Family: A Challenge to National Action" in reference to the report.[58]

The Urban League was Moynihan's staunchest supporter among civil rights organizations. Long concerned with urban poverty, the League was dominated by middle-class African Americans who hoped to uplift poorer African Americans economically and morally. They saw male-headed nuclear families as symbols of racial progress and concurred with Moynihan's depiction of lower-class African American life as marked by a "tangle of pathology." Tellingly, the most common Urban League criticism of the report was that Moynihan treated African American families without differentiation as *the* Negro family. By stressing that better-off African Americans hued to middle-class standards, Urban League leaders affirmed their own dignity and status. Unlike civil rights leaders inspired by left-wing views of equality as the abolition of class injustice, Urban League leaders were more likely to agree with Moynihan's ideal of "equality of results" for African Americans that meant a class distribution similar to that of other ethnoracial groups.

They affirmed Moynihan's depiction of lower-class African American life as marked by a "tangle of pathology." Urban League president Whitney Young was one of the report's strongest advocates. In an October 1965 installment of his weekly column (widely syndicated in black papers), Young proudly trumpeted the report's long quotation from his 1964 book, *To Be Equal*. For Young, *The Negro Family* signaled that "President Johnson intends to hit hard on the issue of the Negro male" by introducing the kinds of jobs, training, education, and housing programs that Young advocated in his domestic Marshall Plan.[59] Young toned down his praise after the report was criticized. In a January 1966 column, he decried the report's misuse by conservatives and criticized its implication that *all* African Americans suffered from family "pathology." Nevertheless, Young continued to back Moynihan. He maintained that critics misunderstood the "real message of the report": the need to alleviate black male unemployment's "effects which go beyond the economic, harming the social fabric of family life."[60]

Other Urban League leaders backed Moynihan. Chicago chapter officials discussed the report in two special meetings and welcomed it for drawing attention to an issue that already concerned them.[61] Moynihan received letters of support from directors of the Cleveland and Detroit chapters. The latter began a research project on the "Detroit Low-Income Black Family" that followed Moynihan's lead, despite his concern that *The Negro Family* "puts all Negroes of all classes regardless of their economic, social, or cultural status together."[62]

Urban League officials appreciated the report's focus on Northern cities. Southern civil rights leaders, however, criticized its call for a new stage of civil rights struggle for falsely implying that African Americans had achieved formal equality. In 1965, despite successful litigation and legislation, many Southern schools and other public facilities remained segregated. The federal government had not yet vigorously enforced equal employment measures, many communities still denied African Americans the vote, and no national law had been passed to prohibit housing discrimination. Thus, an aide to Vice President Hubert Humphrey incensed civil rights leaders when, during a private conference, he cited the Moynihan Report to deflect their demands for more federal registrars to enforce voting rights in the South. Family structure, the aide implied, was a more serious problem than disenfranchisement.[63]

In the run-up to the November White House Conference, the National Association for the Advancement of Colored People pressed the administration to remain focused on achieving full legal and political rights for African Americans, the organization's long-standing goals. Despite seeing value in "recent emphasis on . . . family disorganization, weakened social values, and ghetto demoralization," NAACP officials advised conference planners not to divert energy from "'purely' civil rights" battles. Talk of a new stage in the movement, they argued, gave the misimpression that civil rights battles were "all over but the shouting."[64] NAACP leaders were also disturbed by the report's implication that they should abandon political protest and focus on racial self-help. In a December newspaper column, NAACP chief lobbyist Clarence Mitchell complained that some administration officials "seemed to think that this writing [the Moynihan Report] was so challenging that civil rights groups should stop picketing, stop marching, stop suit filing, stop lobbying—in fact stop everything that they had done in the past and begin concentrating on improving family life among colored people."[65]

Even civil rights leaders who endorsed the administration's new focus on black family instability were skeptical of the Moynihan Report because they doubted the Johnson administration was fully committed to addressing the problem. Robert Carter, NAACP general counsel, was puzzled by the "great shock" over the Moynihan Report, which he thought told an "old story" that the "pathologies of the ghetto . . . are a result of discrimination." However, Carter doubted Johnson would provide African Americans the economic resources needed to form stable families: "My question is, is the Administration really prepared to do these things? President Johnson's [Howard] speech . . . was very good. The problem is whether or not he is now willing to carry out what he said he would do."[66]

At first glance, it was surprising that Bayard Rustin became a leading critic of Moynihan. The report favorably quoted Rustin's call for achieving the "*fact* of equality." Like Moynihan, Rustin strongly advocated bolstering patriarchal nuclear families through paying all American men a family wage. Rustin was also firmly committed to coalition politics with white liberals. In 1965, he became head of the A. Philip Randolph Institute funded by the major American labor federation, the AFL-CIO. Rustin played a key role advising the organizers of the White House Conference on Civil Rights, acting on behalf of the septuagenarian Randolph, the conference's honorary chair. In fact, he initially endorsed structuring the conference around the topic of "Negro

Family Life" provided that it dealt with measures to secure "the economic stability of the Negro family head."[67]

Had the Moynihan Report unequivocally backed social-democratic measures like those in the Freedom Budget, Rustin would have enthusiastically supported it. (In fact, Moynihan later declined Rustin's request that he endorse the Freedom Budget.)[68] However, as Rustin made publicly clear in two 1966 magazine articles directed at white liberal audiences, he believed the report was "presented in a form guaranteed to promote confusion" and vulnerable to conservative appropriation. Rustin challenged Moynihan's focus on the internal weakness of African Americans as a group. Regardless of Moynihan's good intentions, many whites would interpret its message as: "just have Negroes put their own house in order!"[69] He also doubted Moynihan's commitment to the scale of measures needed to create more black male breadwinners. The report, he thought, was "ambivalent about the basic reforms that are needed." Liberals like Moynihan, Rustin concluded, lacked "the political will to demand that the vast resources of contemporary America be used to build a genuinely great society that will finally put an end to . . . deprivation."[70] For Rustin, attacking the Moynihan Report enabled him to express criticisms of the Johnson administration that he preferred not to voice directly.

Among national civil rights leaders, James Farmer delivered the sharpest attack on the Moynihan Report. Farmer directed the quarter-century old Northern civil rights organization he co-founded, Congress of Racial Equality, and was known for organizing militant direct action tactics such as the 1961 Freedom Rides. In October 1965, Farmer opposed making "family stability" a key item on the White House Conference agenda, believing it to be a secondary issue.[71] In December, he lambasted the Moynihan Report in a two-part installment of his regular column for black newspapers. The report, Farmer concluded, was "the most serious threat to the ultimate freedom of American Negroes to appear in print in recent memory." Farmer thought the document excused government inaction. He derided it as a "massive cop-out for the white conscience" that "clearly implied that Negroes in this nation will never secure a substantial measure of freedom until we learn to behave ourselves and stop buying Cadillacs instead of bread." Attacking the report's objectification of African Americans and the Johnson administration's lack of meaningful action, Farmer declared, "we are sick unto death of being analyzed, mesmerized, bought, sold, and slobbered over while the same evils that are the ingredients of our oppression go unattended."[72]

Compared with King's qualified endorsement of the report and Young's ringing defense of it, Farmer's passionate attack suggests just how differently national civil rights leaders assessed the political dangers and opportunities presented by the report. Yet, the most influential challenge to the Moynihan Report came not from top officials, but from the rank-and-file. Farmer's claim that the report was "fast becoming the scriptural basis for several new forms of bigotry" reflected the critique of William Ryan, a white activist without national prominence who first charged that *The Negro Family* represented the emergence of a new form of racism.

Blaming the Victim

Reading about *The Negro Family* in *Newsweek* made Boston activist and psychologist William Ryan agitated. The report sounded like a new rationalization of African American inequality. On his own initiative, Ryan wrote a long memo disputing Moynihan's findings, dubbed it the "Ryan Report," and addressed to "Anyone Interested." Ryan mailed fifty copies to personal contacts and important figures in the civil rights movement. The memo wound up in the files of every major civil rights organization. As interest grew, Ryan mailed an additional hundred copies by request. In November, the liberal weekly, *The Nation*, published a barely revised version of the Ryan Report as its cover story; the NAACP magazine, *The Crisis*, published a slightly different version in December.[73]

Ryan's background resembled Moynihan's. He was an Irish Catholic, a lifelong liberal Democrat whose politics were shaped by his childhood support for the New Deal, and a World War II veteran who benefited from the GI Bill to become the first person in his family to attend college. However, Ryan's local civil rights activism distinguished his liberalism from Moynihan's technocratic variety. He not only enlisted his psychological expertise in the civil rights cause, but was a member of CORE and well known by local NAACP activists.[74] His experience with widespread racial discrimination in education and housing made him skeptical of Moynihan for discounting racism's role in preserving racial inequality in Northern cities.

Ryan's critique generated the phrase that became inextricably linked to the Moynihan Report controversy: "blaming the victim." Ryan challenged Moynihan's focus on the alleged internal weaknesses of African Americans rather than on systemic racism. *The Negro Family*, he charged, "seduces the

reader into believing that it is not racism and discrimination but the weaknesses and defects of the Negro himself that account for the present status of
inequality between Negro and white."[75] While Ryan did not use the phrase
"blaming the victim" in 1965, composing the Ryan Report led him to write
his influential 1971 book *Blaming the Victim*, which reprised his critique of
the Moynihan Report and identified other instances in which social analysts
ignored systemic roots of social inequality.[76]

Ryan was so alert to the Moynihan Report's dangers because he had already begun to formulate the concept of "blaming the victim." His 1964 study
of the Boston school system for a liberal advocacy organization anticipated
his analysis of Moynihan. Ryan refuted cultural deprivation theory, which
argued that African American schoolchildren's low cultural capital explained
their poor academic performances. As one school official told Ryan, "We don't
have inferior schools, we've been getting an inferior type of student."[77] Ryan
charged that by focusing on black students' alleged defects, cultural deprivation theorists rationalized the paucity of resources allocated to majority-
black schools. "The schools," he claimed, "are culturally depriving rather than
that the children are culturally deprived." The "de facto segregated education" common in Northern cities was "inherently unequal," and students suffered from "outright prejudice and neglect on the part of teachers and school
authorities."[78] Moynihan's argument that *family* was the key to racial inequality struck Ryan as similar to what one school official told him regarding black
schoolchildren: "the problem is with the parents."[79] Ryan also thought the
language of "cultural deprivation" simply updated racial stereotypes: "The
term 'cultural deprivation' is rapidly becoming itself a stereotyped term,
almost equivalent to 'Negro.' . . . This term differs little, if it all, from the now
largely-discarded theoretical basis for opposing school integration: innate
Negro inferiority."[80]

Ryan viewed the Moynihan Report through the lens of cultural deprivation theory and saw it as recasting long-standing stereotypes of African Americans in sociological guise. He contended that the report "encourages the
development of a burgeoning form of subtle racism." He faulted Moynihan
for emphasizing out-of-wedlock births among African Americans without
delving into the context of institutionalized discrimination that created them.
Moynihan gave ammunition to journalists engaged in "the popular new sport
of Savage Discovery . . . savages are being discovered in great profusion in the
Northern ghetto—the favorite being the promiscuous AFDC mother with a
litter of illegitimate brats." Ryan feared that there was "serious danger that

the popularizations of the 'Moynihan Report'—if not the document itself—will provide fat fodder for this new racist ideology." He was particularly troubled by Theodore White's "offensive discussion of 'biological anarchy' and 'zoological tenements' in Negro slums," which he recognized was based on *The Negro Family*.[81]

Ryan also challenged the reliability and suitability of Moynihan's statistics. He anticipated later critics who questioned whether out-of-wedlock births accurately measured "family instability" and "family breakdown." He especially questioned the accuracy of the report's data on out-of-wedlock births, echoing concerns that Bureau of Labor Statistics officials expressed privately to Moynihan. Ryan thought racial bias distorted Moynihan's government-collected data. For example, Moynihan neglected facts that African Americans, as compared with whites, had reduced access to birth control, abortion, and adoption, and more likely lacked the economic resources for marriage. (While unwed white mothers during this period were frequently pressured to surrender babies for adoption, African American women had few such opportunities.)[82] Ryan pointed out that government data underreported out-of-wedlock births for whites, who more easily convinced medical authorities to overlook parental marital status. He similarly challenged Moynihan's claim that the majority of violent crimes in the U.S. were "probably" committed by African Americans, contending that Moynihan's uncritical use of arrest rates ignored widespread racial profiling by police. To Ryan, Moynihan's data, skewed by institutional racism, falsely attributed racial inequality to African Americans' cultural weaknesses.

Ryan criticized as "copping a plea" Moynihan's attention to the legacy of slavery and racism and neglect of contemporary racism: "Liberal America today is pleading guilty. . . . to the savagery and oppression against the Negro that happened 100 years ago, in order to escape trial for the crimes of today." Like Moynihan, Ryan advocated jobs programs and other measures to reduce racial inequality. Unlike Moynihan, Ryan did not conceive of such programs as efforts at improving African Americans' competitiveness. Instead, Ryan argued for direct reparations to African Americans "analogous to legal and theological concepts of restitution." "For the millions of grown and half-grown Negro Americans who have already been damaged," he argued, "we must compensate for the injury we did to them."

Ryan participated in a growing radicalization of the civil rights movement, which reacted against the limitations of liberal policy. He pointedly claimed that the new racism was "accepted by liberal and conservative alike."

And he expressed an increasingly common frustration among civil rights activists that the Johnson administration substituted talk for action: "We seem to be spending more energy on *explaining* [racial] inequality than in doing something about it."[83] That Ryan's critique resonated so strongly suggested that many others in the civil rights movement were also predisposed to view the Moynihan Report with suspicion.

Given his lack of national stature, Ryan needed prominent allies to amplify his critique of Moynihan. His memo achieved influence largely through the National Council of Churches (NCC), the major organization of mainline Protestantism in the U.S. and a pillar of establishment liberalism. Anna Hedgeman, a well-connected veteran civil rights activist at the Council, distributed Ryan's report to scores of politicians and civil rights leaders. Hedgeman already disliked Glazer and Moynihan's *Beyond the Melting Pot*. She was also likely critical of the report's emphasis on male family dominance. The only woman on the planning committee for the 1963 March on Washington, Hedgeman pushed for greater involvement by women in civil rights leadership.[84]

Hedgeman worked for the Commission on Race and Religion, which the NCC established in 1963 to support civil rights struggles in the South. By the summer of 1964, the New York-based Commission redirected their attention to the North, where they recognized that the struggle for racial equality required employment, housing, and antipoverty measures. Council members needed no convincing to see racial inequality in socioeconomic terms, but they proved key opponents of Moynihan's attempt to formulate the next stage of civil rights policy around family stability.[85]

Hedgeman forwarded the Ryan Report to the second most influential critic of the report: Benjamin Payton, a rising star in civil rights and Protestant circles. Payton, an African American, was educated at Harvard Divinity School, Columbia, and Yale. In 1963, at thirty-one, he was appointed director of the Office of Religion and Race of the Protestant Council of the City of New York, a citywide ecumenical organization with strong ties to the NCC. Concerned by newspaper coverage of *The Negro Family*, Payton began drafting a critique before he received a copy of the Ryan Report, which he relied on to finish. On October 14, Payton sent hundreds of copies of his paper, "The President, the Social Experts, and the Ghetto: An Analysis of an Emerging Strategy in Civil Rights," to contacts in universities. Payton's memo served as the basis for resolutions adopted by the New York Pre-White House Conference Planning Group, which met on November 9 and decided to press for the removal of "family stability" from the conference agenda. As with Ryan, Payton's pointed attack on the Moynihan Report indicated growing discontent with the Johnson administration and Moynihan's brand of liberalism.[86]

It is obvious from his footnotes that Payton had not read *The Negro Family*, which he erroneously claimed had not been publicly released. Instead, Payton based his analysis on press reports and Ryan's memo. Payton's reliance on second-hand information produced an effect similar to the childhood game of grapevine, where players whisper a phrase in another's ear and it becomes increasingly distorted. For example, Payton proposed as *alternatives* to the Moynihan Report measures that Moynihan advocated such as jobs programs targeted at black men. Nevertheless, it is incorrect to conclude that there were no "intellectual grounds" for Payton's critique.[87] Payton did more than simply articulate the common civil rights criticism that Johnson failed to honor his Howard speech commitments with adequate policies. Like Ryan, Payton argued that Moynihan's emphasis on improving black social structure neglected racist policies. For example, Payton regarded policies that aided the growth of suburbs as detrimental to African Americans. Shifting industry to the suburbs drained jobs from central cities where African Americans were concentrated. Meanwhile, suburban authorities, careful to employ a color-blind "rhetoric of liberalism," found ways to exclude African American residents. "Racial antagonism," Payton observed, "is expressed not only through the use of bomb and burning cross, but through control of zoning, subdivision, and building regulations."[88]

Payton challenged the technocratic nature of Moynihan's liberalism by advocating the democratic participation of ordinary individuals. To Payton, the Moynihan Report embodied how out of touch policy-makers were. "The important moral issue at stake," Payton asserted, "is whether social experts can relate to private citizens *as persons* or merely *as objects*."[89] Payton voiced a growing discontent with how white liberals had dominated racial discourse. Likely drawing on Ralph Ellison's recently published critique of *An American Dilemma*, Payton singled out for criticism Gunnar Myrdal's assertion that black culture was a "pathological" variant of white American culture. Payton claimed that white liberals such as Myrdal and Moynihan were "unable to appreciate the need for local community action on the part of *Negroes themselves*." They saw African Americans not as agents in their own right but as objects to "be acted upon, by the social experts, the federal government, and patron benefactors."[90] In contrast, Payton advocated the local involvement of African Americans in federally funded social programs. He sought programs "harnessed under Negro leadership but with larger and more relevant national resources and co-operation."[91]

Payton's memo articulated a growing anger among African American leaders at the power high-placed white experts such as Moynihan had to define African American life. It anticipated his embrace of a pluralist, non-separatist version of Black Power that stressed African Americans building an independent political and intellectual base. In 1966, Payton co-wrote a statement by black ministers published in the *New York Times* that initiated the Black Theology movement.[92] Like Payton, some white liberals increasingly recognized the need for African Americans to lead the ongoing struggle for black equality. Just a month after writing his memo, Payton took charge of the NCC's Commission on Race and Religion because of concern that the commission had previously been white-dominated.[93]

The crucial role played by the NCC in opposing the Moynihan Report suggests an overlooked religious dimension to the controversy. The leading journal of liberal Protestantism, *Christianity and Crisis*, also joined the fray. In December 1965, it printed Payton's "New Trends in Civil Rights," which updated his critique of *The Negro Family* after he read the report.[94] In February 1966, *Christianity and Crisis* printed "Fissures in the Civil Rights Movement" by Robert Spike, who preceded Payton as head of the NCC Office on Race and Religion. To Spike, the Moynihan Report symbolized the moral bankruptcy of consensus liberalism. He sided with African Americans "infuriated by benevolent and patronizing attempts to improve their personhood (defective because of their pathological family life)." Moynihan's promised "panacea" of bolstering black family stability hid "how cold the power-brokers are to spending real money to help the millions of Americans devastated by our crippling discrimination." Declaring "a revolution in human freedom can not be engineered," Spike seconded Payton's critique of technocratic liberalism and allied himself with "those who see no good thing coming out of the white liberal schemata, those who want far more radical solutions," such as SNCC militants and the growing white New Left. Spike's essay demonstrated how the Moynihan Report controversy spurred the rapid radicalization of some liberals.[95]

Some contemporaries recognized the controversy's religious subtext. Moynihan confided to a Jesuit sociologist that his report had "hit a Protestant nerve."[96] The NCC role in discrediting the report prompted leading Protestant theologian Harvey Cox to worry that the dispute would be seen as a "Catholic versus Protestant controversy."[97] In fact, Catholics were more likely to share Moynihan's view of the family as the basic unit of society, to view it as a proper subject of government policy, and to accept without question the male-breadwinner family model. Liberal Protestants more likely worried that government family policy imposed morality through state intervention. Lacking the tradition of Catholic social teaching, Protestants such as Payton missed the report's possible social-democratic implication of universal family allowances. Instead, they incorrectly assumed Moynihan advocated programs to reform African American family morality through social work.

The dispute hardly divided neatly along Catholic/Protestant lines, and the prominent role of liberal Protestants in attacking the report revealed a growing rift in liberal Protestantism. Conflict over the Moynihan Report exacerbated divisions between those aligned with militant social movements, like Payton and Spike, and those who continued to seek pragmatic social reforms in the tradition of Reinhold Niebuhr, the most influential American postwar theologian. When Moynihan wrote to Niebuhr to protest his treatment by Payton and Spike, Niebuhr temporarily resigned from the magazine he founded, *Christianity and Crisis*, and withdrew his name from the masthead.[98]

The report's early civil rights critics pioneered the concept of "institutional racism" that would shape subsequent analysis of the report. Unlike many later critics, however, they shared Moynihan's views that social pathology marked lower-class African American life and that male breadwinners should head families. None noted the positive value in African American family structures that deviated from the patriarchal nuclear family norm, as did future critics. Tellingly, Rustin, Farmer, Ryan, and Payton contrasted the Moynihan Report unfavorably with the work of E. Franklin Frazier. While Moynihan's later critics attacked Frazier for initiating a pejorative analysis of African American social pathology, his early critics believed that Frazier (but not Moynihan) advocated the kind of social-democratic programs needed to rebuild male-headed black families. Farmer challenged the notion that Moynihan was the first to speak candidly about the problems of African American families, asserting that civil rights leaders for a decade had been trying to force white Americans to see "the plight of American Negroes . . . as a hard fact of life."[99] He employed pathologist language in insisting that many African Americans experienced a "living Hell." Unlike later critics who recognized African American agency, Ryan saw poor African Americans as victims. His objection was to *blaming* the victim. In a 1967 article, Ryan even referred to the "tangle of pathology . . . that accompanies ghetto poverty," using the same phrase notoriously associated with the Moynihan Report.[100]

Rustin, Farmer, Payton, and Ryan offered biting criticisms of the Moynihan Report, but notably none called Moynihan a "racist." In fact, nearly all Moynihan's early critics refrained from questioning his motives or character. Ryan clarified that his concern was with the report's possible uses, not Moynihan's motivations. He claimed he had "no reason to consider Dr. Moynihan himself any variety of racist or to doubt the compassionate nature of his intentions."[101] Rustin declared that it was "unfair to charge Moynihan with being a racist, open or covert" and Payton averred that "the errors of the report are not rooted in any racial hostility on the part of the authors."[102] Even Farmer's quip that Moynihan "did not consciously intend to write a racist tract" differed from later charges that Moynihan was an outright racist.[103]

Civil rights activists and leaders rightly focused not on Moynihan's intentions but on the report's impact upon the struggle for racial equality. Those critics who judged *The Negro Family* more of a danger than an opportunity pioneered the concept of "institutional racism." They saw not just the prejudice of the individual racist and the injustice of Jim Crow-style discrimination, but a broader and more systemic oppression. Moynihan's critics perceived a racism that rendered ostensibly objective government statistics racially biased and allowed a liberal advocate of civil rights to write a report that breathed new life into age-old racial stereotypes.

"One of Those Things Everyone Talks About"

Though the two most important critiques of *The Negro Family* circulated initially as unpublished papers, interest in the Moynihan Report spread well beyond intellectual and political elites. The GPO sold more than 70,000 copies of the report, an extraordinarily high number given that it lacked the marketing and distribution resources of commercial publishers. Several major publishing houses approached Moynihan about printing the report, including one that wanted to combine his text with photographs of poor African Americans in the manner of James Agee and Walker Evans's classic, *Let Us Now Praise Famous Men.*[104]

The Moynihan Report sank deeply into American consciousness. More than five hundred people turned out for a 1966 discussion of the Moynihan Report organized by an African American sorority in Chicago.[105] High school students wrote term papers about it. In a 1965 U.S. Court of Appeals case, Jewell Mazique, wife of a prominent African American doctor in Washington, D.C., cited the report. She claimed that allowing her husband to divorce her would contribute to the "deterioration" of the African American family, of which Moynihan had warned.[106] References to the report appeared in unexpected places. A theater critic claimed that George Bernard Shaw's controversial play, *Major Barbara*, was "the Moynihan Report of 1905."[107]

Hundreds of Americans wrote directly to Moynihan, either to obtain a copy of the report or to comment on media coverage of his views. Moynihan received letters from ministers, doctors, judges, social workers, teachers, librarians, high school and university students, city and state politicians, businesspeople, housewives, servicemen, and prisoners. A Prudential executive wanted several copies of the report to help survey the insurance market for African Americans. A Lutheran church official requested twenty copies for an adult education program, and the Oklahoma Human Rights Commission sought a dozen copies to distribute.[108] Ordinary citizens felt that simply procuring a copy of the report offered them access to important public policy deliberations from which they had been excluded. The report could not be obtained in the usual bookstores and libraries, and media reports continually referred to it as "secret" or "suppressed." As a woman from Rutherford, New Jersey, wrote to her priest, "For years now, it seems, I've been hearing about the Moynihan Report. It's one of those things everyone talks about and our brain-washed public is not permitted to see."[109]

Many private letters to Moynihan reflected the two major interpretations of the report evident in public debate: urging either "national action" or racial self-help. One citizen understood it as a blueprint for a government "program to attack poverty in the ghetto."[110] A San Jose city official described it as "a study of the social effects of poverty and unemployment."[111] Others emphasized the need for African Americans to solve their own problems. A man who claimed to be one-quarter black described the report as a wake-up call for African Americans "laboring under the delusion that everything must be done for them and they are not to do anything for themselves."[112] African American writer Abie Miller praised Moynihan for advocating racial self-help: "The real reason why the 'militants' jumped on you . . . is that your report hinted in the direction of the 'unthinkable': that there might be some things that we, ourselves, should do for ourselves, in addition to what we are asking others to do for us."[113]

Hate mail Moynihan received from white supremacists confirmed *The Negro Family*'s claim that the "racist virus in the American bloodstream still

afflicts us."[114] Though scientific racism had been discredited a generation earlier, many whites still believed that blacks were biologically inferior. One letter-
writer lectured Moynihan, "all men are *not* created equal and it is morally
wrong to preach it." He claimed that the decolonization of Congo proved that
Africans were "savages" who needed to be ruled by whites.[115] Similarly, a
letter signed "one of your haters" informed Moynihan that African Americans would be cannibals were it not for white tutelage.[116] An anonymous letter accused Moynihan of being a race traitor for concerning himself with black
families' welfare. It asked, "why don't you marry all of those poor negro
women and be a da da to their kids that seem to bother you so much?"[117] Another anonymous letter concluded simply, "Yes, I believe niggers, Irish, and
kikes are all in the same rotten class. You are a commie bastard and a pig."[118]

White Southerners challenged whether Moynihan, a Northern liberal, was
qualified to understand African Americans. For example, a South Carolin-
ian claiming his family's "slave-owning ancestry" as the basis of his authority asserted, "white society is not responsible for the African heritage that still
influences the lives of many slum dwellers. You cannot kill tribal memories
in a generation."[119] A Louisiana resident lectured, "To think that federal control, passing laws, or whatever bureaucratic foibles you manufacture can make
the negro advance many generations in a few short years is downright ridic-
ulous."[120] The quantity of hate mail Moynihan received was minimal compared to that garnered by African American public figures. Still, as he received
letters proclaiming him a traitor to the white race, he must have wondered
how anyone could accuse his report of fostering racism.

Other letters suggested that the report offered ammunition to white racists. Educator and writer Jonathan Kozol reported in a private letter forwarded
to Moynihan:

> One encounters repeatedly the bitter phenomenon of white bigots re-
> lying upon Moynihan to support or buttress their ugly views of Ne-
> gro people. I have run into this so frequently that it is almost
> axiomatic . . . that people who do not like Negroes, who do not want
> to place blame on the schools, and who above all are unhappy with
> the idea of integration . . . turn immediately to Moynihan—sometimes
> distorted, sometimes not—to provide academic ammunition.[121]

Some letters to Moynihan confirmed Kozol's fear and the apprehensions of
Ryan and others that the report helped construct a newer, subtler form of

racism that relied on sociological and cultural explanations rather than biological ones. A Gaithersburg, Maryland, resident interpreted the report as
contrasting middle-class "suburbanite" culture based on "education, employment, and the ideal of monogamous marriage" with a lower-class African
American culture based on "low-education and illiteracy, unemployment, and
the matriarchal family or illegitimacy." He enclosed a speech by Booker
T. Washington, a past African American leader who famously advocated
racial self-help.[122]

Though eugenics, like scientific racism, was intellectually discredited after World War II, many ordinary Americans recommended the sterilization
of some African American women in response to Moynihan. Following a 1966
Moynihan essay in *Look*, a woman from Charlottesville, Virginia, concluded
in a letter to the editor that contraception "would have prevented the unfortunate existence of those hordes of illegitimate children born daily to mothers with only animal-instinct intelligence." A resident of Spokane, Washington,
proposed that any woman who bore children out of wedlock should be per-
manently sterilized.[123] That a major national magazine printed these letters
suggested that their views were not considered too extreme. In fact, several U.S.
states operated mandatory sterilization programs for welfare recipients (publicly understood to be disproportionately African American). In a 1965 poll,
20 percent of Americans favored mandatory sterilization of unwed mothers
on state relief.[124]

Some advocated making birth control available to lower-class African
Americans out of genuine concern for their welfare. As one woman wrote to
Moynihan, African Americans "may be poor, but they are not stupid; very
few would choose the danger and pain of an abortion over the convenience
of the pill."[125] Yet, many who simply called for making birth control more
widely available on a voluntary basis voiced a strong prejudice against African Americans and the poor. One writer expounded, "Many families would
not be poor if they were to limit the number of their children to *their* earning power, or even in proportion to their health and general intelligence."[126]

Some sterilization advocates blamed liberals for providing "monetary in-
centive to frequent spawning," but others thought Moynihan agreed with
them.[127] He did not. Moynihan retorted to one advocate of forced sterilization for unmarried mothers that the idea was "perfectly reasonable, provided
that for every black mother sterilized we castrate one middle class male."[128]
Moynihan's Catholicism left him conflicted over the question of birth
control. He did not accept the Church's position, but he believed govern-

ment should support Americans if they wanted to raise large families. However, like other liberals, he noted the connection between poverty and family size. For that reason, Moynihan proposed expanded voluntary birth control programs aimed at African Americans in the memo he wrote to Lyndon Johnson offering policy proposals based on his report.[129] However, Moynihan never advocated this solution as forcefully as he did family allowances, which would have provided additional support to large families. The Johns Hopkins University demographer Margaret Bright, whom Moynihan consulted while drafting of the report, admonished him for not pushing birth control: "a concerted public effort should be to get as many 'takers' for birth control as possible among Negro women. It would be much more profitable than picking up the pieces after all the damage is done." She warned, "People will know you are Catholic, and you will be considered as wearing blinders as far as one little relatively simple solution is concerned."[130]

Moynihan's discussion of the large numbers of black children born out-of-wedlock inevitably raised the question of birth control. When the White House was still planning to structure its civil rights conference around the family, it consulted Fredrick Jaffe of Planned Parenthood. Though Jaffe strongly advocated making birth control available to more African Americans, he cautioned that discussion should occur "in terms of a long-standing and discriminatory denial of access to family planning services." Jaffe specifically worried that Theodore White's depiction of "biological anarchy" would invite eugenicist responses that would deepen African American distrust of white-led birth control efforts.[131]

Some readers sought to apply Moynihan's insights into African Americans to other groups. Richard Titmuss, a London School of Economics professor and an architect of the British welfare state, praised its discussion of the effects of unemployment and underemployment on families. He saw its relevance for immigrants to Britain, and shared the report with others on the National Committee for Commonwealth Immigrants, including government ministers.[132] Mario Obledo, state director of the League of United Latin American Citizens for Texas, praised Moynihan's report on African Americans and suggested that he write a similar study of Mexican Americans. "The Mexican-American minority group," Obledo informed him, "is perhaps in a more ready-made explosive situation than has already been shown by Negro Americans." Despite the criticism the report had garnered, this major civil rights leader thought establishing that his group's social pathology was on par with that of African Americans would help the case for Mexican American equality.[133]

Given the criticism Moynihan received for lumping all African American together, objectifying them, and fostering racist stereotypes, it is surprising that some African Americans found validation in the report. "I am one negro in confinement that can back you up," wrote Paul Douglas Ware, an inmate at a prison mental asylum near Philadelphia, who wrote Moynihan to request a copy of the report after reading about it in magazines.[134] Ware was no doubt flattering Moynihan, who was only one of several public figures to whom Ware appealed for help. Nevertheless, Ware found a striking sense of affirmation in *The Negro Family*. "I am one of the statistics that make up the Case for National Action," Ware wrote after reading the copy Moynihan sent him. "When you speak about the illegitimate that's me, when you speak about those that drop out of high school, fail the Armed Services test, frustrated males, victims of broken homes, life without a father all of this is me."[135] When Ware was later incarcerated at Holmesburg Prison, Moynihan sent him additional copies of his report, which Ware later reported were used in group therapy in his prison's psychiatric ward.[136]

Writing from a New Orleans hospital, Dorothy M. White informed Moynihan that the report nearly brought her to tears with its statistics "vividly picturing the life I have lived as a Louisiana Negro."[137] An African American resident of Durham, North Carolina, praised Moynihan for his plan to create more black male breadwinners. She told him, "the fact that the Negro woman is better educated than the Negro man has affected me, and too many of my peers, having relegated me to the rank of spinsterhood."[138] She even offered to compile information on her family to help Moynihan with his research. These letter-writers felt their individual experiences as African Americans were confirmed by Moynihan's sociological generalizations, a surprising contrast to many African Americans' resentment at having been the subjects of studies conducted by privileged white Americans.

As these letters indicate, Moynihan's call for restoring "family stability" appealed to many African Americans. However, even some African Americans who shared this goal were insulted by what they viewed as Moynihan's patronizing attitude. In 1965, white liberal psychiatrist Robert Coles engaged a black Georgia minister in a discussion of the Moynihan Report's merits. Coles suggested that the minister should appreciate *The Negro Family* since it echoed his own preaching for strengthening male-headed black families. The minister disagreed, believing the report singled out African Americans for their family problems. Coles insisted that the report detailed African American family problems to call for national action. To the minister, though, "It was a call to white people. It didn't speak to Negroes."[139] African Americans, he claimed, "want what is *due* to them, rather than pity and sympathy." He asserted, "if you have to make people look *bad* or broken up before you can get the country to give them what they should have by right, then that's the same old racism and segregation at work."[140] Above all, the minister questioned whether white liberals' commitment to addressing black family problems was genuine. "If we knew that the Congress was going to vote the billions we need to clean up our slums," he reasoned, "then we could have overlooked a few people seeing us in a bad light."[141]

The exchange between Coles and the minister encapsulated the issue at the heart of the initial dispute over the Moynihan Report: whether it bolstered or undermined the case for national action to tackle race-based economic inequalities. However, by criticizing Moynihan's condescending view of African Americans, the minister foreshadowed another issue that would make the controversy so enduring. He anticipated the full-blown critiques of white liberalism that emerged by the end of the decade. For the Black Power movement of the late 1960s and 1970s, the Moynihan Report demonstrated how uninformed white elites exercised disproportionate power to define African American life.

CHAPTER 4

The Death of White Sociology

"It is amazing," wrote Ralph Ellison in 1967, "how often white liberals, possessing little firsthand knowledge of any area of society other than their own, eagerly presume to interpret Negro life." The Moynihan Report prompted the celebrated African American novelist to challenge the cultural authority of white intellectuals whose claims of "instant knowledge" about African Americans gained wide acceptance through "some mystique of whiteness." "[L]ike absentee owners of tenement buildings," he claimed, white liberals such as Moynihan "exploit the abstract sociological 'Negro' as a facile means of getting ahead in the world."[1] Ellison's metaphor of economic exploitation highlighted the disproportionate power that white intellectuals held to define African American social life. As his 1967 comments suggest, the Moynihan Report controversy revolved around not only *how* to understand racial inequality but also *who* had the right to represent African American social life.

Ellison's attack on liberal white racial experts resounded widely in the late 1960s and 1970s. Moynihan made a compelling target because *The Negro Family* positioned him as the nation's most vocal academic and media authority on African Americans. Because of his perceived racial expertise, he received a professorship at Harvard in 1966 and a post in the Nixon administration in 1969. The Black Power movement rejected the power Moynihan and other white elites in government, media, and academia had to define African American life. A new generation of scholars influenced by Black Power claimed the authority to construct sociological knowledge of African Americans. Advocating "Black Sociology," they charged that white-dominated scholarship reflected inherent bias. African Americans, they thought, brought valuable and overlooked perspectives to the study of African American life. As one Black Sociologist put it, African American scholars had the necessary " 'field experience' in being Black."[2]

Challenges to white racial expertise often simultaneously rejected "pathologism," the postwar intellectual paradigm that emphasized the damaged nature of African American social and cultural life. Liberals employed social pathology to highlight racial inequality, but critics argued that distorted depictions of African American life reinforced racial inequality by denying blacks' their full humanity. To critics, the Moynihan Report embodied pathologism's defects. Ellison, for example, attacked the report as the prime example of how white sociologists forced African Americans "to accept a negative and damaging image of themselves."[3] Black Sociologists similarly argued that pathologism was racist and called for the demise of "white sociology." They claimed that African American culture, far from being a pathological variant, was on par with and in many ways superior to Euro-American culture. One Black Sociologist even rejected the goal of "equality" altogether as "a near synonym for integration that means having the same life chances as white people." "White people," he complained, "have been the standard for all of our goals."[4] However, by making the defense of African American culture the central issue, some critics of pathologism diverted debate away from economic inequality.

Racial Experts

"Whether you like it or not," one Massachusetts resident wrote Moynihan in 1967, "you are now the Head Commissioner for Negro Affairs in America."[5] The Moynihan Report turned its author into a leading U.S. racial expert and placed him at the pinnacle of a network of academics, journalists, government officials, and foundation officers studying African American life. Moynihan, who demonstrated little knowledge about African Americans as late as 1963, became a leading national authority on the subject. According to one scholar, in 1970 Moynihan was the fourth-most influential expert on African Americans, trailing only Malcolm X, James Baldwin, and Eldridge Cleaver.[6] In the late 1960s, urban uprisings and the growing radicalization of parts of the civil rights movement created demand for racial experts to interpret such developments for political elites and the wider public. From 1965 to 1969, for example, the Ford Foundation, a leading liberal philanthropic organization, spent $100 million on programs related to "rights for minorities."[7] Moynihan was handsomely rewarded for his racial expertise. He was a popular speaker for university convocation and commencement addresses.[8] The

Eastman Kodak Corporation hired him as a consultant to help resolve a dispute regarding the company's failure to hire more African Americans at its Rochester, New York, facilities.[9]

In 1966, Moynihan was appointed to a professorship at Harvard that affirmed his status as a racial expert. Harvard's press release cited his authorship of *The Negro Family*.[10] This post marked a meteoric rise in academic rank for Moynihan, an assistant professor at Syracuse University six years earlier. Moynihan was recruited to direct the Harvard-MIT Joint Center for Urban Studies. Founded in 1959 with a Ford Foundation grant, the center supported interdisciplinary study of cities.[11] It played a leading role in developing racial expertise to influence public policy and public opinion. By the late 1960s, as uprisings spread across American cities, "urban studies" became a euphemism for the study of urban lower-class African Americans. "For the present, the urban Negro is, in a fundamental sense, *the* 'urban problem,'" confessed James Q. Wilson, who preceded Moynihan as Joint Center head.[12] An African American critic caustically defined the "urban affairs institute" as a place "where white people study and make recommendations on what should be done about Negro ghettos."[13]

After the *The Negro Family*'s release, Moynihan built influence in elite government, foundation, and journalistic circles. He maintained contacts in the Johnson administration, and he testified before Congress. The Carnegie Corporation, the major philanthropic foundation that had earlier funded Myrdal's *An American Dilemma*, asked Moynihan's advice on funding research on African Americans. Carnegie paid Moynihan $2,000 to prepare a memo for foundation heads on "the principal issues in the Northern urban Negro problem."[14] Major publishers competed to offer Moynihan a contract for a book that would expand on *The Negro Family*, which he wrote but never published. National print and television media frequently called him to discuss the spreading urban rebellions. *Time* ran Moynihan's image on the cover of a 1967 issue about "the problems of the cities."[15] In 1968, *Life* ran a feature, "Idea Broker for the Race Crisis: A Troubled Nation Turns to Pat Moynihan," so fawning that its author later publicly apologized. The article claimed that recent riots "vindicated" the *The Negro Family*'s analysis and praised Moynihan's "forward thinking" as "the best hope . . . for any sort of long-term solutions short of out-and-out civil war."[16]

Like many of his critics, Moynihan believed black scholars needed to take charge of the sociological study of African American life. "I feel the time is past when white men can tell black men what is wrong with them," Moynihan wrote to a fellow white sociologist in 1967.[17] Moynihan urged foundations to fund a new cadre of African American social scientists. Unlike his critics, Moynihan did not believe the recruitment of African American scholars would alter the content of racial knowledge. Rather, he hoped African American scholars would lend credibility to the existing paradigm. They would thus be better positioned to convince African Americans to confront family instability and social pathology. If only a black man had written *The Negro Family*, Moynihan implied, it might have been widely accepted.[18] Moynihan also portrayed himself as following in the footsteps of African American scholars who had similarly analyzed black family pathology. For example, he was instrumental in the 1970 reprinting of W. E. B. Du Bois's 1908 sociological study, *The Negro American Family*. Moynihan wrote the foreword in which he declared, "young black students should have it made clear to them that the beginnings of scholarship in this great area of American studies were in fact the work of Negro American scholars."[19]

From his post at Harvard, Moynihan rallied support in the academy. When *The Negro Family* came under attack, other racial experts saw their authority threatened and rushed to Moynihan's defense. Moynihan's academic supporters sought to protect scholars' ability to present objective findings on sensitive topics such as African American family life without having their intentions impugned or their views distorted. Moynihan's defenders compared the dispute to the post-World War II Red Scare in which intellectuals became targets of suspicion. For example, Harvard psychologist Thomas Pettigrew saw William Ryan's critique of the Moynihan Report as "the opening shot of a wave of McCarthyism within the Civil Rights Movement."[20] Pettigrew recalls his alarm at attacks on Moynihan that were "ignorantly anti-social science." Typical of Moynihan's other scholarly defenders, Pettigrew disliked the report's hyperbolic rhetoric and lack of statistical rigor but felt that Moynihan's analysis was essentially sound.[21] Because Moynihan cited Pettigrew's work in *The Negro Family*, Pettigrew felt his own interpretation of African American life was under attack.

Prominent African American psychologist Kenneth Clark also portrayed the controversy as an "academic freedom issue."[22] "Pat Moynihan and every qualified social scientist," he declared, "must have absolute freedom to explore, analyze, and communicate his findings and ideas concerning any social problem."[23] Clark never wrote a planned article examining the controversy, but he publicly vouched for Moynihan's antiracist intentions and substantiated the report's depiction of African American life: "He [Moynihan] highlights the total pattern of segregation and discrimination. Is a doctor responsible for the disease simply because he diagnoses it?" Clark character-ized Moynihan's critics as a "wolfpack operating in a very undignified way." When Clark proclaimed, "If Pat is a racist, I am," he revealed the extent to which his support for Moynihan defended his own work.[24] After all, Moyni-han borrowed the notorious phrase "tangle of pathology" from Clark. Those who thought Moynihan promoted a new form of sociological racism likely thought Clark did as well. Indeed, in the late 1960s, Clark came under fire from other African American intellectuals for his characterization of Har-lem. To critics such as Ralph Ellison and Albert Murray, Clark's *Dark Ghetto* so exaggerated Harlem's problems and ignored its rich cultural life that it reinforced negative racial stereotypes.[25]

Sociologist Lee Rainwater was Moynihan's staunchest supporter. For nearly five decades, scholars have turned to Rainwater and William Yanc-ey's landmark 1967 book, *The Moynihan Report and the Politics of Contro-versy*, which remains an indispensible source. *The Politics of Controversy* was not simply an objective study of the controversy, but an intervention in it. It was written principally to defend the Moynihan Report and its model of social science. At the time, Rainwater directed a major research study of a notorious housing project in St. Louis, Pruitt-Igoe. As a leading patholo-gist, Rainwater was personally implicated by criticism of Moynihan. At the *Daedalus* conference on "The Negro American" the two men met and iden-tified each other as allies. At Rainwater's invitation, Moynihan delivered a talk at Washington University in November 1965, at the zenith of the politi-cal firestorm over *The Negro Family*. In Rainwater's office following the talk, Moynihan suggested to Rainwater and graduate student William Yancey that they write a book on the controversy. Moynihan was centrally involved in the writing of *The Politics of Controversy*, providing Rainwater and Yancey with a list of people to interview and even writing letters of introduction to friends such as Johnson aide Harry McPherson.[26]

Yancey wrote the first draft of the book, which Rainwater and Yancey then revised together. Eager to publish while public debate raged over *The Negro Family*, they worked at breakneck speed. They completed most of the book in the first six months of 1966 and published it in early 1967. Though Rainwater had the most at stake in the controversy, Yancey, a fieldworker on Rainwater's Pruitt-Igoe project, did most of the research. Yancey spent a week in New York City and Washington, D.C., interviewing major govern-ment officials, civil rights leaders, and intellectuals involved on all sides of the dispute. Yancey also collected for reprinting the controversy's key documents, including *The Negro Family*, which for the first time became easily accessible (no longer requiring a special purchase through the Government Printing Office).[27]

The Politics of Controversy did more than document the debate; it defended Moynihan. It portrayed Moynihan as a sound social scientist and a well-intentioned liberal who was unfairly attacked and bore little responsibility for the controversy. According to Rainwater and Yancey, Moynihan's ideas were misunderstood because of the government's inept release of the report, sensationalistic media coverage that portrayed black family instability as an individual problem rather than a social one, and the tumultuous political environment that followed the Watts riots. Even their presentation of documentary sources intended to vindicate Moynihan. While Rainwater and Yancey gave equal space to Moynihan's critics in the book's appendix, they printed *The Negro Family* and Johnson's Howard speech toward the beginning, after their first three chapters, to ensure readers would interpret the report along their lines. Critics' works appeared at the end when readers may have already been convinced that Moynihan's opponents misunderstood his intentions.

Rainwater's defense of his authority as racial expert lay at the heart of *The Politics of Controversy*. Rainwater and Yancey were "puzzled and concerned" by sharp criticism of the Moynihan Report.[28] In the two decades between Gunnar Myrdal's 1944 publication of *An American Dilemma* and the 1964 Civil Rights Act, white liberal social scientists believed their work contributed to racial equality. Now Moynihan, a white liberal whose report drew heavily on postwar social science, had been sharply criticized by civil rights activists. Social scientists, Rainwater and Yancey determined, could no longer assume their work to be "morally unambiguous since they knew that they were attacking the citadels of a discriminatory power."[29] The moral obligation of scholars was to tell the truth, regardless how uncomfortable or embarrassing that might prove for African American leaders or lower-class African Americans. No matter how sympathetic social scientists were with the cause of racial equality, they needed to resist the "constant pressure . . . to tailor their findings to preferred civil rights strategies." Otherwise, they would produce "apologetics and not social science."[30] Presenting the Moynihan Report as reflecting a scholarly consensus, Rainwater and Yancey believed criticism of *The Negro Family* posed a serious threat to the public stature and political significance of social scientific research.

The Politics of Controversy implicitly endorsed a top-down model of social science in which experts advised policy-makers and informed citizens.
Rainwater and Yancey defended sociologists' ability to produce objective
knowledge, insisted on the relevance of sociological insight for policy-making,
and criticized media outlets for simplistic and sensationalized reporting of
sociological research. They argued that social scientists and government officials needed to take greater care when publicizing their research, citing the
inept release of the Moynihan Report as a case in point. In their narrative,
controversy resulted not from the content of Moynihan's report but from the
incompetent way it was publicized.[31]

Rainwater's interpretation of the Moynihan Report controversy was self-
serving. He dismissed the possibility that social scientists might draw different conclusions about lower-class African American life than had he and
Moynihan. Rainwater seemed unaware that whatever degree of consensus
once existed about Moynihan's views on African American families was fast
disappearing. Thus, *The Politics of Controversy* did not defend scholarly autonomy so much as a particular sociological paradigm: pathologism.

Rainwater was a leading pathologist. His influential 1970 book, *Behind
Ghetto Walls*, resulted from the major research project he directed at the Pruitt-
Igoe housing project funded by a $750,000 grant from the National Institute
of Mental Health to produce "a basic analysis of the conditions underlying
the pathological behavior currently found in urban public housing."[32] Rainwater employed several graduate research assistants to observe Pruitt-Igoe
residents and collect their life histories. Despite repeated entreaties from his
graduate researchers, Rainwater spent little time directly interacting with
Pruitt-Igoe residents.[33] Thus, even though Rainwater's approach was ethnographic, it remained impersonal. The cover photo of *Behind Ghetto Walls* encapsulated Rainwater's perspective. The camera looks out from a top-floor
apartment through a broken glass window across a barbed-wire fence toward
a depressing expanse of concrete high-rise buildings. A sole African American figure appears in the distance below.

Rainwater portrayed the lives of his subjects so harshly that even fellow
pathologist Kenneth Clark thought he confused "the issue of social justice
and social pathology with a sort of normative pornography type description
of the Negro poor and his predicament."[34] For Rainwater, lower-class African American culture had "some elements of intrinsic value and many more
elements that are highly destructive to the people who must live in it."[35] In
Pruitt-Igoe, Rainwater found "a community of persons who think poorly of

each other, who attack and manipulate each other, who give each other small comfort in a desperate world."[36] Like Moynihan, Rainwater redirected scholarly attention from the direct effects of white racism toward perceived flaws in African American social structure. The problems of poor African Americans, Rainwater contended, only indirectly resulted from "white cupidity." Instead, white racism "created situations in which Negroes do the dirty work of caste victimization."[37]

Like Moynihan, Rainwater identified family as the "crucible of identity" for poor African Americans: "the caste-facilitated infliction of suffering by Negroes on other Negroes and on themselves appears most poignantly within the confines of the family."[38] Like Moynihan, Rainwater saw the lower-class black family as marked by instability and matriarchal dominance. While he saw that this family structure helped lower-class African Americans function in their environment, he thought it an unhealthy adaptation that perpetuated low socioeconomic status. It "prepares and toughens its members to function in the ghetto world, at the same time that it seriously interferes with their ability to operate in any other world."[39]

Like other liberal sociologists, Rainwater emphasized pathology to call for social programs aimed at eliminating the poverty he saw as its root cause. Critics saw a contradiction between Rainwater's unrelentingly negative depiction of lower-class African Americans and his call for antipoverty programs. However, Rainwater, Moynihan, and other pathologists thought it necessary to demonstrate the depths of the social problem in order to justify reform. Rainwater shared Moynihan's commitment to the family wage: "An equitable society should not require its families to achieve median income by forcing women and children to enter the labor market."[40] He advocated more extensive economic reforms than did Moynihan. He called for a massive redistribution of income to guarantee every American family an adequate income. Had Johnson officials truly understood "the problems Moynihan put on their desks," Rainwater and Yancey claimed, they would have realized that "the back wages due the Negro community dwarf any current domestic program."[41] Rainwater and Yancey sharply criticized Lyndon Johnson for failing to live up to his Howard speech commitments. In fact, they alleged that Johnson officials deliberately fostered discontent over the Moynihan Report to distract civil rights leaders from Johnson's inaction. (Moynihan did not share this view.)

Rainwater rejected Black Power's strategy of mobilizing African Americans for autonomous political action. Lower-class African American culture,

Rainwater implied, had little of value and blacks would be best off assimilating to middle-class American norms. *The Politics of Controversy* criticized SNCC militants who "found after they had integrated the lunch counter they didn't like the menu."[42] Rainwater also intimated that middle-class Americans must lead the political charge to eliminate poverty because constructive change was unlikely to emerge from the profoundly damaged and destructive individuals described in *Behind Ghetto Walls*. In fact, Rainwater and Yancey claimed that Black Power advocates criticized the Moynihan Report so strongly because it undermined their strategic rationale. "The Moynihan thesis," Rainwater and Yancey concluded, was "deeply embarrassing to those who wish to build Negro political power, since emphasis on pathological processes within the Negro community tends to vitiate the claims of those who would maintain that Negroes . . . are on the road to amassing great power."[43]

When Rainwater and Yancey wrote *The Politics of Controversy*, defending social scientists' autonomy to portray African American social life upheld the intellectual authority of a white-dominated profession. For instance, no members of Moynihan's Joint Center on Urban Studies were African American. The casual racism exhibited by white liberals reflected the absence of African Americans from networks of racial experts. Moynihan held a joke identification card as an "honorary Negro" to protect him from violence in case of a race riot.[44] The editors of *Trans-action*, a journal co-founded by Rainwater to convey sociological ideas to a broader public, privately referred to a special issue on African American life as their "Spade Special."[45] At a 1966 meeting of a Seminar on Poverty chaired by Moynihan that gathered Rainwater and other prominent white experts on African Americans, a participant circulated an anonymous note. "If we came clean and said what we're really trying to do is improve the Negro ghetto subculture," it suggested, then the government would replace the OEO (Office of Economic Opportunity) with CONGO (Council of Negro Ghetto Opportunity). Among a community that rejected scientific racism and advocated racial integration, this joke connected the perceived inferiority of poor African Americans to African roots. In case anyone had missed the punch line, Moynihan later typed and circulated the note to seminar participants.[46]

Unsurprisingly, white liberal racial experts such as Moynihan and Rainwater were unprepared for the mounting challenge to their authority. African American activists in Boston targeted Moynihan and the institution he headed. In 1967, the MIT-Harvard Joint Center received $6 million from the

Ford Foundation to study urban African Americans. At the press conference announcing the grant, an African American worker who had helped prepare the event space boldly questioned why money went to elite white universities for research rather than directly to African Americans. Later that week, a group of community leaders in Roxbury, an African American neighborhood in Boston, called for a national boycott of participation in research sponsored by the Joint Center. The Center, they charged, was not sincerely interested in the problems of Roxbury and other African American neighborhoods; it wanted only to secure the new research funds opened in response to urban rebellions. Furthermore, they accused Joint Center researchers of acting without the consent or input of African Americans they studied and of lacking competence "to assess or evaluate the research needs of the black community." They specifically challenged Moynihan's authority as director of the Joint Center. Moynihan's research, they alleged, showed that "his racist attitudes override social scientific objectivity" and that his "characterization of black culture as 'Pathological' indicates an inability to recognize the true beauty, warmth, dignity, and soulfulness of black people as we relate to one another; and an unwillingness to confront the racist nature of this society."[47] Roxbury protestors articulated an opposition to white liberal racial experts that was increasingly prevalent in the late 1960s with the growth of Black Power.

Bang! Bang! Mr. Moynihan

"The reason we are in the bag we are in isn't because of my mama, it's because of what they did to my mama."[48] Stokely Carmichael, leader of SNCC, denounced the Moynihan Report in a famous 1966 speech which popularized the slogan "Black Power" and signaled the radicalization of one segment of the civil rights movement. Part of what distinguished the Black Power movement from the earlier phase of the civil rights movement was its insistence on racism's deep embedding in American consciousness and society. Carmichael and Charles Hamilton coined the phrase "institutional racism" in their 1967 book, *Black Power*, to denote how African Americans were systematically oppressed in ways far less obvious than overtly discriminatory laws.[49]

Carmichael echoed William Ryan's attack of *The Negro Family* for blaming the victim and providing new rationalizations for racial inequality. He also attacked the Moynihan Report as epitomizing the illegitimate power whites held to portray black life. In his "Black Power" speech, Carmichael criticized the 1966 White House Conference on Civil Rights spawned by the Moynihan Report and boycotted by SNCC. He charged that white officials holding forth on the problems of black families was insulting: "They called conferences about our mamas and told us that's why we were where we were at." Carmichael protested how whites had stripped African Americans of their ability to represent themselves. African Americans, he claimed, should refuse to discuss their family problems with whites. "I don't play the dozens with white folks," he declared, criticizing civil rights leaders "sitting up there talking with Johnson while he was talking about their mamas."[50]

Carmichael's demand for African American self-representation was the central stance of the Black Power movement. As Carmichael put it, African Americans must "struggle for the right to create our own terms to define ourselves and our relationship to the society, and to have these terms recognized."[51] Black Power leaders demanded more than economic equality. They sought cultural equality that would allow them to define African American social reality. Though embedded in a long tradition of black nationalism and black radicalism, Black Power emerged in the mid-1960s just as the Moynihan Report began circulating. The Black Panther Party was founded in 1966, the same year as Carmichael's speech. Politically amorphous and never a complete departure from the civil rights movement, Black Power nevertheless reflected a new mood in African American politics. It advocated that African Americans build autonomous political power, rather than serving as junior partners in coalitions led by white liberals. It emphasized the value of a distinctively African American culture with African roots. The slogan "Black is Beautiful" captured efforts to overturn a white-oriented aesthetic by valuing dark skin and kinky hair.

Leaders such as Carmichael employed a new rhetoric to appeal to lower-class African Americans. Their bold and provocative language advertised their disregard for offending whites. Some leaders found it liberating to no longer cater to white sensibilities. "For once," Carmichael proclaimed, "black people are going to use the words they want to use—not just the words whites want to hear."[52] While early civil rights critics of *The Negro Family* did not call Moynihan a "racist," Black Power advocates had no qualms about doing so. For example, in 1969, Rev. Douglas Moore denounced Moynihan as a "plantation boss" and an "outright racist."[53] Black Power advocates scorned white intellectuals who had arrogated the right to interpret African American life. The militant Philadelphia NAACP leader Cecil Moore attacked "intellectual phonies and white intellectuals from the North." Black Power advocates also challenged African American leaders who allied with white liberals. One protest sign at the 1966 White House Conference on Civil Rights read, "No More "Cullud' Leaders and 'White Experts' on US."[54]

Black Power intellectuals criticized the arrogance of Moynihan's claims about African Americans. Amiri Baraka claimed that African American musicians captured black social life far better than distant white experts. For example, rhythm-and-blues musician Junior Walker's song "Road Runner" explained the break-up of African American couples in ways "all more precise and specific than the Moynihan Report."[55] In his 1968 book, *Look Out Whitey! Black Power's Gon' Get Your Mama*, Julius Lester took aim at Moynihan in a chapter entitled "Bang! Bang! Mr. Moynihan." Of course, Lester did not literally mean African Americans should shoot Moynihan, but rather urged them to target Moynihan's cultural authority. For Lester, Moynihan epitomized the white liberal who "generally turned out to be more white than liberal whenever blacks assert themselves." Like other Black Power advocates, who often collapsed distinctions between white supremacists and white liberals, Lester posited that "Moynihans" who pretended to ally themselves with African Americans were more dangerous than open segregationists. Thus, he vowed, "it will be the Moynihans we go after first rather than the southern sheriff." To Lester, Moynihan's pretension to racial expertise proved that whites thought "they are greater authorities on blacks than blacks themselves." African Americans could not trust whites, Lester maintained, "until they stop going to the Daniel Moynihans to learn about blacks, but come to the ghetto to learn for themselves."[56]

Whites in the burgeoning New Left formed a receptive audience for the Black Power critique of liberal white expertise. For example, Walt Shepperd criticized Moynihan as representing a "new paternalism" among whites who presumed to interpret urban African-American experience they hardly knew. Shepperd edited *Nickel Review*, one of many underground newspapers that sprang up in the late 1960s to express a growing countercultural and New Left sensibility. In a 1967 review of Rainwater and Yancey's *The Politics of Controversy*, Shepperd lambasted middle-class white sociologists for misrepresenting African American culture. He approvingly quoted an anonymous Harlem poet: "Mr. Moynihan, if you come into my neighborhood talking that shit, I'll beat your brains out with my Louisville Slugger." Shepperd believed that he and his white readers, unlike out-of-touch white liberals, grasped the value of African American culture. Alluding to the chorus of "Ballad of a Thin Man," a Bob Dylan song about the failure of a middle-aged conformist to understand youth counterculture, Shepperd asked, "Something is happening here and you don't know what it is, do you Mr. Moynihan?"[57]

Not all Black Power advocates responded negatively to the Moynihan Report. Daniel H. Watts, editor of the black nationalist publication, the *Liberator*, praised Moynihan in an editorial on the 1965 White House Planning Conference on Civil Rights. Watts derided civil rights leaders present at the conference, mocking Martin Luther King as the "Self-annointed One" and Whitney Young as "White House-Court Jester (the curly hair one)." Surprisingly, he defended Moynihan as the "one man at the conference possessing a *possible* blueprint for meaningful change." Watts and Moynihan engaged in a cordial exchange of letters following the publication of Watts's article.[58]

The report appealed to Black Power advocates invested in restoring black male familial authority; they shared Moynihan's disdain for "matriarchal" family structures. The Nation of Islam (NOI), a religious organization that advocated black nationalism, endorsed Moynihan's family model while rejecting the notion that liberal experts could solve African Americans' problems. The NOI influenced Black Power leaders, especially through its one-time spokesperson, Malcolm X. Long before Moynihan published his report, NOI leaders expressed concern with ghetto pathology. Unsurprisingly, then, *Muhammad Speaks*, the NOI organ and the highest-circulating black newspaper, cheered Moynihan's documentation of high rates of illegitimacy and female-headed families among African Americans. The paper praised *The Negro Family* for giving "substance to some of the Honorable Elijah Muhammad's contentions and claims" and printed a long article with detailed quotations from the report.[59]

In 1967, NOI minister Louis Farrakhan, who later led the NOI and organized the 1994 Million Man March, conducted an interview with Moynihan published in five installments of *Muhammad Speaks*. The newspaper respectfully described Moynihan as "aptly rated as perhaps the greatest . . . American sociologist."[60] Farrakhan and Moynihan largely agreed on family ideals. For example, Farrakhan grilled Moynihan on whether birth control and sterilization programs directed at African Americans were forms of racial genocide. The Catholic Moynihan partly agreed, replying, "When the issue of birth control is used as a device to solve the problem of poverty by limiting the number of persons who are born, I think we get awfully close to that in our thinking."[61] However, the juxtaposition of radically different worldviews produced comic moments: Moynihan asserted that some crime would always exist, because, "As you [Farrakhan] know, there is a devil in the world."[62] (Presumably, Moynihan did not mean the white devil of NOI mythology.)

While they agreed on creating more male-headed African American families, Farrakhan rejected the notion that liberal elites such as Moynihan could be entrusted with the task. In an article reacting to the interview, he deduced, "the United States government is at a complete loss in its attempt to solve the problems of 25 million black people." The government had no real programs for addressing black male unemployment and "rebuilding black families." However, citing its support of birth control measures, Farrakhan alleged the government had "a program to cut down the birth rate of black babies." Pointing to Moynihan's call to draft more African American men into the army, Farrakhan reaffirmed Elijah Muhammad's warning about "the government's wicked intentions against the black people of America." Farrakhan argued that African American family problems could be best addressed through self-reliance. "For 35 years," he declared, "the Honorable Elijah Muhammad has warned us that in the final analysis, we would have to unite and depend on ourselves."[63] Ironically, the racial self-help strategy advocated by the Nation of Islam replicated the white conservative agenda.

Surprisingly, one of the most prominent critics of white liberal expertise in the late 1960s was a liberal integrationist who rejected black nationalism and insisted on the fundamental Americanness of African American identity. Ralph Ellison derided white intellectuals who claimed that their ethnicity granted authority to write about African Americans. Criticizing Moynihan's scholarly collaborator for enacting a kind of intellectual blackface, Ellison deadpanned, "Burnt cork or no, I'm afraid that Mr. [Nathan] Glazer makes a pretty sorry Negro."[64]

Ellison criticized white liberal intellectuals as part of a broader opposition to pathologism. In 1964, he famously printed a review of Myrdal's *An American Dilemma* that he wrote twenty years prior but shelved out of fear it would undermine Myrdal's positive contributions toward discrediting racism. Ellison challenged Myrdal's application of white American norms to African American culture and his argument that African American culture deviated from white culture only because of the effects of racism. In contrast, Ellison posited that African American subculture should be confronted on its own terms and understood as containing inherent value. Ellison memorably asked, "can a people . . . live and develop for over three hundred years simply by reacting? Are American Negroes simply the creation of white men, or have they at least helped to create themselves out of what they found around them?"[65]

Though Ellison criticized white experts, his primary targets were African American pathologists. Sociologists such as E. Franklin Frazier and Kenneth Clark, he contended, perniciously influenced African American writers including Richard Wright and James Baldwin to portray African American life in wholly pejorative terms. For example, Ellison was disturbed by Baldwin's description of "piss in the halls and blood on the stairs" in Harlem. Ellison recommended that African Americans write from personal experience instead of drawing from social science, which was unable to faithfully represent black life: "If a Negro writer is going to listen to sociologists. . . . If he accepts the clichés to the effect that the Negro family is usually a broken family, that it is matriarchal in form and that the mother dominates and castrates the male . . . well, he'll never see the people of whom he wishes to write."[66] Ultimately, Ellison charged African American pathologists with adhering to a "white" perspective. Their reliance "upon outsiders—mainly sociologists—to interpret our lives for us" affirmed his own authority to speak for African Americans while denying that of African American intellectuals such as Clark and Baldwin who also claimed to speak from personal experience.[67]

Ironically, Ellison, who celebrated American culture as a mixture of Euro-American and African American traditions, portrayed sociology as a white construct imposed upon African Americans. Despite Ellison's idiosyncratic stance, he influenced a new generation of African American social scientists who sought to overturn pathologism and offer the indigenous expertise on African American life called for by Black Power leaders. Unlike Ellison, these scholars sought to use sociology to construct competing images of African Americans.

Black Sociology

African American sociologist Joyce Ladner attacked the Moynihan Report as the quintessential example of "[t]raditional sociological analyses" that "portrayed Blacks as disorganized, pathological, and an aberrant group."[68] Surprisingly, Ladner was one of Lee Rainwater's doctoral students. She felt a sharp disconnect between her sociological training and her personal experience; similar feelings were shared by many African American scholars of her generation who studied at universities where blacks previously had been largely excluded. Born in 1943, Ladner grew up in Hattiesburg, Mississippi. As a student at historically black Tougaloo College in the early 1960s, she became a civil rights activist. She worked under leaders such as NAACP activist Medgar Evers, who was assassinated by a white supremacist in 1963. Ladner's experience taught her about the deeply institutionalized nature of American racism and the positive resources African Americans possessed for community mobilization. Consequently, she rejected Rainwater's pathologism. After Ladner completed her dissertation in 1968, she and Rainwater became so estranged that they lost contact for two decades.[69] Ladner's first book, *Tomorrow's Tomorrow*, which emerged from doctoral research she conducted for Rainwater's Pruitt-Igoe study, offered an entirely different portrait of lower-class African Americans. To Ladner, Rainwater's research and the Moynihan Report typified "white sociology," the demise of which she heralded in the landmark collection of Black Sociologists' work she edited in 1973, *The Death of White Sociology*.

Black Sociology emerged in the late 1960s as part of the Black Studies movement that transformed the academic study of African Americans. Influenced by Black Power calls for racial self-representation, African American students demanded universities include African and African American material in their curricula and hire black faculty. The long and contentious 1969 student strike at San Francisco State University was the most dramatic contest of hundreds in American universities. Black Studies programs facilitated the entry of a new generation of African American scholars into white-dominated universities. Though Black Studies proponents wanted autonomous departments and programs, they also transformed existing academic disciplines.[70] Sociology was a particularly ripe terrain of struggle, given its key role in constructing representations of African Americans and the earlier prominence of African American sociologists such as W. E. B. Du Bois, E. Franklin Frazier, and Charles Johnson. In 1968, the Black Caucus formed within the American Sociological Association (ASA). Its demand for changing sociological perspectives on African Americans produced heated conflict at ASA annual meetings; similar clashes occurred in leading professional organizations in political science, psychology, and other disciplines.[71] In 1969, Nathan Hare, who directed the Black Studies program at San Francisco State before being fired for his role in the student strike, co-founded the journal *The Black Scholar*, the leading forum for Black Sociology. Eventually, Black Sociology produced its own textbook, Robert Staples's *Introduction to Black Sociology*, first published in 1976.[72]

The Death of White Sociology began with an epigraph from *Ebony* editor and Black Studies proponent Lerone Bennett: "It is necessary for us to develop and maintain a total offensive against the false universality of white concepts, whether they are expressed by William Styron or Daniel Patrick Moynihan."[73] This quote likened the Moynihan Report to Styron's 1967 novel about a famous slave revolt leader, *Confessions of Nat Turner*, which used the first-person perspective to narrate Turner's experiences. Black Studies scholars railed against the white novelist's depiction of Turner's damaged psychology.[74] Several essays in *The Death of White Sociology* similarly took *The Negro Family* as evidence of white sociologists' failure to convey the reality of black life. For instance, Nathan Hare considered the report a classic example of how "ideology influences interpretation."[75] Hare thought *The Negro Family*'s pervasive white bias promoted racial stereotypes and failed to see African American culture on its own terms. Similarly, Albert Murray, a cultural critic and close friend of Ralph Ellison, derided the Moynihan Report as "the stuff of which the folklore of white supremacy is made." Like other sociological works, he claimed, the report was a "propaganda vehicle to promote a negative image of Negro life in the United States."[76]

Black Sociologists reevaluated prevailing norms of scholarly objectivity. According to Charles Hamilton, "The black social scientist in this country is a member of a race that is subjected and oppressed. . . . It is impossible to be 'objective' about that, any more than it is possible for a white social scientist, who has benefitted directly or indirectly from racial oppression, to be 'objective.'"[77] Black Sociologists challenged Rainwater's reading of the controversy, which pitted social scientific autonomy against political pressures. One contributor to *The Death of White Sociology* described Rainwater and Yancey's *The Politics of Controversy* as a "whitewash" of the Moynihan Report controversy. (Presumably, the pun was intended.)[78] Black Sociologists argued that the sociologist's standpoint decisively affected his or her knowledge. Thus, African Americans were best positioned to understand African American social life. Moreover, Black Sociologists believed their scholarship should actively advance African Americans' welfare. According to Ladner, "Black sociologists must act as advocates of the demands the masses are making for freedom, justice, and the right to determine their destinies."[79] The founders of Black Studies hoped not only to establish a new academic field but also to foster Black Power. As Ladner quoted Hare, their goal was to unite "the Black academy and the street."[80]

Calling for white sociology's death was a rallying cry that allowed Black Sociologists to present themselves as unified, but hid tensions inherent to building a Black Sociology. While *The Death of White Sociology* pinpointed white racial experts' pretensions, it obscured complex racial dynamics involved in producing sociological knowledge. Taken literally, the concepts of "white" and "black" sociology suggested a crude essentialism in which race determined perspective. For the most part, Black Sociologists did not argue that one had to be black to depict African American social life accurately. In fact, *The Death of White Sociology* included contributions by whites. White scholars could contribute to Black Sociology provided they familiarized themselves with African American perspectives. However, Black Sociologists denounced white scholars such as Moynihan who generalized on the basis of statistics with little direct personal experience of African Americans. They also stressed that if sociology remained white-dominated, it could only produce biased knowledge of African Americans. Some white scholars sympathetic to Black Sociology concluded that studying African American life was best left to blacks. Citing Moynihan as a negative example, Ira Katznelson concluded, "Only a very rare white with extraordinary sensibilities could accurately convey the black experience" and "white scholars have no role to play in solving internal black community disputes."[81] However, claiming that black scholars could best study African Americans risked limiting them to the study of race, a restriction that had long frustrated African American intellectuals.[82]

Black Sociologists tended to depict the tradition of white-dominated sociology in monolithic terms that hardly did it justice. For example, in his contribution to *The Death of White Sociology*, Abdul Alkalimat (Gerald McWorter) viewed the history of sociology as one long string of ideological justifications for racism. He saw no difference between scientific racists of the late nineteenth century and Myrdal-inspired postwar social scientists who contributed to civil rights gains.[83] Elsewhere, he argued that white scholars, regardless of context, were "apologists for whatever racist practices exist."[84] Even more circumspect Black Studies scholars portrayed a unitary "white sociology." Ladner even accused "white sociology" of mutually exclusive faults: ignoring the distinct culture of African Americans *and* accentuating African American difference to deny potential assimilation.

The concept of "black" sociology implied that all African American scholars shared or should share the same perspective. Consequently, Black Sociologists were uncertain how to regard leading African American pathologists

E. Franklin Frazier and Kenneth Clark. *The Death of White Sociology* included texts by Frazier and Clark and so recognized the historic contributions of African American scholars. However, both intellectuals were key sources for the Moynihan Report, and Clark had been one of its leading defenders. Their work challenged Black Sociologists' attempts to label pathologism as inherently "white" and antipathologism as authentically "black." Some Black Sociologists concluded that despite lifelong activism for African American equality, Frazier's and Clark's sociological contributions came at the expense of African Americans. For example, Alkalimat attacked "black intellectuals acquiescing to a white social science." He described Frazier as "a brother who was strong enough to collect a lot of important data but [who] fell victim to theory based on the racist, white liberal ideology."[85] Albert Murray, singled out Clark as one of the "prominent Negro spokesmen . . . who employ, repeat, and even extend the imagery of white supremacy."[86] Hence, debates over Black Sociology were not solely about who controlled sociological knowledge, but also about which ideas best reflected African American experiences.

Attacks on white bias concealed different ideas of objectivity among Black Sociologists. Some thought Black Sociology would produce a truly universal knowledge, either by rebalancing the previous focus on Europeans and European culture alone, or because African Americans had a privileged access to the truth as members of an oppressed group. Others, however, viewed scholarship as fundamentally political and challenged the very concept of objective knowledge. They wanted Black Sociology to strengthen the political cause of Black Power. For some contributors to *The Death of White Sociology*, science was "inevitably a handservant to ideology," while others warned of the limitations of "Black propaganda."[87] In addition, some contributors emphasized the distinctiveness and autonomous character of African American culture, while others such as Albert Murray stressed the racially mixed, "mulatto" nature of American culture as a whole. Black Sociology took many forms.

The Black Sociology movement did not last much beyond the 1970s. Nevertheless, despite internal tensions, it transformed sociology. Even William Yancey, co-author of *The Politics of Controversy*, challenged negative depictions of African American social life. Through his work on the Pruitt-Igoe project, Yancey reached different conclusions about lower-class African American culture than Rainwater. Yancey found a positive sense of community and identity among Pruitt-Igoe residents that he felt many poor whites lacked. After reading *Behind Ghetto Walls*, Yancey wrote Rainwater in surprise at how much they disagreed. In 1971, Yancey co-wrote an article, "Uncle Tom and Mr. Charlie," to challenge "hypotheses of Negro self-hatred and Negro pathology."[88] He specifically criticized Rainwater. The Moynihan Report controversy, he now claimed, revealed that highlighting African American pathology undermined the case for economic justice. The article's publication in a leading academic journal, the *American Journal of Sociology*, suggested the impact of Black Sociology on mainstream sociological discourse.

Black Sociology, and the larger Black Studies movement, transformed the intellectual climate of American universities in ways that crucially affected the long-term reception of the Moynihan Report. For example, in 1975, African American students at Stanford University protested the selection of Moynihan as commencement speaker. Honoring Moynihan, they insisted, conferred legitimacy upon him as a racial expert. They objected to Moynihan's role in the Nixon administration but mainly protested his authorship of *The Negro Family* a decade prior. Eminent African American scholar St. Clair Drake rallied Stanford faculty members in support of the student protest, drafting a letter signed by nearly all the members of the Anthropology Department.

Interestingly, when the Moynihan Report first appeared, Drake was not so opposed. In 1965, he prepared a long memo on *The Negro Family* for African American leaders and researchers in Chicago. Though Drake criticized conceptual flaws in the report, he defended Moynihan's motives as "above suspicion" and noted the report performed a "useful service" by highlighting the impact of black male unemployment on families.[89] By 1975, though, Drake was riled that *The Negro Family* made Moynihan an "instant expert" on African Americans who, without scholarly distinction, obtained a professorship at Harvard.[90] Drake's path to Stanford had been more arduous. Born in 1911, he was part of a generation of African American scholars who were largely excluded from universities like Harvard and Stanford. Though a celebrated scholar, noted for his work on the African Diaspora and his co-authorship of a classic 1945 study of African Americans in Chicago, *Black Metropolis*, Drake spent most of his career teaching at Roosevelt University in Chicago. In 1969, when Drake was nearly seventy, Stanford invited him to direct its new Black Studies program. African American scholars were suddenly in short supply as white-dominated universities sought to meet student demands for Black Studies programs. As Drake sarcastically commented, universities that denied him a position his whole career recruited him now that "the kids are ready to burn the place down."[91] Drake's personal experience left him outraged that Harvard appointed Moynihan on the basis of a single report, particularly one that Drake considered a sloppy work of social science.

In 1975, supporting the Stanford student protest, Drake rejected Moynihan's claim to racial expertise as "very dubious."[92] He now labeled the Moynihan Report as "bad social science," a "prime example of pseudo-scholarly support for racist ideas," and a case of "middle-class Eurocentric bias."[93] Moynihan, he claimed, showed little interest in African American scholars' work and displayed an intolerably patronizing "father knows best" attitude toward African Americans as a whole.[94] For Drake, Stanford's choice of commencement speaker undermined standards of social scientific discourse and posed an "affront to Black people."[95] The Stanford community, he contended, should recognize that their university was now "a multi-cultural, multi-racial institution" that should account for "the sensitivities of ethnic students . . . when selecting speakers."[96] Despite protests, Moynihan delivered the commencement address. Clearly, Moynihan's racial expertise retained authority on college campuses by 1975. Reports of white sociology's death were greatly exaggerated, but its objectivity no longer went unchallenged.[97]

Black Families and White Social Science

Leading Black Sociologist Andrew Billingsley sought "the overthrow of the current ruling elite in social science which is largely composed of white males over forty."[98] In his contribution to The Death of White Sociology, "Black Families and White Social Science," Billingsley criticized Moynihan and white liberal sociologists. His article's subheadings read "Arrogant Analysis by White Liberals," "Blacks Are Black, Social Science is White," and "The Best Studies of Black Families are by Black Scholars." The Moynihan Report, Billingsley charged, was "conceived, executed, and reported out of the white middle class perspective in social science, with no meaningful participation by black people."[99] To Billingsley, pathologists did not only observe pathology; they created it. Social scientists such as Moynihan who harped on negative aspects of black social life, Billingsley claimed, helped produce poor self-esteem among African Americans. The problem was not the black family, but rather "the white racist, militaristic society, which places higher priority on putting white men on the moon than putting black men on their feet on this earth."[100]

The family was a pivotal terrain for battles over who had the authority to characterize African American life. Stressing positive adaptive features of

African American families undermined the whole discourse of social pathology. The issue of family particularly dramatized the need for African American self-definition. To Black Power advocates, any group unable to interpret its own family structure to the outside world lacked the cultural power required for its welfare and advancement. The topic of family also highlighted the need for black perspectives in a white-dominated research field. African American social scientists had personal experience that nearly all whites lacked: living in a black family.

A common misconception holds that the Moynihan Report controversy suppressed research on African American families. The opposite is true. Some of Moynihan's sharpest critics credited his report with spurring research on African American families. One estimate counted over fifty books and over five hundred articles published on the topic during the 1970s.[101] Disproving *The Negro Family* became something of a cottage industry for scholars, who combated Moynihan's interpretation of the African American family as part of a broader war against pathologism.

One leading publication, *Journal of Marriage and Family*, published so many articles on the topic it might have been renamed *Journal of Refuting the Moynihan Report*. A 1978 special issue of that journal on "Black Families" summed up transformations in the field since *The Negro Family*: scholars now viewed African American families as "adaptive" rather than "pathological." This relabeling defined African Americans positively; scholars embraced what guest editors termed a "nonpejorative" perspective of African American families "possessing a value system, patterns of behavior, and institutions which can be described, understood, and appreciated for their own strengths and characteristics."[102] However, "adaptive" and "pathological" were not mutually exclusive descriptions. Moynihan and Rainwater viewed matriarchal African American family structure as an adaptation to poverty and racism, but believed it impeded economic and social advancement. Antipathologists, however, questioned whether sociologists should evaluate African American families in terms of attaining (white) middle-class norms. Instead, they argued, sociologists should consider African American families' capacity to promote group survival in a racist society. They challenged Moynihan for presenting "black Americans from the perspective of their presumed failure to respond 'adequately' to the promise of America."[103]

The Moynihan Report never represented a social scientific consensus on the African American family. Some established scholars, such as Howard University sociologist Hylan Lewis, questioned Moynihan's conclusions as soon as the report became public. Lewis prepared the agenda paper for the family panel of the 1965 White House Planning Conference on Civil Rights. Though Lewis's text did not name either Moynihan or *The Negro Family*, any knowledgeable reader would have recognized the paper as a critical response to the report. Lewis worried that Moynihan contributed to alarmism about African American families and perpetuated racial stereotypes. Though he shared concern about the high percentage of female-headed families, he thought that the rise in the rate of such families from 18.8 percent in 1949 to 23.2 percent in 1962 reported by Moynihan hardly signaled a "crumbling" black family structure. While Lewis saw the two-parent household as ideal, he noted the positive adaptive features of single-parent homes. Most important, Lewis noted similarities between lower-class African American families and lower-class white families. He criticized the Moynihan Report's failure to control for income level when comparing African American and white families. If the main problem was poverty rather than race, Lewis suggested, then it was a mistake to use family structure to explain racial inequality.[104]

Later critics of Moynihan often built on Lewis's insights, though they discarded his cautious tone. By 1970, even otherwise dry scholarly articles on African American families polemically attacked the report. For example, one article concluded a careful, nuanced dissection of the report: "The Moynihan research is a political weapon . . . used for white control of black people . . . . Research on blacks . . . can serve either as a means of control of blacks by whites, or as a means of resistance to such control."[105]

Andrew Billingsley's career illustrates key shifts in interpretations of African American families. A professor of social work at the University of California, Berkeley, he shared much of Moynihan's perspective when he began researching African American families. In a 1965 article coauthored with his wife, Amy Tate Billingsley, he remarked, "Many of the social problems about which social work is concerned are related to patterns of family disorganization and instability, in which Negro families are overrepresented." The Billingsleys advocated strengthening the African American family to "better carry out its major responsibilities of socialization and social control."[106] However, Billingsley constructed his 1968 book, *Black Families and White America*, as a critique of pathologism and the Moynihan Report. He now contended that Moynihan's alarmist focus on matriarchal families obscured the fact that most black families were "stable, conforming, and achieving, and cause no problems to anybody." Contra Moynihan, Billingsley described the African American family as "absorbing, adaptive, and amazingly resilient."[107] Calling for African American self-definition, Billingsley declared, "Negro people . . . must begin to define themselves and not accept the negative definitions which have been handed down by white people . . . leadership in this effort must come from within rather than from outside the Negro community."[108]

Antipathologism's growing influence was epitomized by the about-face of the National Urban League, where Billingsley had served as a research fellow. The Urban League had once been Moynihan's most reliable source of support among African Americans. By 1969, however, its president Whitney Young was no longer proud to have been quoted in *The Negro Family*. In the late 1960s, Young repositioned the Urban League in response to challenges by African American radicals. Young even embraced the phrase "Black Power," though mostly to repackage his longstanding advocacy of racial uplift and extensive federal antipoverty programs. Young attacked the Moynihan Report in his 1969 book, *Beyond Racism*: "Of all the distortions about Negro life in America, one of the most damaging has been the constant concern by white academic 'experts' . . . with the lack of stability of *the* Negro family." (Young's observation that some of these experts came "from broken families themselves" was a snipe at Moynihan.)[109] Young declared, "the black ghetto is more than a tangle of pathology," and highlighted the "resilience and strength shown by black people, and the fantastic successes they have wrought from a hostile environment."[110] In 1972, National Urban League research director Robert Hill published an influential pamphlet that emphasized, as its title indicated, *The Strengths of Black Families*. In a clear link to earlier criticisms of *The Negro Family*, Hill's mentor was Dorothy K. Newman, the Bureau of Labor Statistics researcher who was an early internal critic of the Moynihan Report and in 1968 produced a document at the Bureau colloquially known as the "counter-Moynihan Report Report."[111]

Though antipathologists chose a common target in the Moynihan Report, they disagreed about how best to characterize American families. One scholar astutely identified two competing alternatives to pathologism. The "cultural equivalent" perspective held that most African American families conformed to wider American norms, while the "cultural variant" perspective viewed African American families as diverging from American norms but equal or superior to them.[112] An established middle-class-led organization, the Urban League articulated the former perspective. For example, instead of focusing on the quarter of African American families headed by women, Young claimed, researchers should recognize that "the majority of all poor black families could manage to hold themselves together and meet every test of middle-class American standards for respectability is remarkable."[113] Among the "strengths" of African American families Hill cited were mainstream American values as "work," "achievement," and "religion."

Notwithstanding Billingsley's occasionally radical rhetoric, he too mostly hewed to the "cultural equivalent" perspective. He identified "sources of achievement" among African American families, revealing his roots in the social work tradition and his middle-class definition of achievement. Billingsley argued that "strong family life" led to achievement, though he did not equate a strong family with the nuclear family model.[114] Despite challenging ruling social scientific elites, Billingsley was embedded in mainstream scholarship. For example, *Black Families in White America* employed the sociological model of leading mainstream scholar Talcott Parsons. Bizarrely, Billingsley even cited the work of Moynihan supporters Rainwater and Pettigrew as providing "rays of hope."[115]

The "cultural variant" perspective's leading advocate was the indefatigable Robert Staples, who from the late 1960s published countless essays on African American families. Staples collaborated with Billingsley; for a time, he, Billingsley, and Joyce Ladner were colleagues at Howard University. Nevertheless, Staples thought Billingsley shared too much of Moynihan's perspective. He criticized Billingsley for devoting so much attention to affluent, two-parent African American families. Billingsley, he complained, shared "mostly the view of the middle-class sociologist who accepts middle-class norms, concludes that most black families share middle-class value orientations and prescribes action to eliminate poverty to bring disadvantaged black families into conformity with the modal middle-class family." In contrast, Staples upheld "the positive values in much of lower-class life."[116]

Whereas Billingsley represented the changed Urban League perspective, Staples reflected the influences of Black Power and the New Left. He was politically active in both CORE and the antiwar movement. Staples straddled the worlds of mainstream scholarship and radical politics, holding key editorial roles at both *Journal of Marriage and the Family* and *Black Scholar*. As with other African American family scholars of his generation, Staples felt the Moynihan Report poorly represented his experience. Born in Roanoke, Virginia, Staples grew up in a stable two-parent lower-middle-class family. In 1965, he entered a doctoral program in family sociology at the University of Minnesota, where he planned to study sexuality. He recalls that the "perfect storm" of publicity generated by the report redirected his attention to family structure. Suddenly there were not enough black experts on African

American families to meet the demand. Much of what Staples wrote on African American families was by request. For example, a white book editor suggested that Staples edit his influential anthology, *The Black Family*, first printed in 1971 and since published in six editions.[117] Were it not for the Moynihan Report, Staples would never have become a leading scholar of African American families. In fact, Staples credits the Moynihan Report with drawing attention to the study of African American families. He claims that although Moynihan had "no background, sensitivity, or training" in the subject, he brought visibility to the topic that it otherwise would not have received.[118]

Staples questioned white racial experts' authority. Rainwater's Pruitt-Igoe research illustrated for him how white social scientists exploited African American graduate researchers and falsified African American social life: "a white sociologist . . . did a study of lower-class black families in a housing project. He visited the housing project only twice, once just driving by it. His graduate students, mostly black, gathered the bulk of the data. He then wrote a book which depicted these people as the most wretched people in society."[119] Staples also questioned African American pathologists. In a contentious exchange in the *Black Scholar*, Staples attacked an article by psychologist Clemmont Vontress that described self-hatred and other disorders among African American men. "Brother Vontress," Staples claimed, had written "the Moynihan report reincarnated: another scholar, this time a black one, had introduced a brief indictment of slavery and racism to justify his subsequent slander of the black population."[120]

New interpretations of African American families sparked by the Moynihan Report controversy spread well beyond the field of sociology. Alex Haley's bestselling 1976 novel, *Roots*, adapted as a popular television mini-series in 1977, recounted the strengths of black families in the face of slavery and ongoing racial oppression. Some viewed *Roots* as a refutation of the Moynihan Report. For example, African American historian Benjamin Quarles praised the mini-series for revealing that "the black family . . . is not the 'tangle of pathologies' Moynihan called it."[121] African American photographer Carrie Mae Weems compiled her first major body of work, *Family Pictures and Stories* (1978–1984), in response to the Moynihan Report. Weems photographed members of her extended family engaged in everyday activities. The personal knowledge the images conveyed, Weems asserted, offered insights absent in sociological generalizations by distant outsiders such as Moynihan. Unlike antipathologist accounts that portrayed only the strengths of black families, Weems's photographs offered unvarnished portraits of her family. Still, Weems felt her empathetic photographs acknowledged the humanity of her African American subjects that the Moynihan Report had denied them.[122]

The controversy also reverberated in the revitalized field of African American history. A new generation of scholars refuted claims that slavery stripped African Americans of agency and culture associated with Stanley Elkins's work, which lost credibility because of its association with the Moynihan Report.[123] The new scholarship celebrated slave resistance and the robustness of slave culture. Historians discredited *The Negro Family*'s assumption that slavery devastated African American cultural and family life. Eugene Genovese, for example, debunked the "myth of the absent family" in his influential 1974 book, *Roll, Jordan, Roll*.[124]

Herbert Gutman wrote that his pivotal 1975 book, *The Black Family in Slavery and Freedom*, was "stimulated by the bitter public and academic controversy surrounding Daniel P. Moynihan's *The Negro Family*."[125] Like Robert Staples, Gutman likely would never have written on African American families but for the Moynihan Report controversy. In the mid-1960s, Gutman was best known as a labor historian. The left-wing Gutman supported the militant wing of the civil rights movement and shared its critique of the report as a rationalization of racial inequality. He saw an opportunity to disprove Moynihan's thesis by drawing on the work of Laurence Glasco, an African American graduate student working under his supervision at the State University of New York at Buffalo. Gutman asked Glasco to mine his recently computerized data from the 1855 Buffalo census for information about African American families. What Glasco found overturned the standard view; in his sample, the majority of African Americans lived in two-parent families. Gutman sought not only to correct the historical record but also to counteract the Moynihan Report's damaging political effects. As Glasco recalls, Gutman saw these results as a chance to "thrash the Moynihan Report."[126]

Gutman confronted Moynihan with the results of his research in a personal letter that enclosed a co-authored paper with Glasco that argued that their data disproved Moynihan's view on slavery's effects on African American families. To Gutman's dismay, Moynihan was unperturbed. The report's argument about slavery, Moynihan replied, "was not at all central to my thesis."[127] In fact, Moynihan claimed that Gutman's evidence on nineteenth-century African American family resilience only strengthened his report's thesis about the destructive effects of twentieth-century urbanization and male unemployment on contemporary African American families. Moynihan invited Gutman to meet in a bar and continue their discussion over drinks. He even cited Gutman and Glasco's paper in a 1970 essay.[128] Disappointed by Moynihan's casual deflection of his argument, Gutman conceded in his reply to Moynihan that African American families became destabilized "two generations later [after slavery] in the immigrant city."[129]

Though the Moynihan Report prompted *The Black Family in Slavery and Freedom*, Gutman never satisfactorily explained how his history disproved Moynihan's analysis of the deleterious effects of urbanization and unemployment on African Americans after the Great Migration.[130] Gutman wrote he found no "evidence that the black family [ever] crumbled or that a 'pathological' culture thrived."[131] However, ending his narrative in 1925 left little basis to judge Moynihan's depiction of contemporary African American families. (Eugene Genovese was on surer ground in *Roll, Jordan, Roll* when he criticized the "ill-fated Moynihan Report" solely for projecting "the story of the twentieth-century black ghettos backward in time and . . . assumed a historical continuity with slavery days."[132]) Gutman's choice to primarily attack Moynihan's short government report rather than the more substantial scholarship of E. Franklin Frazier underlines the Moynihan Report's preeminence as a target for left-wing scholars of the era.

Nevertheless, Gutman's major contribution to the reinterpretation of slavery struck a blow against pathologism. He rejected the notion that slavery created a "fatherless matrifocal . . . family," a view that he noted even many of Moynihan's critics shared.[133] Reflecting the influence of Black Power, Gutman emphasized the resilience of African American culture and the importance of seeing African Americans as agents, not just as victims of white racism. Like sociological critics of Moynihan, Gutman stressed African American agency and cultural strength: "Enslavement was harsh and constricted the enslaved. But it did not destroy their capacity to adapt and sustain the vital familial and kin associations and beliefs that served as the underpinning of a developing Afro-American culture."[134]

Since Moynihan's critics acknowledged his report fostered research on African American families, Moynihan in turn might have credited their criticism with making his report a canonical text in the study of African American families. For example, Staples's anthology, *The Black Family*, contained an entire section, "The Moynihan Report: Challenge and Response," which reprinted the report's chapter, "The Tangle of Pathology." Critics perpetuated the sociological abstraction, "the black family," which stressed racial difference at the expense of distinctions in social class. Thus they bolstered a tendency to discuss economic inequality in primarily racial terms. Because of their shared "history of racist oppression," Staples declared, "Black families cannot be compared, objectively, with white families. There is no evidence to indicate that Black and white families share the same experiences, even if they belong to the same socioeconomic group."[135] Billingsley too insisted that lower-class black families had more in common with middle-class black families than with lower-class white families.[136]

Antipathologists ignored the insights of Moynihan's early critics such as Hylan Lewis, who emphasized the diversity of African American family structure based on class and noted similarities between African American and white families at the same income levels. Instead, Black Sociologists' comparisons between middle-class white families and lower-class black families conflated race with class. Many civil rights critics of Moynihan has sought to direct debate to jobs, education, and racial discrimination instead of family. Yet the new generation of scholars of the African American family fought on the terrain defined by the Moynihan Report. Since the 1980s, Moynihan Report supporters such as William Julius Wilson have frequently charged that 1970s scholars ignored the topic of African American families. In fact, by keeping the subject alive in the 1970s, Black Sociologists ironically helped pave the way for Wilson's revival of pathologism in the 1980s.

Defining opposition to the Moynihan Report in terms of the shortcomings of "white social science" in misrepresenting "black families" obscured the question of what social functions the family should serve. The Moynihan Report united Black Sociologists in challenging its conclusions, but they had different notions of the family and how to study it. Some agreed with Moynihan about restoring the familial authority of African American men, while others combined Black Power with women's liberation. African American intellectuals proved just as divided as other Americans about family ideals. The emergence of feminism and other challenges to the nuclear family norm undermined the male-breadwinner ideal and added a vital element to debate over the Moynihan Report.

CHAPTER 5

Feminism and the Nuclear Family Norm

In 1970, African American poet June Jordan wrote "Memo to Daniel Pretty Moynihan":

> You done what you done
> I do what I can
>
> Don't you liberate me
> From my female black pathology
>
> I been working off my knees
> I been drinking what I please
>
> And when I vine
> I know I'm fine
> I mean
> All right for each and every Friday night
>
> But you been screwing me so long
> I got a idea something's wrong
> with you
>
> I got a simple proposition
> You takeover my position
>
> Clean your own house, babyface.[1]

A crucial figure in the Black Feminist movement, Jordan articulated what was by 1970 a common criticism of *The Negro Family* that emphasized its patriarchal ideals and its racial paternalism. Rejecting the report's portrayal of "female black pathology," Jordan celebrated African American women, averring that she was "All right for each and every Friday night." Her poem made Moynihan an archetype of white male domination. "You been screwing me so long" evokes the history of white male sexual exploitation of African American women dating from slavery. Jordan's closing injunction to the baby-faced Moynihan to "clean his own house" conveyed multiple meanings: white experts should stop making arrogant pronouncements about African American families; African American women working as domestic servants were fed up with their economic exploitation; and middle-class whites should address flaws in their own families.

The report was as much about normative family structure as about racial inequality. Moynihan consciously promoted "the values of a self-supporting, nuclear family, in which the male is normally the principal and, for some periods, the only wage earner."[2] While *The Negro Family* was immediately contentious, few early critics questioned its male-breadwinner model. Civil rights leader Bayard Rustin proclaimed that one of the report's ideas "we can all accept" was "that the Negro family can be reconstructed only where the Negro male is permitted to be the economic and psychological head of the family."[3] An otherwise critical editorial in the liberal Protestant journal *Christian Century* agreed: "When Moynihan states that . . . an inordinate number of Negro families are matrifocal and that such a society humiliates and debases the Negro male he is saying nothing new, nothing prejudicial, and nothing debatable."[4] By 1968, however, Moynihan recognized that the nuclear-family norm he promoted had become controversial. He now complained about "social radicals" who failed to grasp that "the 'middle class family' . . . is as much a biological necessity as it is a cultural inheritance."[5]

Feminists challenged the report as justifying gender inequality. Already in 1965 a few feminists questioned the report's implication that policy-makers should target job opportunities for black men at the expense of black women. A few years later, radical feminists attacked the report as a brief for patriarchal domination. Black Feminists proved among the report's most influential and comprehensive critics. To them, Moynihan propagated a pernicious myth of black "matriarchy" that combined racism with sexism. They noted that many African American male activists shared Moynihan's idea that achieving racial equality required black men to be patriarchs. According to Michele Wallace, Moynihan duped black men into confusing patriarchy with equality: "Your problem, buddy, he seemed to suggest, is this black woman of yours. You want to be equal but, if you're a man, you must do something about her first."[6]

Not only feminists challenged Moynihan's family ideal. Countercultural critics rejected the report's equation of masculinity with breadwinning; others questioned Moynihan's association of masculinity with military service. Anthropologists argued that equality entailed recognizing African Americans as part of a distinct subculture on par with that of other Americans. Understanding African American families solely as products of social inequality denied them their full humanity. In her classic 1974 refutation of the Moynihan Report, *All Our Kin*, which also rebutted Oscar Lewis's "culture of poverty" theory, Carol Stack combined a left-wing critique of liberal antipoverty measures, a challenge to the nuclear family ideal, and a call to view the family in cultural terms. Like many other feminists, Stack recognized the tangle of racial, gender, and class inequality.

The Desirability of Patriarchy

Pauli Murray was outraged when she first read about the Moynihan Report in *Newsweek*. She correctly understood that Moynihan endorsed increasing economic opportunities to African American men at the expense of jobs available to African American women.

Born in 1910, Murray spent her career combating both the racial discrimination of Jim Crow and the gender discrimination she termed "Jane Crow." A single African American woman frustrated by the male monopoly of her chosen profession of law, Murray identified with "the class of unattached, self-supporting women for whom employment opportunities were necessary to survival . . . the ones most victimized by a still prevalent stereotype that men are the chief breadwinners."[7] Writing to *Newsweek*'s editor, Murray questioned Moynihan's assumption that black women claimed a "disproportionate share" of white-collar and professional jobs versus black men. Talk of African American "matriarchy," she complained, did "a grave disservice to the thousands of Negro women in the United States who have struggled to prepare themselves for employment in a limited job market which . . . has severely restricted economic opportunities for all women as well as for Negroes." Unlike Moynihan, Murray applauded African Americans' relatively gender-equal educational attainment, particularly since so many African American women served as heads of family. African American women's economic achievements, Murray insisted, did not cause African American men's low economic position. "[I]t is bitterly ironic," she protested, "that Negro women should be . . . censured for their efforts to overcome a handicap not of their making and for trying to meet the standards of the country as a whole."[8]

Newsweek refused to publish Murray's letter. In fact, Murray's critique of "Jane Crow" was largely submerged during early public debate about the Moynihan Report. Nevertheless, Murray foreshadowed feminist challenges to the male-breadwinner ideal that would crucially affect the Moynihan Report controversy. *The Negro Family* became public at the moment second-wave feminism emerged. In 1963, Betty Friedan disputed the male-breadwinner/female-homemaker model in her bestselling book, *The Feminine Mystique*. Friedan singled out for attack a book cited in *The Negro Family*. Moynihan's report quoted anthropologist Margaret Mead's *Man and Woman* as proof that the adult male's role in every human society is "to provide food for some female and her young."[9] Friedan lambasted Mead for making culturally determined gender roles seem natural and for glorifying "women in the female role—as defined by their sexual biological function."[10]

In the mid-1960s, feminists organized to demand equal access to employment and to challenge systematic gender discrimination that reserved the best jobs for men on the grounds that they were the primary supporters of their families. Murray and others argued that the 1964 Civil Rights Act would only benefit African American women if it prohibited both racism and sexism. While the act did prohibit gender discrimination in employment, feminists had to pressure the Equal Employment Opportunity Commission (EEOC) to fully enforce it, as administrators initially focused solely on racial discrimination. In 1966, Murray, Friedan, and others founded the National Organization for Women (NOW) to push employment rights for women. The mainstream feminism NOW represented is sometimes mistakenly regarded as elitist, solely concerned with securing rights for affluent white women. The campaign for equal employment opportunities, however, benefited all women workers, especially those who could not rely upon the family wage system.[11]

Some feminists initially supported the Moynihan Report. Dorothy Height, leader of the National Council of Negro Women (NCNW), at first welcomed its publication. Moynihan quoted Height in *The Negro Family*: "If the Negro woman has a major underlying concern, it is the status of the Negro man and his position in the community and his need for feeling himself an important person . . . in order that he may strengthen his home."[12] *The Negro Family* so impressed Height that she distributed dozens of copies to contacts. It inspired the November 1965 NCNW convention, which featured the theme, "The Negro Woman: New Roles in Family and Community Responsibility." The convention call mentioned the Moynihan Report as positive impetus for discussion.[13] However, in the face of growing criticism from civil rights and feminist activists, Height quickly backed off her support for Moynihan. By December 1965, Moynihan complained, "Even dear Dorothy Height has turned on me!"[14]

Mary Dublin Keyserling helped change Height's mind with her keynote address at the 1965 NCNW convention. She headed the Women's Bureau in the Department of Labor since 1964 when she replaced Esther Peterson, a Moynihan ally. Keyserling was part of a small network of white feminist opponents of the Moynihan Report who served in the Johnson administration. They generated resistance to *The Negro Family* behind the scenes, but rarely voiced their criticisms openly. In her 1965 address, for example, Keyserling did not mention Moynihan or the report. Instead she disputed the claim in a recent *Daedalus* article that black women were "overemployed" in comparison with black men, omitting Moynihan's name as the author. Keyserling's roots were in a different liberal tradition from Moynihan's. She had been integral to a circle of left-liberal feminists in the 1930s and 1940s who worked within government to combat gender inequality as well as class and race inequality. Though she moderated her views because of McCarthyism, her critique of Moynihan demonstrated that she still connected these various forms of injustice.[15]

Like other feminists, Keyersling offered a different vision from Moynihan of how to help lower-class women. Instead of creating male-headed nuclear families, she believed, public policy should improve women's wages so they could better support families on their own. Though Keyserling worried about "family breakdown" among African Americans, she thought it absurd to cite the wage labor of African American women as its cause. Rather, African American women's economic contributions were a "stabilizing and enriching factor" for families. She quoted with alarm the head of a Washington, D.C., job-training center: "We are not encouraging women. We're trying to reestablish the male as the head of the house." Contrariwise, she asserted that it was particularly important to provide job opportunities to African American women since so many of them had low-wage jobs and provided crucial economic support to their families. She pleaded, "let us not fall into the error of believing that we solve an unemployment problem by trying to take one group of people out of jobs they are now in and which they need desperately, in order to open employment opportunities for others."[16]

Other feminists complained privately about the Moynihan Report. Elizabeth Wickenden, an Office of Equal Opportunity consultant with strong connections in the government welfare establishment, attributed the failure of the 1965 White House Conference on Civil Rights to uproar over the report. "Women's groups," she recounted, "felt it emphasized the plight of the Negro male at the expense of the Negro woman and hence carried anti-feminist overtones."[17] The report similarly irked Catherine East, career civil servant and contributor to the President's Commission on the Status of Women. East confidentially forwarded her highly annotated copy of *The Negro Family* to contacts outside government. To East, Moynihan not only cooked up the new racism identified by his civil rights critics but "seasoned [it] with a generous measure of anti-feminism." In her view, the report represented a "new momism" that blamed strong women for family problems. Writing to a liberal Protestant minister, East asserted that Moynihan's Catholicism led him to see "one-parent homes" as "pathological."[18]

The Moynihan Report also alarmed Martha Griffiths, Democratic Representative from Michigan and key proponent of the feminist Equal Rights Amendment. In a letter to Secretary of Labor Willard Wirtz publicized in the press, Griffiths protested, "It is high time to disperse the syrupy miasma flowing from the Moynihan report that 'Negro women have it good,' when the facts are just the opposite and produce detrimental effects on their economic progress." Griffiths slammed the Department of Labor for focusing exclusively on African American male unemployment, ignoring similarly high rates of joblessness among African American women. The male-breadwinner ideal, she contended, precluded training programs for women that would benefit families in poverty: "this world has been dominated for so long by the myth 'nice women stay at home and rear their families supported by nice men' that the men who make the laws never face reality and the knowledge that in a large number of instances women are supporting families, and the only way you can ever give those families proper protection is to give the women adequate training and decent jobs."[19] When Moynihan learned of Griffiths's letter, he requested a copy. Misreading her opposition as misunderstanding, Moynihan tried to convince her that "part of the outburst against that report of mine came from a kind of fire-breathing feminist type who is fighting against attitudes that simply no longer exist."[20] Moynihan was so steeped in family wage ideology that he could not comprehend why feminists objected to targeting job opportunities at African American men.

In 1965, Pauli Murray blamed gender discrimination for inhibiting women workers who were "trying to meet the standards of the country as a whole." A few years later, radical feminists questioned these standards. For them, the Moynihan Report represented a broader problem: a system of patriarchal control extending from the boardroom to the bedroom. Armed with the slogan, "the personal is political," radical feminists formed consciousness-raising groups throughout the country to discuss how individual problems resulted from patriarchal oppression. Their critique of the male-breadwinner family model surpassed that of earlier feminists, who hoped to make female-headed families economically viable but avoided directly challenging patriarchy. Unlike early feminists such as Betty Friedan, radical feminists such as Kate Millet and Shulamith Firestone criticized all forms of male domination, pointing to its sexual roots.[21]

A radical feminist critique of the Moynihan Report emerged from a surprising source: a 1971 position paper commissioned by NOW, the bastion of mainstream feminism. Merrillee A. Dolan's "Moynihan, Poverty Programs, and Women—A Female Viewpoint" castigated the male-breadwinner family: "His entire report is a strong statement on the desirability of patriarchy. It is a plea for the government's poverty policies to strengthen the patriarchal system and leave women to the mercy of a man's economic support." That no one yet had publicly criticized the report as a "pure slander of women" proved "just how patriarchal our society is." The opposition of NOW to the Moynihan Report indicates that the organization was not solely concerned with the problems of well-off white women. Dolan's report emerged out of NOW's "Women in Poverty" taskforce, which she headed.[22]

Aileen Hernandez, the African American who succeeded Friedan as NOW president, commissioned Dolan's paper. Hernandez felt that the male-breadwinner ideal of *The Negro Family* ensured that women did not benefit from government antipoverty measures. "So many of [Moynihan's] damaging notions," Hernandez informed Dolan, "have formed the basis of the federal policies which either ignore women altogether or actually worsen their circumstances."[23] "Don't write about blacks," she told Dolan, instructing her to instead analyze "Moynihan's infamous study" in terms of "women in poverty and how the ideas of Moynihan have permeated the poverty programs' *man*power training."[24] Dolan did as Hernandez requested, but also went beyond her remit and passionately assaulted patriarchal authority in general.

Born in 1941, Dolan established herself in the 1960s as a leading feminist in New Mexico where she worked as a state investigator combating job discrimination and implementing affirmative action programs. Her concerns typified late 1960s feminism, as she fought for abortion rights and against sexual abuse of women. Dolan's campaign against sexual violence reflected the motto, "the personal is political," as male relatives had abused her sexually as a child.[25] Dolan's judgment of the Moynihan Report was unequivocal: "nearly everything imaginable is wrong with it." Her paper reflected the influence of African American feminists (including Murray, whom she cited). It was especially inspired by the welfare rights movement, which called attention to the economic exploitation of poor women, especially African Americans. Dolan absorbed the movement's attention to poverty's structural causes: "People are poor for one reason—the economic system in the United States is not structured to eliminate poverty, and it is not intended to be. It depends upon a cheap reserve of labor—extracted primarily from women and minorities and especially minority women."

Dolan saw the Moynihan Report as an attempt to impose the patriarchal family model upon poor African American women. Unlike earlier feminists such as Murray, Dolan maintained that denying women equal economic opportunities was part of a broader system of male domination. "Government meddling in women's lives to try to force them to hook male 'breadwinners,'" she declared, "is certainly totalitarian, even if it is done through economic coercion measures." Contra Moynihan, Dolan advocated policies to enable female financial self-sufficiency so that a woman could make her "own decisions about how and with whom she shall live (and sleep)." On Moynihan's failure to support child care centers, Dolan remarked, "Moynihan would prefer to avoid this expensive proposition and force women to compete for mates—no matter their personal preference." Again taking her cue from African American feminists, Dolan challenged Moynihan's language of "illegitimate" births, claiming the term should be abandoned as it "degrades both women and children who are not the property of a man" and prized "legal status on a piece of paper" above the actual love and care a child received.

Though African American poverty genuinely concerned Dolan, she most vigorously objected to Moynihan's assumption of male dominance. She described the male-breadwinner family that Moynihan idealized as a form of "slavery," an analogy few African American feminists would have made. The nuclear family entailed "the male holding the economic strings and there-fore power over the female whose job is house-cleaning, babysitting, and pro-viding sex services." To Dolan, the report's passage arguing that men needed to "strut" just like roosters did was a classic example of sexist analogy to the animal kingdom. Moynihan was a misogynist who "thoroughly dislikes and resents" women. Dolan mocked Moynihan's endorsement of military service for African American men: "According to Moynihan . . . women are so ter-rible that it is a fantastic relief to get away from them. Never mind that the service is experiencing explosive racial problems. It is still better than being around women."

Dolan projected onto the Moynihan Report her concern with "the ob-scene exploitation of the female body." Like other feminists, Dolan politicized sexual violence against women. Dolan contended that Moynihan's pushing women to depend economically on male breadwinners was "forcing women to sex." By denying women the means to economically support themselves, she alleged, Moynihan drove women into sex work: "Women who are des-perate to earn a living, if they are young and pretty enough, are economically forced to work as topless or topless-bottomless 'go-go girls,' in joints controlled by gangsters."

Ultimately, Dolan questioned Moynihan's fundamental assumption that the "white middle class family [is] a desirable goal." Moynihan and other post-war liberals thought the middle-class family embodied the American Dream. In contrast, Dolan painted a bleak picture of American nuclear families pop-ulated by tyrannical husbands and miserable wives addicted to alcohol and tranquilizers. Moynihan's ideal family model was hardly stable: "One looks at the high divorce rate . . . and the undercurrents of tension and hatred . . . and wonders what Moynihan means. . . . Violence in such families, both phys-ical and psychological, is not at all rare." Dolan endorsed countercultural young Americans who "seem to be saying that all is not lovely and 'stable' even if daddy is bringing in the bread and mommie is staying at home wait-ing on daddy and the kids."[26]

Feminists recast middle-class white men, epitomized by Moynihan, as the dominant oppressive force in American society. Unlike Dolan, who wrote at the behest of a major national organization, Linda Driver of Kalamazoo, Mich-igan, wrote on her own initiative an exposé of the Moynihan Report, "A White Man's Myth Explored." Though Driver called what she sent Moynihan an "open letter," likely no more than a few people read her analysis. Neverthe-less, her response reflected a popular 1960s analysis of the Moynihan Report that addressed racism and sexism while challenging white male patriarchy. Though Driver was white, she was clearly influenced by Black Power ideals and rhetoric. Citing Stokely Carmichael and Amiri Baraka, she derided the Moynihan Report as "permeated throughout with the sanctimonious odor of THE MAN's (i.e., Mr. Charley's, Big Daddy's, Uncle Sam's), approval." Driver criticized Moynihan's paternalistic stance toward African American men: "Give the black man 'equal' jobs, Mr. Moynihan says, and you'll make him a man in the eyes of the black woman, his black babies, and even—God be praised for such benevolence—in the eyes of the white man." Like Dolan, Driver saw Moynihan's report as an assertion of white male dominance over both African Americans and women: "I've been here for over three hundred years, just like that black man, [a]nd I've been the victim as he is the victim of the same oppressor—the white male." Driver unfavorably contrasted the male-breadwinner family model to the "alleged matriarchal family" which preserved "the American Negro's perception of himself as a human being, capable of human experiences and relationships—relationships that count— that are real—not fake ones based on the socio-religious pattern of the white middle class ideal marriage thing, where it seems the bond of family unity is not so much love as it is legality." In the late 1960s, feminists such as Driver were not the only vocal critics of the nuclear-family norm. They were joined by a growing number of men who rejected the Moynihan Report's equation of masculinity and breadwinning.[27]

I Am a Man

In 1968, black sanitation workers on strike in Memphis carried posters reading "I Am a Man" that powerfully conveyed their demand to be treated with dignity. Like many participants in the Moynihan Report controversy, the men who held these signs associated masculinity with breadwinning and saw men's inability to support their families as an indictment of economic inequality. By the late 1960s, however, critics challenged the Moynihan Report's conception of masculinity that valorized financially supporting a wife and children. Though most debate over the Moynihan Report focused on its portrayal of femininity, its model of masculinity also invited challenge.

Moynihan's ideal of middle-class masculinity rankled the late 1960s counterculture, which decried the competitive middle-class "rat race" as stifling and inauthentic. The counterculture popularized a broader post-World War

II concern pervading the works of middlebrow writers and the pages of *Playboy*: middle-class white men were losing their virility. The icon of the American Dream—the successful male executive—was a repressed, conformist "organization man." Though the critique of middle-class masculinity targeted the inauthentic corporate workplace, countercultural men also disparaged the housewife as an agent of emasculation whose desire for home and family constrained the male breadwinner's individuality. The late 1960s witnessed accelerating postwar male revolt against the breadwinner ethic; increasing numbers of men openly rejected the notion that they must be family patriarchs in order to be fully masculine. One hippie commune proclaimed in 1967, "The . . . betty crocker miss clarol family institution is a death form. Marriage, responsibility for children, alimony are death.' "[28]

New Left critic Marcus Raskin alleged that matriarchy was hardly just an African American problem. "The problem of maleness or momism," Raskin asserted, "is not something upon which Negroes have a monopoly." Writing for the left-wing Catholic publication, *Ramparts*, Raskin claimed, "Many of our readers are painfully aware of the castrating Jewish, Irish, or Italian matriarch." Raskin observed that no one in the Johnson administration devised plans to "rebuild the Jewish, Irish and Italian family by restoring manhood to Jewish, Irish and Italian men." While Raskin agreed that matriarchal family structure hindered African Americans, he criticized the Moynihan Report for seeing middle-class family values as the solution: "It is only the foolish who would think that the middle-class is the be-all and end-all of existence. It is hardly something that has to be emulated."[29] To Raskin, liberals eager to aid African American men's competitiveness actually trapped them in a repressive rat race: "What now seemed necessary was to get the Negro ready for these goodies. He was to prepare himself to run that race of opportunism which his white American brethren had become so adept at running."

Underground journalist Walt Shepperd concurred. He denounced Moynihan for projecting concern with his own masculinity onto black men. Middle-class white men were matriarchy's real victims: "the notion of matri-focal Negro families is a projection by the white middle-class of its own true character. A glance at the Sunday funnies (a window on the suburban mind) shows Blondie and Lucy chopping at the gonads of Dagwood and Charlie Brown."[30] Shepperd suggested that all the traits that anthropologist Oscar Lewis listed as part of a "culture of poverty" aptly described the affluent American middle class: alcoholism, violence, authoritarianism, fatalism, male chauvinism, and a female martyr complex. Though Shepperd criticized "male chauvinism,"

he was hardly a feminist given his anxiety about strong women emasculat-
ing men.

African American writer Albert Murray similarly questioned whether
middle-class masculinity was worth emulating. Moynihan, he claimed, "implies without so much as a blush that all the repressions, frustrations, and
neuroses of the white Organization Man add up to an enviable patriarchal
father image rather than the frightened insomniac, boot-licking conformist."
To Murray, white women were the true matriarchs. Moynihan made "no mention at all of the incontestable fact that the aggressiveness of white American
women is such that they are regarded as veritable amazons not only in the
Orient but also by many Europeans and not a few people at home."[31]

Moynihan's opponents questioned his premise that black men particularly suffered from sexual identity problems. Black Sociologist Robert Staples
praised the greater "sexual permissiveness of black people" and their refusal
of a sexual double standard where "white women lack the same sexual freedom as white men."[32] He identified with the sexual liberation movement,
which found the middle-class family ideal stifling and repressive. "The sexual
norms of the Black community," he argued, "should be revealed and accepted,
with gratitude that Blacks avoid the sexual neuroses of White America."[33]
Although Staples countered presumptions that black men suffered sexual
disorders, he replicated stereotypes about oversexualized African American men: "Their sexual expression derives from the emphasis in black
culture on feeling, on releasing the natural functions of the body without
artificiality or mechanical movements. In some circles this is called 'soul'
and may be found among people of African descent throughout the world . . .
black men do not moderate their enthusiasm for sex relations as white
men do."[34]

Male homosexuality was an important subtext in discussions of black masculinity prompted by the Moynihan Report. Moynihan relied on a postwar
tradition of social science that saw black men as especially prone to homosexuality because of their inability to play conventional patriarchal roles.[35]
Like most liberals of his time, Moynihan took heterosexual norms for granted;
homosexuality was considered a disorder by the American Psychiatric Association until 1973. Though the Moynihan Report did not mention homosexuality, it linked masculinity to supporting a woman financially. In his 1966
report to the Carnegie Foundation, Moynihan feared that black male homosexuality endangered his goal of increasing the number of black male breadwinners. Moynihan bemoaned the loss of "sexual identity" among the

disproportionately high number of African American men in prison. Worried that prison authorities were abandoning attempts to "segregate" homosexuals, Moynihan speculated, "The likelihood that one of the first experiences of a young prisoner . . . is to be forced to submit to the homosexual uses of older inmates suggests that this could be an important ingredient in family disruption among lower class Negroes." Consequently, Moynihan urged Carnegie to sponsor "a determined look at the role of homosexuality in the prison system" as part of its research program on African Americans.[36]

Many postwar social scientists believed African Americans were particularly likely to be gay because they lacked masculinity. By the late 1960s, however, critics increasingly rejected the ideas that black men were emasculated and that homosexuality constituted a lack of masculinity. Ralph Ellison, for example, challenged both assumptions: "The Moynihan Report complained that Negroes don't strut anymore. Why, Negro faggots are the struttingest people I know."[37] Robert Staples contested the notion that black men were "latent homosexuals."[38] (However, Staples's conflation of heterosexuality with masculinity reinforced heteronormativity.) The Moynihan Report never became the target for gay men that it was for feminists. Nevertheless, the gay liberation movement undermined Moynihan's male-breadwinner family ideal. Gay advocacy of sexual privacy rights also made any attempt to encourage a particular family model for Americans through government policy appear coercive.[39]

To many critics, Moynihan's plan to bolster the masculinity of African American men by drafting them into the army was the report's most disturbing aspect. The escalation of the Vietnam War after 1965 dramatically altered the context of Moynihan's suggestion. Although he never enthusiastically supported the war and had turned against it by 1967, Moynihan continued to push for the army to recruit more African American men because soldiering was historically "a path of upward mobility for those born rude and poor." Even as Johnson escalated the war, Moynihan recommended, "every Negro youth from a deprived background, either urban slum or rural backwater, ought to serve a period in the armed forces in order to train them in the 'national standards' needed to succeed in American society.[40] Moynihan felt military service would pave the way for African American success as it had for him and other white ethnics who served during World War II. He also viewed returning African American war veterans as racial role models: "When these Negro G.I.s come back from Viet Nam, I would meet them with a real estate agent, a girl who looks like [African American actress] Diahann Carroll, and a list of jobs. I'd try to get half of them into the grade schools, teaching kids who've never had anyone but women telling them what to do."[41]

Moynihan's logic shaped government policy. In 1966, Secretary of Defense Robert McNamara announced Project 100,000 to enable those who failed the selective service exam to enter the armed forces. The program was based on suggestions Moynihan made in his 1963 government report, *One-Third of a Nation*. To publicize the program, the Department of Defense claimed that military service would aid disadvantaged Americans. In fact, they mainly needed more men to fight in Vietnam. In practice, the program failed as an antipoverty measure but succeeded in ensuring that working-class and black Americans bore the brunt of fighting in Vietnam. In most cases, the promised training was not carried out, and Project 100,000 recruits suffered twice the death rate of American troops as a whole.[42]

By the late 1960s, many Americans doubted that American masculinity required serving the nation in wartime. New Leftist Raskin questioned Moynihan's claim that an African American in the army would "feel like a man." Rather the military was an "authoritarian system," analogous to slavery as it imposed "dehumanization, emasculation, and blind obedience."[43] Army discipline would emasculate black men rather than empower them. The radical white psychiatrist Joel Kovel similarly castigated Moynihan's martial masculinity in his influential 1970 book, *White Racism*. The report, Kovel contended, "exhorted the black man to use his State-granted virility for the greater glory of all in the service of our military."[44] Like Raskin, Kovel saw the military as the quintessential example of how hierarchical institutions suppressed individuality:

> the Moynihan Report proclaimed the military as perhaps the best way to black manhood. Yet what kind of manhood is so fostered by military life? Isn't it simply the mechanized—indeed, robotized—reduction of humanity to selfless tools of the will of culture, the grinding of both white and black into gray? Nowhere in our culture is there less freedom, less autonomy, less originality, joy and affirmation; nowhere is there more cold calculation, more mindless regimentation, more dullness, more banality.[45]

Kovel identified the Moynihan Report as an example of "metaracism" (similar to institutional racism) which renounced racial prejudice but affirmed the oppressive social system—embodied by the imperialist war in Vietnam—that had earlier been sustained by scientific racism.

The Vietnam War's unpopularity and the racial disparity among its casualities made African American leaders increasingly skeptical of the military as an effective means of social advancement and eroded popular African American belief that the "right to fight" in the American military demonstrated citizenship. Moynihan complained that African American men were underrepresented in the armed forces, but they were overrepresented in Vietnam War fatalities. In 1965, for example, though less than one in ten soldiers was black, one in four combat deaths was African American. Forty-one percent of recruits under Project 100,000 were African American; the majority were assigned to the infantry and sent to Vietnam. In addition, African Americans experienced racial bias from local draft boards and army entrance exams that disproportionately assigned blacks to combat roles. The Selective Service punished African American activists by drafting them, most famously in the case of boxer Muhammad Ali.[46] Black Power leaders in particular criticized the exploitation of African American soldiers and the war itself, which they viewed as part of the same imperialism that oppressed blacks at home. The 1966 Black Panther Party platform called for African American exemption from military service and Stokely Carmichael exclaimed, "A mercenary is a hired killer and any black man serving in this man's army is a black mercenary, nothing else."[47]

The Nation of Islam long opposed American militarism (its leader Elijah Muhammad was jailed for refusing to register for the World War II draft). Nation of Islam minister Louis Farrakhan confronted Moynihan over his suggestion that more black men join the military in his multi-part interview for *Muhammad Speaks*. Moynihan agreed when Farrakhan asked, "If you have a greater proportion of blacks carrying the burden of an unpopular war, don't you think the government's commitment to the blood of these black soldiers should be to improve the sickening conditions under which black people have to live in the continental United States?"[48] However, Farrakhan rejected the notion that African American men should fight a war to receive equal status in the United States. "It is absolutely criminal," Farrakhan declared, to offer military service as the route to economic advancement "after the government forgot about the health, education and welfare of black people all these years."[49]

The images that illustrated Farrakhan's interview underscored the Nation of Islam's opposition to Moynihan's martial masculinity and the war.

Alongside one installment appeared a collage of three images: a photograph of Moynihan striking a thoughtful pose in his office chair; a cartoon of Uncle Sam enlisting black men into the army; and a drawing of a black man pointing a gun at a defenseless Vietnamese woman and her two children.[50] Another illustration depicted the Grim Reaper standing over a mass Vietnamese grave. Beside him stands a black man wearing a suit. Below is a caption of Moynihan's statement in the interview, "as long as we are at war in Asia, there are going to be plenty of jobs in America."[51] These images directly tied Moynihan's advocacy of African American advancement through the military to the murder of Vietnamese civilians.

Critics of Moynihan's militarist masculinity often advocated his patriarchal ideal of the family. The Nation of Islam, for example, fully endorsed the male-breadwinner model. It simply rejected Moynihan's means of achieving it. Elijah Muhammad preached, "The woman is man's field to produce his nation."[52] Such sentiments drew the ire of Black Feminists, who directly attacked Moynihan's patriarchal ideals.

Black Feminism and the Matriarchy Myth

"Just as black men were busiest attacking Moynihan," Michele Wallace complained, "they were equally busy attacking the black woman for being a matriarch."[53] Wallace was only twenty-seven years old when she wrote *Black Macho and the Myth of the Superwoman,* the 1979 book that was widely reported in the mainstream media and landed her on the cover of the feminist *Ms.* magazine. She was the daughter of artist Faith Ringgold, who brought attention to the history of white male sexual exploitation of African American women with her *Slave Rape Series* paintings in the early 1970s. Wallace popularized a decade of Black Feminist commentary on the Moynihan Report by attacking its racial paternalism and male-breadwinner ideology. She faulted Moynihan for reviving the "myth of the superwoman": the notion that African American women were powerful "matriarchs" who held disproportionate authority in their families and communities. The report, Wallace maintained, activated hostility toward African American women among African American men. Moynihan "bared the black man's awful secret for all to see—that he had never been able to make his woman get down on her knees."[54] To Wallace, African American men's ready acceptance of Moynihan's thesis explained why the struggle for black liberation had been derailed by the pursuit of "Black Macho."

Wallace followed other African American feminists who battled the Moynihan Report in a proxy war against the patriarchal ideals of African American men. By criticizing the Moynihan Report, Black Feminists such as Frances Beale challenged the black male radical who "when it comes to women . . . seems to take his guidelines from the pages of the *Ladies' Home Journal*."[55] *The Negro Family* provided an indirect target for Black Feminists wary of alienating black male radicals, whom they saw as crucial allies in the fight against racism. Highlighting black male radicals' commonalities with Moynihan would force them to reexamine their gender ideology. Far from being part of a distinctively African American culture, Black Feminists argued, patriarchy was simply the white middle-class ideal. Black Feminists pointed out that African Americans who complained about "emasculation" and "matriarchy" agreed with Moynihan. Joanna Clark compared "the brother nattering away about how we've been lopping off balls long enough, it's time to stand aside" with "people like Glazer and Moynihan carrying on about our matriarchy and [urging black women to] confine ourselves to standing behind the man of the family."[56] For Black Feminists, the Moynihan Report illustrated the interconnected oppression of African Americans, women, and the poor. They found its racism, sexism, and defense of capitalism inextricable; thus they pioneered the idea of "intersectionality"—interactions between different forms of oppression.[57]

Black Feminism grew out of the Black Power movement and shared its demands for racial self-definition and challenges to institutionalized racism. Its grounding in Black Power differentiated it from the earlier work of African American feminists such as Pauli Murray and Aileen Hernandez, who similarly stressed connections between racial and gender oppression. Black Feminists believed that neither male-led Black Power organizations nor the white-led feminist movement adequately represented African American women's concerns. The first Black Feminist organization, the Black Women's Liberation Caucus, coalesced in 1968 within the Black Power organization, SNCC; in 1969, it split off and became the Third World Women's Alliance. A series of short-lived organizations formed over the subsequent decade, including the National Black Feminist Organization (1973) and its offshoot, the Combahee River Collective (1975).[58] Perhaps the most significant Black Feminist organization was the National Welfare Rights Organization (NWRO), founded in 1966, which derived its energy from an activist rank-and-file of African American women who deposed the organization's male leadership in 1972. In pushing rights for welfare recipients, NWRO powerfully connected race, gender, and class oppression. Its leader, Johnnie Tillmon, an African American woman, simultaneously attacked the male-breadwinner ideal and the political and economic oppression of African American women. She criticized AFDC, the federal program providing aid to single mothers, as "a supersexist marriage" in which "You trade in *a* man for *the* man."[59]

Black Feminists debunked the myth of an African American "matriarchy." Though the Moynihan Report was the most prominent recent manifestation of the matriarchy thesis at the time of Black Feminism's emergence, the idea had deep roots in American history and culture. In the 1960s, African American women remained one of the most stigmatized groups in American society. For example, Louisiana Senator Russell Long publicly referred to a group of African American welfare rights protesters as "brood mares."[60]

The Moynihan Report resonated with stereotypes of African American "matriarchy" in a 1967 *Parade* magazine article, "Negro Problem: Women Rule the Roost," which quoted extensively from *The Negro Family*. According to its author, Hollywood reporter Lloyd Shearer, the root of African American problems was African American women's unnatural power over their men. Shearer opined, "The reason Negro men so frequently desert their families is that they feel inferior to their women. They feel inferior, because they are inferior—educationally, economically, morally—and this omnipresent inferiority breeds hostility." Two illustrations demonstrated Shearer's point. One presented photographs of African American women celebrities including Lena Horne and Eartha Kitt with the caption, "All of the above were or are married to whites, a vital fact which points up the rejection of the Negro male by his own women and undercuts his status." The other, a photograph of a policeman arresting a black man during a recent riot, was captioned, "Negro male hostility, born of rejection." The juxtaposition of images suggested that African American women's rejection of African American men was the root cause of ghetto uprisings.[61]

Black Feminists believed that by portraying male dominance as necessary to black empowerment, African American men reinforced popular stereotypes apparent in Shearer's article. Many Black Power leaders sought to combat the "emasculation" of African American men, a problem they believed dated from slavery and was exacerbated by black women's power in their families and communities. For example, in his bestselling *Soul on Ice*, Black Panther Party leader Eldridge Cleaver declared, "We shall have our manhood. We shall have it or the earth will be leveled by our attempts to gain it."[62] While Cleaver pinpointed white supremacy, he also targeted black women; a character in his book suggested that black women served as "silent allies" of white men in the emasculation of black men.[63] Unlike Moynihan, Cleaver did not advocate middle-class breadwinning, but he did insist on male dominance. Some Black Power leaders promoted patriarchal ideals as part of an authentically African tradition to which African Americans should return. For example, Maulana Karenga, leader of the black nationalist organization US who popularized wearing dashikis and invented the holiday Kwanzaa, pronounced, "What makes a woman appealing is femininity and she can't be feminine without being submissive."[64]

Many African American women also accepted that racial progress required prioritizing African American men's advancement. When Black Feminist Inez Smith Reid surveyed African American women, she found many agreed with a respondent who suggested that African American women should "stand by our men and try not to take the leading role." A beautician she interviewed who said, "I don't think that the men should be listening to what Moynihan and others say" nevertheless asserted that African American women should "save our men because the system has crushed them so bad." Many black women agreed with Moynihan on what an ideal husband should be: "protector, supporter, and companion." For low-wage workers, the idea of a man's financial support was particularly attractive.[65]

Even some Black Studies scholars who criticized the black matriarchy thesis replicated much of the Moynihan Report's gender ideology. For example, in an influential 1970 article in *Black Scholar*, Robert Staples attacked Moynihan and others for promoting "The Myth of the Black Matriarchy." The myth, Staples alleged, was a "cruel hoax," part of a "white ruling class" strategy to divide and conquer African American men and women.[66] Staples's claim that gender tensions among African Americans owed to outside oppressors absolved black men of sexism. While Staples attacked Moynihan for overstating matriarchal dominance in African American communities, he too figured racial inequality in terms of African American men's inability to assert family dominance. "Many black men," Staples complained, "have not been permitted to become the kings of their castles" because of the "inordinate power" held by black women. Employment discrimination, Staples asserted, affected black men more than black women.[67] Unlike Moynihan, Staples thought black manhood could best be achieved through political rebellion. He positively cited the "voluntary" accession of black women to "almost exclusively" male leadership in the civil rights movement and insisted that "black females" in movement organizations "inevitably defer to some competent black male, an act which shows how much they really prefer the dominating position they supposedly have in black society."[68] For Staples, the most important role the African American woman could play in the black liberation struggle was that of a mother, who deserved respect because "From her womb have come the revolutionary warriors of our time."[69]

While Black Feminists agreed with Staples that white elites promoted the black matriarchy myth to divide African American men and women, they disagreed with his gender ideology. Linda La Rue denounced him for implying that "black women will be able to separate their femaleness from their blackness . . . or that male freedom ought to come first; or finally, that the freedom of black women and men, and the freedom of black people as a whole, are not one and the same."[70] Black Feminists thoroughly repudiated the matriarchy myth. For example, in an influential 1969 essay, Jean Carey Bond and Patricia Peery asked, "Is the Black Male Castrated?" Citing African American men's recent history of political resistance, they answered with a resounding "no." Yet they worried that the Moynihan Report had so successfully popularized the matriarchy myth that "even Blacks have swallowed his assumptions and conclusions hook, line, and sinker." They observed, "It is ironic that at a time when Blacks are newly perceiving and denouncing the shallowness of white analyses of the Black experience, many members of the avantgarde are still capable of being mesmerized by racist social scientific thought."[71] According to Bond and Peery, Moynihan promoted the matriarchy myth to divide African Americans, but black men accepted it to assert their supremacy over black women. By claiming emasculation, African American men could insist, "Women must abandon their 'matriarchal' behavior, learn to speak only when they are spoken to, and take up positions three paces . . . behind their men."[72]

Black Feminists thought the notion of an African American matriarchy absurd. Presumably referring to the Moynihan Report, a Black Feminist in Los Angeles told a reporter, "Some white man wrote this book about the black matriarchy, saying that black women ran the community. Which is bull. We don't run no community. We went out and worked because they wouldn't give our men jobs."[73] Bond and Peery suggested, "Black women, domineering or not, have not had the power in this male-dominated culture to effect a coup against anyone's manhood."[74] Black Feminists recognized that Moynihan used

"matriarchy" to normalize male dominance by complaining about roughly
equal levels of educational attainment among black men and black women.
As they pointed out, African American women were the most disadvantaged
group of American workers, earning on average less than African American
men and significantly less than white women. To Brenda Eichelberger, a
founder of the National Black Feminist Organization, "The term 'matriarchy'
connotes power. What power do black women have except to scrub Miss Ann's
floors?"[75]

Black Feminists were also sharp and influential critics of conventional
American gender ideals. Echoing the counterculture's rejection of masculinity as breadwinning, Bond and Peery regarded the middle-class white man
as the truly emasculated one "whose dazzling symbols of power—his goods,
his technology—have all but consumed his human essence."[76] Many Black
Feminists argued that African Americans should not emulate Moynihan's
flawed models of masculinity and femininity. Mary Ann Weathers asserted,
"We do not have to look at ourselves as someone's personal sex objects, maids,
baby sitters, domestics and the like in exchange for a man's attention . . . This
is whitey's thing."[77] Frances Beale observed that the housewife "often leads
an extremely sterile existence . . . as a satellite to her mate . . . a parasitic
existence that can aptly be described as legalized prostitution."[78]

Black Feminist critiques permeated beyond small radical organizations.
Eleanor Holmes Norton, an American Civil Liberties Union lawyer mentored
by Pauli Murray who later became a long-serving U.S. Congress delegate from
the District of Columbia, voiced the Black Feminist critique of the family. In
an essay included in the popular 1970 feminist anthology, *Sisterhood is Powerful*, Norton asked: "Are black people to reject so many of white society's
values only to accept its view of woman and of the family? At the moment
when the white family is caught in a maze of neurotic contradictions, and
white women are supremely frustrated with their roles . . . ?" Worried about
the male-breadwinner model's appeal to black men, Norton urged African
Americans not to create "crepe paper copies acting out the old white family
melodrama." She echoed both feminist depictions of miserable housewives
and countercultural critiques of organization men: "White men in search
of endless financial security have sold their spirits to that goal and begun a
steady emasculation in which the fiscal needs of wife and family determine
life's values and goals. . . . The whole business of the white family—its soft-
ened men, its frustrated women, its angry children—is in a state of great
mess."[79]

Similarly, in her pivotal 1972 study of African American women, *Tomorrow's Tomorrow*, Joyce Ladner rejected the Moynihan Report's contention that African Americans would best progress by adopting middle-class norms. Lower-class African American women could not adopt such norms (because of their lack of economic resources), nor should they. The white middle-class standard, she claimed, "purports to be exemplary" but "is in the process of internal destruction, and there is little within it which seems worthy of being salvaged."[80] For Ladner and other Black Feminists, widespread white rejection of the nuclear family undermined Moynihan's effort to extend that model to African Americans. Ladner pointed to ample evidence of the "bankruptcy" of the white middle-class family: "'tuning out' by thousands of young whites into hippie communes . . . suburban 'swingers' (sex clubs); [and] the absent father who spends so much time away from his home that it [the white middle class] according to the classical definition becomes a 'matriarchal' society."[81]

While criticizing the "white" family, Black Feminists often advanced the "black" family as superior. Like Black Sociologists, they generally compared middle-class white families to lower-class African American ones. Many Black Feminists thought that what Moynihan and others saw as a damaging "matriarchy" was more than a positive adaptation to poverty and oppression: it offered a laudable alternative that all Americans should emulate. Jacqueline Jackson contended, "blacks have had a 'headstart' on whites in developing alternative forms of marital and familial life . . . whites are patterning themselves after blacks, not the other way around."[82] Ladner similarly saw the lower-class black family as embodying the virtues of distinctively African American culture. The "spiritual, aesthetic quality of Black culture," she reflected, "offers this society the basic humanistic values which have disappeared through the process of neo-colonialism and its rapid technological advancements."[83] Ladner cited the appeal of African American culture to whites who viewed "the 'soul ideology' as their personal salvation and seek to emulate Black life-style whenever possible."[84] White Americans, she found, emulated African American attitudes toward sexuality and out-of-wedlock births to break free from repressive and sterile legalistic norms. For example, African American women served as "role models" for the increasing number of white women who had babies out of wedlock, including celebrities Mia Farrow and Vanessa Redgrave.[85]

According to Ladner, all Americans should imitate African American gender roles, better described as "egalitarian" than as "matriarchal." She claimed that African American women in some ways benefited from not attaining middle-class femininity. They were "liberated from many of the constraints the society has traditionally passed on women" because they could not be housewives subjected to the authority of their husbands. "Although this emerged from forced circumstances," Ladner maintained, "it has nevertheless allowed the Black woman the kind of emotional well-being that Women's Liberation groups are calling for."[86] However, Ladner's desire to challenge the pejorative tradition in sociology and to celebrate the strengths of black families limited her feminism. She overlooked the fact that fathers who left unmarried women with the sole burden of child-raising exercised male privilege just as much as men who insisted on being patriarchs.

Ladner's claim that African American women were already "liberated" implied that Moynihan correctly argued that African American women had more power in their communities and families than white women did in theirs, a tenet of the matriarchy myth. Unlike Ladner, however, other Black Feminists considered the relative powerlessness of African American women. For Norton, African American women were "'liberated' only from love, from family life, from meaningful work, and just as often from the basic comforts and necessities of an ordinary existence." She continued, "There is neither power nor satisfaction in such a 'matriarchy,'" but "only the bitter knowledge that one is a victim."[87] Michele Wallace ridiculed Ladner's notion that African American women were more liberated than white women: "It is a mockery to say . . . that black women have higher status in their community than white women in theirs. As far as I have been able to tell, black women have no status at all in the black community, particularly since the sixties. Their presence there is at best good-humoredly tolerated."[88] Influenced by radical white feminists such as Robin Morgan and Pat Mainardi, Wallace openly blamed black men for the oppression of black women. Similarly, bell hooks, in her major work *Ain't I a Woman*, begun in 1973 and published in 1981, pointed to pervasive sexism in the African American community: "It was never the black female having so much power in the home that alienated some black men, but that she had any power at all."[89]

This debate about whether African American women were already liberated reflected a broader tension within Black Feminism between either stressing African American women's achievements to counter racial stereotypes or emphasizing the serious nature of oppression they faced. As with Black Sociology, there was a strong desire to present a unified Black Feminist ideology, but there was a considerable diversity of views among Black Feminists and more disagreement than historians often portray.[90] Black Feminists, however, were not the only ones to contest the matriarchy myth; anthropologists too sought alternate understandings of non-nuclear African American families that viewed them as part of viable subculture.

All Our Kin

In 1966, graduate student Carol Stack received a phone call from Professor Oscar Lewis. He invited her to meet him the next day for breakfast to introduce her to an important visitor. The tall, debonair man she met at the University of Illinois faculty club was Daniel Patrick Moynihan. As Stack listened to Moynihan and Lewis talk, she realized the significant impact social science could have on public policy. Stack had just begun her ethnographic study of families in a poor urban African American neighborhood. But she had no inkling that the resulting book, *All Our Kin*, would become a classic refutation of both Moynihan's report and Lewis's "culture of poverty" theory.

Moynihan and Lewis had only recently become acquainted. Though some critics attacked the Moynihan Report as a "culture of poverty" theory, the phrase does not appear in *The Negro Family*. Moynihan later claimed when he wrote his report, "I had never . . . even heard of 'the culture of poverty.'"[91] Nevertheless, key similarities between the analyses of Moynihan and Lewis led the two men to identify as allies and for their work to be frequently linked. Like Moynihan, Lewis suggested that poverty could be self-perpetuating. Lewis used the phrase "culture of poverty" in a 1959 study of a Mexican village, *Five Families*, and expanded the concept in later works, especially his 1966 National Book Award-winning study of poor Puerto Ricans, *La Vida*.[92] Lewis defined the culture of poverty as "a way of life, remarkably stable and persistent, passed down from generation to generation along family lines."[93] Its characteristics included female-headed families, alcoholism, domestic violence, early sexual initiation, and a strong present-time orientation.

Like the Moynihan Report, the "culture of poverty" was ideologically promiscuous. Even Lewis was confused about its meaning and privately ambivalent about its use. Lewis was a socialist who thought political rebellion by the poor would cure the culture of poverty; he supported the goals of the Cuban Revolution. Though he meant to dramatize the human costs of economic inequality, he risked dehumanizing the poor just as pathologists did. By arguing structural inequality caused the culture of poverty yet the family perpetuated it, Lewis, like Moynihan, provided both a powerful argument in favor of government action and a rationalization for inequality. Socialist Michael Harrington popularized the term in his bestselling exposé of poverty, *The Other America*, but it was also used by conservatives such as Edward Banfield who argued that poverty's cultural origins rendered it immune to political solutions.[94] Like the Moynihan Report, the culture of poverty became a lightning rod for critics who disputed pathologist depictions of the poor.

When Stack met Moynihan, she barely knew who he was. When she emerged from her fieldwork a few years later, however, she immersed herself in the debates surrounding the report. Moynihan's name only appears a few times in *All Our Kin*, a short and engaging book that conveyed much of its analysis through narratives of ordinary individuals. But any alert reader could tell that *All Our Kin* sustained a critique of the Moynihan Report and the social scientific tradition it represented. Published in 1974, *All Our Kin* integrated several themes voiced by critics of the Moynihan Report: the positive values of a distinctive African American culture; feminist interest in capturing the perspectives of African American women; rejection of the normative nuclear family model; and a left-wing perspective on capitalism and the welfare system.[95]

Just as Joyce Ladner rebelled against the sociological training of her doctoral adviser, Lee Rainwater, Stack rejected the views of Lewis, who served on her dissertation committee until his untimely death in 1970. Much like Ladner's generation of African American sociologists, Stack found that her personal experience contradicted the scholarly consensus on lower-class families. She drew different lessons from her ethnic background than Moynihan had from his. Stack was born into a tight-knit working-class Jewish family that she remembers as vibrant and supportive. She was also influenced by a tradition of Jewish sympathy with African Americans. Her father grew up near Harlem and identified with African Americans. Raised in Los Angeles, Stack often accompanied her father on his bread truck delivery route through Watts, where she remembers observing extended family networks, with multiple generations socializing together outside their homes. The first high school graduate in her extended family, Stack attended the University of California, Berkeley. There, she was shocked to find that sociologists described poor American families, white and black, as "pathological" and "disorganized." After majoring in philosophy, Stack resolved to enter graduate school to study lower-class African American families. During her doctoral work, she absorbed many of the late 1960s cultural transformations wrought by feminism, the Black Power movement, the New Left, and the counterculture.

Stack's experiences as a woman in a male-dominated profession and as a single mother also influenced her perspective. She enrolled at the University of Illinois because her husband, John, was appointed to a professorship in physics there. As a faculty wife, she had to convince the anthropology professors to take her seriously as a scholar. Stack and her husband divorced soon after moving to Illinois when their son, Kevin, was only six months old. When she conducted her ethnographic research, Kevin went along. This experience gave Stack a more critical perspective on the nuclear family ideal as she came to see marriage as a form of "selling out." Undoubtedly, being a single mother helped Stack bond with the female African American welfare recipients she observed.[96]

Dissatisfied with the sociological literature, Stack chose to study poor African American families from an anthropological perspective. Rather than relying on statistical generalizations, as Moynihan did, Stack forged intimate relationships with her subjects as a participant-observer. She sought to capture their perspectives and understand how their behavior formed part of a coherent subculture that differed from mainstream American culture. Stack participated in a revival of anthropological study of African Americans, a field that had lain dormant since the 1940s studies of Melville Herskovits, Horace Cayton, and St. Clair Drake. One model for her work was Elliot Liebow's *Tally's Corner*, published in 1967. Liebow's study illuminated the dignity, complexity, and humanity of a group of African American men who congregated at a street-corner in Washington, D.C. It enabled readers to empathize with "Tally" and other lower-class African American men in ways not possible from reading Moynihan's depersonalized statistics. Nevertheless, like Moynihan, Liebow viewed poor African American men as failed breadwinners. "Street-corner men," Liebow claimed, shared the same ideal of masculine success—supporting a family—as other Americans, but lacked the job opportunities needed to fulfill it. Moynihan endorsed Liebow's conclusions by providing a laudatory blurb for the book's cover.[97]

Anthropologist Charles Valentine also influenced Stack by arguing that poor African Americans formed a subculture that needed to be understood on its own terms. Valentine was a professor at Washington University in St. Louis, where he was a colleague of Lee Rainwater and a teacher of Joyce Ladner. Valentine began his career as a scholar of Melanesian culture, but switched directions in the 1960s toward studying poor people in the United

States, especially African Americans. His new interest was motivated by his upbringing in a poor white family, his marriage to an African American woman, his active involvement in the civil rights movement, and his residence in a poor African American neighborhood in St. Louis.[98] Valentine encouraged Stack in her research, and Stack cited him frequently in *All Our Kin*.[99] Valentine's 1968 book, *Culture and Poverty* popularized the notion that the Moynihan Report advanced a "culture of poverty" theory. Valentine argued that the subculture of the poor, especially that of the African American poor, could not be understood in terms of the absence of middle-class values, as he claimed Moynihan and Lewis had done. Interpreting poor Americans as having culture, Valentine believed, conferred on them "a basic human worth and dignity."[100] As Valentine explained, culture entailed universality (all peoples have culture), organization (all cultures have coherence), and adaptation (all cultures are adaptations to their environments).

Valentine criticized what he termed the "pejorative tradition" in sociology. He targeted E. Franklin Frazier in particular, helping revive debates from a previous generation between the anthropologist Herskovits and the sociologist Frazier. He also lambasted the Moynihan Report for revealing "all too clearly that the purpose of such so-called social science . . . is not to illuminate human variety or to elucidate social reality . . . [but] is rather to support a set of class-bound prejudgments about a troublesome element of our society."[101] Valentine especially disliked Moynihan's conception of the family: "Nothing could be more contrary to a whole sphere of understanding established by students of culture, than the statement that the family—meaning of course the conventional middle-class Western family—is absolute."[102] For Valentine, the family structure of poor African Americans was part of a rich subculture and not simply an effect of economic inequality.

The main reason anthropologists had not studied African Americans in the two decades prior was that they had assumed African Americans shared the same values as other Americans. However, African American culture was rediscovered in the mid-1960s, fueled in part by Black Power calls for racial self-definition.[103] By the late 1960s, a growing group of scholars agreed with Joyce Ladner that "the culture of the Black community represents an autonomous social system that departs markedly from the dominant middle class."[104] Anthropological study of lower-class African Americans also revived because scholars adopted an increasingly critical perspective on mainstream American values. Cultural anthropologists had long studied other cultures to shed a critical light on the U.S. Valentine's call for anthropologists of lower-class African Americans "to achieve sufficient intellectual and emotional independence from the middle class" was meant as both a methodological principle and a moral stance.[105]

In *All Our Kin*, Stack heeded Valentine's call to understand African American social life in cultural terms as well as Ralph Ellison's insistence that "How children grow up is a cultural, not a statistical, pattern."[106] "Statistical patterns," Stack concurred, "do not divulge underlying cultural patterns. This confusion between statistics and cultural patterns underlies most interpretations of black family life."[107] Stack's method involved intense participant-observation of a community of poor African Americans in an urban area in Illinois she called "the Flats," renamed to protect the anonymity of her subjects and universalize the neighborhood. Stack's ethnographic approach differentiated her from Moynihan, who hardly knew any African American families and Rainwater, who relied on graduate students for his fieldwork. Her perspective was face-to-face rather than bird's-eye. She believed the time she took to know her subjects justified how a "young white woman could conduct a study of black family life."[108] Her effort to immerse herself in African American life won her the acceptance of Black Studies scholars. The *Journal of Black Studies* praised Stack "for her openness 'to see' as have few white Americans, including eminent scholars who consider themselves Afro-American 'experts.'"[109]

Stack's reliance on ethnographic observation and life history grounded her rebuttal of the Moynihan Report. Examining how poor African American families lived, Stack contested Moynihan's statistical assertion that single women headed a high percentage of poor African American families. Most households defined as "single-mother" in government statistics were in fact multigenerational. Residents of the Flats, she showed, participated in close-knit extended kinship networks. Parental roles played by individuals in the white middle class, she maintained, were shared throughout the community. A baby's "mama" might not be its biological mother, especially if the woman was considered too young to take primary responsibility for raising a child. Even though children might not live with their biological fathers, they typically had father figures and were connected to patrilineal kinship networks. Child-raising was a communal, rather than individual, responsibility demonstrated by the practice of "child-keeping," whereby children went to live for periods with kin. According to Stack, "These predictable, stable child-keeping patterns provide a commanding contrast to the characterization of the black family life as 'broken' and 'disorganized.'"[110] Hence, Stack dismissed stereotypical views of African American families as "deviant, matriarchal, and broken."[111] Recognizing that African American families possessed a distinctive culture meant they could not be uncritically contrasted to the "white middle-class model."[112] It was significant that Stack's contacts in the Flats were women. Stack was a pioneer in examining poor African Americans from a female perspective. Like the Moynihan Report, most previous scholarship had focused on African American men. Along with Joyce Ladner's *Tomorrow's Tomorrow, All Our Kin* initiated social scientific scholarship on African American women, building on Black Feminism.

All Our Kin revealed the distance debate over African American families had traveled since the early days of the Moynihan Report controversy. In a review, the white psychiatrist Robert Coles, who once tried to convince an African American minister of the Moynihan Report's merits, praised *All Our Kin*. He especially recommended it to "white middle-class readers" ignorant of poor African Americans' lives.[113] Stack challenged not only Moynihan, but also Moynihan's most influential early critic, William Ryan, who claimed that African American pathology resulted not from family structure but from poverty and discrimination. To Stack, the question was not whom to blame for victimizing African Americans, but whether pathology adequately described African American social and family life. Like Moynihan, Ryan failed to ask "what role the ties of kinship or friendship play in the black community, who socializes the children born in the ghetto, what folk criteria qualify a woman to give birth or to raise a child, or what may be the adaptive functions of sexual unions and multiple household kin networks."[114] Versus Ryan, Stack perceived that the urban African American family "embedded in cooperative domestic exchange, proves to be an organized, tenacious, active, lifelong network."[115]

All Our Kin contained more than a hint of skepticism about the middle-class family norms idealized by Moynihan. To Stack, the cooperative ethic of poor African Americans was superior to the atomic individualism typifying mainstream American values. "In contrast to the middle-class ethic of individualism and competition," Stack observed, "the poor living in the Flats do not turn anyone down when they need help."[116] Stack's readers must have wondered whether the cooperative extended kinship structure of African American families was more than just a "profoundly creative adaptation to poverty," but also offered virtues the nuclear-family model lacked.[117]

There were inherent dangers in the new anthropological view of the lower-class African American family best articulated by Stack. Using the tools of anthropology, a discipline formed to study peoples considered primitive and exotic, risked accentuating the otherness of poor African Americans even more than the Moynihan Report had. For example, citing past scholarship on Native Americans, Valentine asked, "Can we now accomplish the same achievement with our more familiar exotics, the savage underclass at home— the potentially predatory nomads who wander with the seasonal cycles of our crops, the pockets of primitive mountain folk still living by a coal-age culture, or the marauding hostile tribes on the frontiers of our inner cities?"[118] Stack relied on classic anthropological concepts developed to describe non-Western cultures, such as Marcel Mauss's idea of "gift exchange" to explain cooperative kinship networks in the Flats, which to Stack bore "striking resemblance to patterns of exchange . . . in non-Western societies."[119]

There was also a risk in equating African American culture as a whole with the culture of poor African Americans, just as Black Sociologists had often equated the "black family" with the lower-class family and the "white family" with the middle-class family. Even though readers of *All Our Kin* would have understood that the book discussed a specific class of African Americans, at times it equated "Black" with "poor"; for example, its title referred to a "Black community." Seeing that lower-class African Americans possessed a deep-rooted culture also implied that escaping poverty would be difficult. In fact, Stack concluded that, despite their effectiveness in surviving poverty, kinship networks inhibited class mobility for Flats residents. Cooperative kinship networks prevented geographic mobility, discouraged marriage, and made it difficult for individuals to accumulate capital, since resources were quickly absorbed by the needs of kin. Ironically, this insight replicated Oscar Lewis's argument that the culture of poverty was an obstacle to class mobility.

Focusing on culture could occlude the race-based economic inequalities Moynihan and other pathologists highlighted. Recognizing that poor African Americans possessed a rich familial and cultural life potentially undermined the need for national action. For example, in his 1970 ethnography of urban African Americans, *Positively Black*, folklorist Roger Abrahams identified the main problem African Americans faced as the "ethnocentrism" of the "culture-blind white liberal" he claimed Moynihan typified. "[T]he black problem," he asserted, "really *is* a white problem, a white failure of understanding."[120] Pleading for Americans simply to recognize the existing rich culture of African Americans, such anthropological work anticipated a form of multiculturalism that celebrated the cultural accomplishments of ethnoracial minorities but ignored economic inequalities. Arguing that lower-class African American subculture possessed an authenticity middle-class white Americans lacked also risked romanticizing poor African Americans.

Stack, however, combined an anthropological view of poor African American families with a left-wing critique of the American economic and political system that impoverished them. She challenged Moynihan's liberalism, claiming that African American poverty resulted not from an inability to compete in the marketplace but from the exploitation of workers inherent in capitalism. "[T]he present economic order in the United States," she maintained, "is dependent upon cheap labor and economic racism that confines Blacks to low-skilled jobs, low wages, and unsatisfactory employment."[121]

Stack's argument reflected the socialist revival in American scholarship during the 1960s and 1970s. She particularly relied on the work of Frances Fox Piven and Richard Cloward, who offered a left-wing critique of welfare in their influential 1971 book, *Regulating the Poor*. Cloward and Piven were intellectual architects of the welfare rights movement. Involved in the initial planning for the War on Poverty, Cloward was radicalized by his experience in a community action program that convinced him that only massive redistribution of wealth could alleviate poverty.[122] In an influential 1965 paper, Cloward and Piven advocated expanding relief rolls to produce political pressure to enact a national guaranteed income system. In *Regulating the Poor*, Piven and Cloward argued that welfare and other forms of poor relief maintained social and economic inequality. The capitalist system, they asserted, benefited from what Karl Marx termed a "reserve army of the unemployed": a class of poor people who served as surplus labor in times of economic expansion and at other times depressed wages as an oversupply of labor. Far from benefiting the poor, then, relief agencies in fact managed "the regulation of marginal labor and in the maintenance of civil order."[123]

Cloward and Piven revisited the Moynihan Report's much-discussed "scissors" chart to show how welfare cases rose even as black male unemployment rates fell. Moynihan interpreted this finding to mean that African American pathology was becoming self-perpetuating. For Moynihan, rising welfare cases suggested an increase in female-headed families eligible for benefits. Cloward and Piven, however, convincingly discredited Moynihan's assumption that welfare rolls expanded simply because more people qualified for assistance. In fact, the "welfare explosion" of the 1960s was a response to the political disorder created by African American demands for equality: government officials turned to poor relief to defuse unrest. Piven and Cloward agreed with Moynihan that urban migration and high rates of unemployment destabilized urban African American families and advocated jobs programs for male African Americans so they could be family breadwinners. Nevertheless, their view of welfare deliberately reinforcing a hierarchal class system sharply differed from Moynihan's meritocratic understanding of the American economy.

Stack drew on Piven and Cloward's work to show that welfare policies by design reduced the social mobility of the poor, undermining attempts to form nuclear families and to accumulate capital. "Wealth inequity" rather than family structure, Stack deduced, was at the heart of African American poverty. Versus Moynihan and other liberals, Stack contended that reforms that encouraged individual class mobility were doomed. A radical redistribution of wealth was needed. According to Stack, the welfare system actually kept residents of The Flats in poverty. She recounted the story of a family who hoped to use an inheritance to purchase a home. Because of their new assets, the welfare office immediately withdrew benefits, making it impossible for the family to gain equity. To Stack, the system denied poor Americans the ability to acquire the capital needed to lift themselves up from poverty.

Stack understood that simply emphasizing the strengths of black families, without also indicating the ways African Americans suffered from racial and class inequality, undermined the case for systemic reform. Still, Stack's economic critique, advanced mainly toward the end of *All Our Kin*, conflicted with her portrayal of lower-class African Americans as possessing a viable subculture. The book's protagonist, the young African American mother Ruby Banks, appeared in the first half of the book as a central participant in a vibrant system of cooperative exchange. At the end of the book, however, readers learned of Banks's discouragement after she married and left the Flats but returned without her husband a year later. Whereas Stack earlier described families in the Flats as forming a viable subculture, at the end of the book she showed they were betrayed by "mainstream values." Stack even argued that forming nuclear families would aid African Americans in escaping poverty and stressed the need to combat black male unemployment. Here she sounded like Moynihan, invoking the lack of male breadwinning as a marker of economic inequality. Ultimately, Stack never fully reconciled her two challenges to the Moynihan Report: recognizing a distinctive African American culture and pressing for radical economic solutions to poverty that transcended the basic framework of competitive individualism.

Better than any other work, *All Our Kin* synthesized the various challenges to the Moynihan Report for its arrogance, dehumanizing pathologism, support for patriarchy, and rationalization of racial-based economic inequality. In the face of these criticisms, Moynihan moved rightward. By the late 1960s, Moynihan became increasingly skeptical of the federal government's ability to enact social reform. He developed into one of the most prominent members of a set of neoconservative intellectuals, one-time liberals who rushed to protect the social order against the growth of left-wing social movements such as Black Power and feminism. For neoconservatives, radical criticism of the Moynihan Report indicated the need to defend bedrock American values such as the nuclear-family norm.

CHAPTER 6

From National Action to Benign Neglect

In January 1969, President-elect Richard Nixon received a memo from a Democrat who would soon join his administration, Daniel Patrick Moynihan. Applying ideas he developed in *The Negro Family*, Moynihan warned Nixon, "Among a large and growing lower class, self-reliance, self-discipline, and industry are waning" as "general pathology appears to be infecting the Puerto Rican as well as the Negro." He observed, "Families are [becoming] more and more matrifocal." Criticizing Great Society liberalism, Moynihan jettisoned his earlier focus on male unemployment: "Much of what is now termed 'the crisis of the cities' is more a moral and cultural crisis than a material one."[1]

Absent the controversy over *The Negro Family*, it is impossible to explain how Moynihan, a liberal Democrat at the start of the 1960s, became a top adviser to a Republican president at decade's end. The report turned Moynihan into a racial expert and led to his appointment as head of Nixon's newly created Council for Urban Affairs. "Urban affairs" was largely a euphemism for African Americans, and Moynihan filtered to Nixon ideas he developed in the late 1960s to defend *The Negro Family* against its critics. Moynihan continued to promote some liberal policies. He lobbied for Nixon's Family Assistance Plan (FAP), a universal family allowance of the kind his report implicitly advocated. Yet, Moynihan justified such reforms with an increasingly conservative logic that stressed shoring up social order against Black Power radicals. In *The Negro Family*, Moynihan employed a vocabulary of social justice *and* social control; under Nixon, he shifted decisively toward the latter.

Moynihan's joining Nixon emblematized the rightward journey of a prominent group of postwar liberals known as "neoconservatives." Drawing on the Moynihan Report, neoconservatives portrayed lower-class African Americans as dangers to social order, analogized African Americans to European immigrants, defended the nuclear family norm, and questioned liberal social engineering. Though they continued to call for reforms to reduce economic inequality, their insiders' critique of liberalism ultimately aided conservatism. Neoconservatives made common cause with leading conservatives such as William F. Buckley, who quickly grasped how the Moynihan Report could serve his purpose. Neoconservatives' influential narrative of the controversy blamed leftists for fracturing the postwar consensus and suppressing honest discussions about African Americans. In a famous 1970 memo to Nixon, Moynihan argued that intemperate discussion of race, rather than failure to resolve persistent inequality, explained racial disharmony. Moynihan advised Nixon that the nation would benefit from a period of "benign neglect" of "the issue of race."[2] Leaked to the *New York Times* in 1970, the memo sparked a firestorm similar to that ignited by the Moynihan Report, all the more heated because of its author's involvement in the prior dispute.

A Casualty of Political Correctness

In their popular 1997 history of American race relations since the civil rights era, neoconservatives Stephan and Abigail Thernstrom dubbed the Moynihan Report "an early casualty of political correctness."[3] The term "politically correct" was not widely used until the 1990s, but the concept's origins partly lie in the Moynihan Report controversy. In the late 1960s, Moynihan defenders already made the point conveyed by 1990s critics of "political correctness": leftists, in their zeal to combat discrimination against minorities, restricted free discussion of sensitive topics.[4] In countless variations, neoconservatives hailed Moynihan for his brave and prophetic engagement with the sensitive topic of African American families and excoriated his left-wing opponents for distorting his ideas and foreclosing necessary debate on African American family breakdown. They portrayed Moynihan, who epitomized the powerful white male whose authority was under attack, as the controversy's principal victim. This narrative appealed to some liberals who believed that fruitless debate over the Moynihan Report derailed economic reforms to benefit poor African Americans. However, demonizing Moynihan's liberal and left-wing critics mainly aided conservatives.

Moynihan's 1967 essay, "The President and the Negro: The Moment Lost," established the neoconservative narrative of the controversy. This first of many texts in which Moynihan offered his version of events appeared in *Commentary*, fast becoming a principal mouthpiece for neoconservatism. Like the report, Moynihan's account of the controversy contained liberal and conservative elements. At first glance "The President and the Negro" redoubled his liberal argument that true equality for African Americans involved not just civil rights but economic parity. Moynihan asserted the report was designed to "persuade the government that public policy must now concern itself with issues beyond the frame of individualistic political thinking." He informed readers of its role in Johnson's Howard University address and linked it to the president's soaring declaration, "freedom is not enough." He defended its focus on family instability: "the subject of family does not, as has been charged, distract from issues like employment, but rather gives them a reality and urgency which normally they do not command."[5] Moynihan also spelled out policy recommendations omitted from the report. These included a family allowance and guaranteed full employment that would benefit all working-class Americans but disproportionately aid African Americans.

Moynihan lamented that the "bold initiative" begun by his report and the Howard speech lay "in ruins" six months later. When Republican gains in the 1966 mid-term elections halted Johnson's Great Society agenda, the reformist moment ended. The result for African Americans, Moynihan claimed, was a "calamity." Adopting liberal historian C. Vann Woodward's analogy that the 1960s witnessed a "second Reconstruction," Moynihan warned, "the nation may be in the process of reproducing the tragic events of the Reconstruction: giving to Negroes the forms of legal equality, but withholding the economic and political resources which are the bases of social equality."[6]

Though Moynihan framed a liberal question—why the moment for reform was lost—he offered a conservative answer. For scuttling necessary social reforms he blamed "Negro leaders unable to comprehend their opportunity . . . civil-rights militants . . . and . . . white liberals." Liberals, Moynihan claimed, "allowed the question of developing a program" designed to address race-based social inequalities "to be superseded by a preposterous and fruitless controversy over a Department of Labor report." He polemicized against the "liberal Left," which "can be as rigid and destructive as any force in American life." He scored liberals for failing to confront black family instability, alleging they responded to his report "by denying the facts of the damage ('the statistics are wrong') and/or denying that the damage was real ('it is a cultural pattern superior in its vitality to middle-class mores')."[7]

Moynihan was especially aggrieved that opponents misunderstood and misrepresented his intentions. He paid his critics back in kind, claiming that they practiced "the scholarship of Che Guevara." Rather than responding to their criticisms' content, he treated them as irrational personal attacks. He characterized his opponents as driven by emotions rather than reason, "caught up in a frenzy of arrogance and nihilism." He claimed that one leading critic of the report, Benjamin Payton, "bordered on the psychopathological." He reductively asserted that his most influential critic, William Ryan, had only "one idea": "that I was obsessed with illegitimacy." Moynihan offensively caricatured Ryan's argument: "white bourgeois females fornicate as much as, or even more than (although not of course so well as), Negro girls."[8] Elsewhere, Moynihan dismissed Ryan as a "notably hysterical ideologue."[9]

For Moynihan, lashing out at his critics fulfilled a psychological need. Deeply hurt by criticism of *The Negro Family*, Moynihan felt singled out with good reason. He and his report became a lightning rod for attacks on white liberals and the Johnson administration. Though "The President and the Negro" presented itself as objective political analysis, it was a deeply emotional essay full of rage and self-pity. Writing it was cathartic for Moynihan. He confided to *Commentary* editor Norman Podhoretz, "If I can just get this published I will feel a vast evil spirit is somehow exorcised."[10] Yet Moynihan must have known that his intervention would only further fan the flames of controversy. Indeed, part of him seemed to relish the attention being at the center of the dispute brought him. If writing "The President and the Negro" helped Moynihan recover from the initial sting of criticism, he never grew tired of recounting his history of the controversy. His narrative also appealed emotionally to white Americans who similarly felt confronted in the late 1960s by the full weight of their racial privilege, particularly liberal whites who had thought themselves allies of African Americans but now found themselves distrusted by civil rights activists.

As an account of the Moynihan Report controversy, "The President and the Negro" was selective at best. It overestimated the lost opportunity for liberal reform. As Moynihan recognized in a more sober moment, the Howard speech proposed no specific policies: "The fact that two Kennedy intellectuals [Moynihan and Richard Goodwin] could slip a big speech past Lyndon Johnson hardly constituted a major national commitment."[11] Moreover, the modest reforms Moynihan hoped Johnson would adopt failed to match rhetorical calls for full racial equality. Finally, the Moynihan Report controversy was hardly the primary reason why such reforms never materialized. Moynihan self-importantly placed the dispute over his report at the center of Johnson's domestic policy-making, specifically discounting the administration's escalation of the Vietnam War as a reason liberal reform stalled. Unpersuasively, Moynihan claimed that the war rendered the administration unable to devise adequate programs but that it would have advocated, funded, and implemented such policies had liberals adopted *The Negro Family*'s analysis.

Personalizing the controversy allowed Moynihan to ignore the substance of critics' charges. By portraying criticism as ad hominem attacks, Moynihan shifted the debate to his character rather than to his ideas. Placing the onus of the controversy on the "liberal Left" overlooked many liberals, including some civil rights leaders, who supported the report. Moynihan speciously alleged that the civil rights movement "had no program for going beyond the traditional and relatively easy issues of segregation and discrimination."[12] He pointedly ignored both Whitney Young's "Marshall Plan" for urban reconstruction, an important stimulus to the Moynihan Report, and the $100 billion Freedom Budget unveiled by A. Philip Randolph and Bayard Rustin at the White House Conference on Civil Rights. Moynihan repudiated Lee Rainwater and William Yancey's argument in *The Politics of Controversy* that the Johnson administration used the Moynihan Report controversy to distract critics from its retreat from the civil rights agenda. Moynihan summarized "The President and the Negro" for Johnson aide Harry McPherson: the "white liberal community" let down the president.[13] Letting the Johnson administration off the hook, Moynihan indirectly absolved white Americans who were willing to grant African Americans civil rights but unwilling to support measures needed to ensure full equality. In this telling, those who most forcefully demanded equality were blamed for the failure to attain it.

Misinterpretations of the report from the right were just as damaging as those from the left, but Moynihan failed to recognize his strategic flaw of highlighting African American family pathology to advocate liberal reforms. He did not acknowledge those who appealed to his report to argue that racial self-help was the only solution to African Americans' problems. Solely concerned with his left-wing opponents, Moynihan appeared oblivious to conservative supporters' use of his report to undermine liberalism. Moreover, by defending himself from charges that he was a "racist," he sidestepped nuanced arguments that the report encouraged subtle forms of racism regardless of its author's intentions. Moynihan defined "racism" solely as bigotry and dismissed out of hand concepts of unconscious or institutional racism.

He never acknowledged how the report was used to reinforce racial stereotypes. For example, journalist Theodore White's description of "biological anarchy" in African American ghettos drew on material provided directly by Moynihan.

"The President and the Negro" illustrated Moynihan's drift toward neoconservatism. It discredited the "liberal Left" as irrational, while suggesting that a reasonable dialogue remained possible with conservatives. Ruing the "moment lost" meant the time for substantial national programs to reduce economic inequality among African Americans had passed. Moynihan even hinted that it would now be civil rights leaders' primary responsibility to address black poverty. African Americans, he asserted, "cannot afford the luxury of having a large lower class that is at once deviant and dependent. If *they* do not wish to bring it into line with the . . . world around them, *they* must devise ways to support it from within."[14]

Predictably, Moynihan's critics contested his version of events. In a letter to *Commentary*, William Ryan asserted that Moynihan's account addressed "false issues." Ryan insisted that his criticism was "conceptual rather than personal" and that no one accused Moynihan of racism. "For him to continue snapping off clever answers to his own straight lines," Ryan retorted, "is neither particularly enlightening nor wholly honest."[15] Bayard Rustin declared, "the undertone of bitterness in Mr. Moynihan's article reflects more than personal pique; it is a political alienation from the Negro movement."[16] Even some of Moynihan's allies disliked "The President and the Negro." Jason Epstein, a liberal publisher who co-founded *The New York Review of Books* and edited Moynihan's planned book-length follow-up to the report, regretted its blanket attack on left-liberals, preferring Moynihan to "confront particular enemies in specific terms rather than categorically as Liberals."[17]

"The President and the Negro" set a template for the dominant narrative of the Moynihan Report controversy, one accepted for decades by neoconservatives, conservatives, the media, and even many liberals. The press widely reported the essay. A *New York Times* editorial endorsed it: "the willingness of the Negro leadership to acquiesce in the extremist attacks on [Moynihan's] report and the president's speech meant a tragic lost opportunity for helping Negro families." In a shocking metaphor that likened the embattlement of white racial experts to the murder of African Americans by lynch mobs, the editorial claimed that Moynihan and Oscar Lewis were victims of an "intellectual lynching."[18] Even before Moynihan published the *Commentary* essay, his perspective was well represented in the media. Starting in late 1965, he used personal connections to see "that columns were written, editorials were written, articles were placed."[19] Press accounts often placed Moynihan's intentions at the center of the controversy and ignored the substance of his critics' charges. For example, an August 1966 story in *Newsweek* declared that "movement ideologues" had misunderstood *The Negro Family* and unfairly abused its author as a "racist."[20]

Rainwater and Yancey's *The Politics of Controversy* offered the most sophisticated and detailed version of the Moynihan-as-victim narrative. One reviewer of the book, with only a hint of irony, captured the mythic underpinnings of their account:

> This is a tale which sociologists will doubtless repeat to their children on dark, stormy nights. Outside the winds will howl and the shutters will bang, to remind the children that mysterious forces, beyond the grace of reason, are astir in the night. Rainwater and Yancey have fashioned a kind of socio-epic. They sing of arms and the Moynihan, wherein an intrepid reformer with friends at court goes forth to slay a dragon (Negro family instability) only to learn that the dragon has friends, too. In the end, the King turns his back on our hero and decides to let sleeping dragons lie.[21]

Many liberal politicians and intellectuals endorsed the myth of Moynihan as martyr. Assistant Secretary of Commerce Eugene Foley told Moynihan, "You have now reached the stature of Socrates, Galileo, Zola's Dreyfuss."[22] Moynihan's Harvard colleague, the famous sociologist David Riesman, confided, "I keep thinking of you as the messenger who brings the bad news and is slaughtered by the Greeks."[23]

The narrative of the controversy proffered by Moynihan's supporters had significant variations and broad ideological appeal. Its crucial importance for neoconservatives was evident in "Race and Truth," an article *Commentary* published nearly a decade after "The President and the Negro." Michael Novak, a white ethnic Catholic and one-time liberal like Moynihan, defended the report against Herbert Gutman's recently published *Slavery and Freedom*. He perceptively criticized Gutman for targeting a short government pamphlet in his scholarly tome and for overstating the extent to which his historical findings disproved Moynihan's thesis. However, Novak expanded his critique of Gutman into a broader claim that the left prevented "truthful discussion of racial matters." He cited the dispute over *The Negro Family* in which Moynihan was "branded as a racist." To Novak, the controversy initiated a new period during which the left intimidated its opponents and suppressed free discussion. In Novak's view, "Intellectual muggers stand ready to discipline those who stray" from liberal orthodoxy. "New extortion rackets function: conform, or take your punishment."[24] Though responding to the appreciable growth of left-wing views in academia, evident in Gutman's book and the growth of Black Studies, Novak vastly overstated the left's power to shape racial discourse. As had Moynihan in "The President and the Negro," Novak overlooked the considerable influence retained by conservatives, neoconservatives, and centrist liberals, especially in mainstream political and media discussion. Exaggerating left-wing influence allowed neoconservatives to present themselves as brave challengers of orthodoxy, rather than what they were: elites with considerable power to shape racial discourse and policy.

Novak dismissed the left-wing perspective that racism was a persistent, institutional system of oppression. Holding African Americans responsible for their own progress, he maintained, was the only "truthful" view of American race relations. Moynihan's sin was that he "did not sufficiently 'exonerate' blacks for their own condition" because "by focusing on the question of family structure, Moynihan implicitly allowed attention to fall on the behavior of blacks toward each other, not on injustices in the system." Helping pioneer a typical conservative argument of the 1980s, Novak alleged that leftists were racists because they denied African Americans' agency when explaining African Americans' low socioeconomic status in structural terms. "If you grant no responsibility or hope for their own advancement to blacks, but treat their needs as in every respect due to a form of victimization, then no one calls you a racist; you are regarded, instead, as a friend to blacks. 'Don't blame the victim' is the slogan of such friendship." He complained, "But if . . . you assert that blacks are equal to whites in potency, moral spirit, dignity, responsibility, and power over their future, and deny that they are mere pawns and victims, then you set off a chorus of alarms and find yourself on treacherous emotional territory."[25] According to Novak, liberals who wanted to use the government to redress deeply rooted racial inequalities were the true "racists."

Liberal Measures, Conservative Logic

Moynihan justified entering the Nixon administration in terms of a hope that Nixon could be a "Tory man" who enacted "liberal measures" like

nineteenth-century British Prime Minister Benjamin Disraeli.[26] Yet it was
Moynihan's increasingly conservative logic that made this liberal veteran
of the Johnson administration an appealing appointment for Nixon. The
charged political atmosphere of the late 1960s exacerbated Moynihan's existing ideological tensions. He moved simultaneously leftward and rightward.
While advancing ever-bolder proposals for economic reform, he increasingly
framed questions of race, poverty, and government in conservative terms.
He affirmed the limits of national action and maintained the need for social
stability.

Moynihan wrote at a remarkably prolific pace during the latter half of the
1960s, publishing countless articles in journals and popular magazines. In
virtually every piece, he touched on the report's central preoccupations of race,
family, and poverty. He repeatedly cited black family instability to explain
contemporary social turbulence. During a volatile period of American history, from fall 1965 to the election of Richard Nixon in 1968, his central activity was defending *The Negro Family*. His major project was a book-length
elaboration of the report. Titled *Toward Equality*, the manuscript developed
the report's argument that family structure explained racial inequality. Moynihan updated his analysis to examine the spread of urban rebellions, the development of Black Power, and the expansion of welfare rolls. Though at times
Toward Equality adopted the score-settling tone of "The President and the
Negro," it offered a more detailed and nuanced response to critics. By
September 1968, Moynihan had drafted a sprawling manuscript over 750
typescript pages long. Though he frequently drew ideas and text from the
manuscript for other writings, including memos he wrote for Nixon, he never
published the book. He shelved it when he joined the Nixon administration
in 1969. Having reentered politics, he no longer needed to cement his scholarly reputation, and he feared that reigniting the controversy over the report
would damage him politically in his new role. Moynihan may also have been
dissatisfied with the state of his manuscript; its rambling and contradictory
nature reflected his confusion during this period. The way its ideas moved
in divergent directions flummoxed one reader, who responded to its chapter
on welfare by asking, "What is your point? Are you attacking the welfare system? The Negroes? The lower class? The upper class?"[27]

From 1966 to 1967, Moynihan organized a seminar on poverty for the
American Academy of Arts and Sciences, a venture that continued from the
Academy-sponsored conference on the "Negro American" where Moynihan
first publicly presented his report's findings. Moynihan recruited leading pov-

erty researchers to participate in the seminar, including Oscar Lewis, Walter Miller, and Lee Rainwater. Seminar participants debated a series of questions, including the validity of the "culture of poverty" thesis and public policies that would best alleviate poverty. They met monthly in the Academy's Edwardian manor house to discuss poverty before retiring to enjoy dinner and claret by candlelight.[28]

As part of his involvement in this seminar, Moynihan joined other 1960s liberals in promoting more expansive anti-poverty programs. Along with ally Rainwater, Moynihan advocated an "income strategy" to reduce poverty, contrasting his position with the "service strategy" of expanded social work and community action that typified Johnson's War on Poverty programs. He favored jobs creation and direct income transfers to the poor. As Moynihan explained, the goal was to "set income floors so that most people live an average life." By eliminating the "uncertainty of income flows," Moynihan hoped to abolish the conditions that produced the lower-class pathology he detailed in *The Negro Family*.[29]

Moynihan invoked conservative logic to justify such policies. Indeed, at the poverty seminar's conclusion Moynihan joked to an audience at the American Academy about how through their deliberations "thirty liberal professors became more conservative."[30] Eschewing the language of economic and racial justice, Moynihan promoted anti-poverty measures that enforced conventional middle-class values and ensured social stability. The poverty seminar directed attention to the poor's behavior. Moynihan argued that instead of trying to organize poor people for democratic participation, as community action programs did, government should strengthen "stabilizing" and "conformity-inducing institutions" such as the police and the schools in order to teach people "to behave."[31]

Even when promoting liberal reforms, Moynihan increasingly posited the inherent limitations of government action. In the poverty seminar, for example, he argued that since intellectuals could come to no consensus about poverty, they could hardly provide adequate knowledge for policy-makers to act effectively. A key tenet of postwar liberalism was that expert knowledge could aid policy-makers in alleviating class and racial conflict. By the late 1960s, liberal social engineering was challenged not only by the left, which favored greater democratic participation, but also by the right, aided by neoconservative intellectuals such as Moynihan. For example, Moynihan advised *Muhammad Speaks*, "I would like to urge anyone reading this interview to get what you can out of government—but don't depend on it. The government tends to oversell itself."[32] (Presumably, readers of the Nation of Islam newspaper needed little prompting from Moynihan to distrust the U.S. government.)

Moynihan's major challenge to liberal social engineering came in his influential 1969 book, *Maximum Feasible Misunderstanding*, which originated as a lecture series in the spring of 1967. It criticized the War on Poverty Community Action Program, which Moynihan alleged "represented the direct transmission of social science theory into governmental policy."[33] Questioning whether social science could provide accurate knowledge for government action, Moynihan mounted a broader critique of liberalism. Liberals' "fatal flaw," he concluded, was, "We constantly overestimate difficulties, overpromise results, and avoid any evidence of incompatibility and conflict."[34] (Using the first-person plural added credibility to his insiders' critique of liberalism.) Moynihan urged chastened expectations for government, which should seek only "the achievement of limited goals."[35] This sounded very different from the case for national action to achieve racial equality he had once made. Indeed, at least one observer saw *Maximum Feasible Misunderstanding* as an allegory for the Moynihan Report, a veiled *mea culpa* in which Moynihan renounced the report's strategy of marshaling social science for an activist government.[36]

By denouncing community action's democratizing effects, blaming intellectual elites for the program's design flaws, and stressing government limits, *Maximum Feasible Participation* strongly appealed to conservatives. Still, it could be read as a brief for an income strategy to combat poverty; Moynihan noted that as a member of the War on Poverty task force he had advocated jobs creation as an alternative to community action. Yet Moynihan claimed that such employment programs would have given "an unavoidably 'conservative' cast to the entire undertaking" by reinforcing the work ethic and assimilating the poor to middle-class American values. By blaming social scientists for the War on Poverty's problems, Moynihan articulated a common neoconservative argument that a "new class" of professionals directed government policies in their self-interest, not out of genuine interest for the disadvantaged. To Moynihan, liberal advocates for the poor were "too willing by half to see public funds, and tax-free private funds, employed on a vast scale to further what was in effect a political agenda of a fairly small group of intellectuals."[37]

Moynihan also questioned liberal social engineering by promoting the Coleman Report, a 1966 government document officially titled *Equality of*

Educational Opportunity. This massive statistical survey, headed by Johns Hopkins University sociologist James S. Coleman, originated in the 1964 Civil Rights Act, which called for a study documenting educational disparities between whites and African Americans. Coleman initially expected to identify resource gaps in African American schools. However, he surprisingly concluded that government spending on education minimally influenced student achievement. Student social background and the social composition of schools, he found, were more significant factors.[38] When government officials ignored Coleman's findings, Moynihan played a crucial role in publicizing them. He recruited Coleman to summarize his findings for *Public Interest.* Along with Thomas Pettigrew, Moynihan convened a series of seminars on the report that met at Harvard during the 1966–67 academic year and led to the publication of a volume of papers coedited by Moynihan. Funded by the Carnegie Corporation, the faculty seminar was a major event on the Harvard campus, often drawing over fifty participants.[39]

Moynihan perceived similarities between Coleman's report and his own, in terms of both the ideas they contained and the debates they sparked. In each controversy, civil rights activists challenged experts' intellectual authority. In Coleman's case, critics believed his report legitimized neglecting the educational problems of poor African American children. Moynihan claimed that, like *The Negro Family,* the Coleman Report had been mistakenly "greeted as a conservative document" and perceived "as threatening to the political coalition that sponsored it."[40] He worried that Coleman, like himself, was "labeled a racist."[41] In Moynihan's view, criticism of the Coleman Report confirmed left-liberals' irrationality and unwillingness to accept scientific authority.

The Coleman Report bolstered the arguments of *The Negro Family.* Moynihan frequently cited Coleman's finding that "the sources of inequality of educational opportunity appear to lie first in the home itself and the cultural influences immediately surrounding the home."[42] Family influence was crucial. Moynihan interpreted Coleman's message in a liberal vein: "employment and income strategies designed to strengthen the home environment of the child and his family have over the long run a chance to produce a great additional component to educational achievement."[43] Nevertheless, the Coleman Report contained conservative implications by highlighting cultural values imparted by families and downplaying differential effects of government investment in schools. Like Moynihan, Coleman shifted focus from resource disparity toward African Americans' inability to compete with other ethnoracial groups. As Coleman wrote Moynihan in a letter shared with the Harvard faculty seminar, the "central problem" was "Negro achievement," not "the white environment." He asked, "How are you going to get the Negroes up to the point where it's a fair fight—where they can compete with whites on equal terms?"[44]

Like Moynihan, Coleman was disturbed by the growth of radicalism and social conflict during the late 1960s. At Moynihan's behest, Coleman wrote to Lyndon Johnson aide Douglas Cater. "I write out of a feeling of terrible unease for my country," Coleman confided, "a feeling that it is experiencing a crisis greater than any in my lifetime." Coleman feared that if the President did not take decisive action "greater and greater polarization will occur . . . the actions of the black extremists will incite reaction among the white extremists."[45] Writing to Moynihan, Coleman worried about the political polarization he saw incited by black militancy and wondered if they and others could "constitute some kind of force for action, some kind of group that would be able to do something."[46] Coleman articulated a fear shared by many postwar liberals, including Moynihan, that the U.S. was descending into social disorder in the late 1960s. What liberals once believed was a stable postwar consensus seemed to be quickly unraveling.

In the late 1960s, Moynihan harped on the threat of social instability, which he argued resulted largely from black family instability. Responding to the growth of Black Power and the spread of urban rebellions, Moynihan amplified the report's warning of the social dangers of African American family break-up. Though Moynihan spoke about these issues in countless venues, including television appearances, he addressed them most frankly in his unpublished book, which argued, "Increasingly the Negro population threatens the stability of the society." Moynihan predicted, "In the period ahead, the most explosive social combination for the United States will be the continuation of demands for black power at the top combined with the persistence of Negro weakness at the bottom." Moynihan applauded certain strains of Black Power that stressed racial pride. However, he was apoplectic about the "resurgence of militant Negro radicalism," which he viewed as basically irrational: "avowedly nihilistic," bent on "rage and destruction" for its own sake, and "moving towards association with Chinese communism."[47]

To Moynihan, Black Power was dangerous because of its potential base among lower-class African Americans. Moynihan professed that in Watts "at the heart of the riot seems to have been young men consciously, exultantly asserting their manhood in the act of destruction and defiance and with no

regrets, no remorse." Moynihan blamed lower-class African American culture for the uprising: "During the riots Negro teenagers began more and more
to display their devastating style of jeering and taunting, a talent learned from
one another in the destructive slum world of the 'Dirty Dozens' but now boldly
turned outwards towards white authority."[48] Moynihan dismissed the notion that urban uprisings resulted from racial injustice. While the Johnson-
appointed Kerner Commission claimed "white racism" as a major cause of
the riots, Moynihan blamed radical leaders and lower-class African Americans. He also justified the disproportionate responses of authorities. He dismissed "routine charges of police brutality" as a precipitating cause of the riots.
Moynihan even claimed that police brutality was not racially motivated.
"Newark police have been clubbing lowerclass persons [of all races] for generations," Moynihan opined about the 1967 rebellion there. "There is nothing to be gained by declaring such behavior inexcusable," he added.[49] Moynihan
also jibed at liberal intellectuals who wanted to correct police brutality. "American intellectuals are cop haters," he explained.[50]

    Moynihan blamed liberals for not averting the social conflicts of the late
1960s. In a widely reported speech at a conference of the Americans for Democratic Action (ADA), a leading liberal organization, Moynihan considered
"The Politics of Stability." He worried that the nation might "not emerge intact" from its "period of political instability." Drawing from his unpublished
book manuscript, Moynihan pinpointed the dangers of an African American "underclass" and "a group of radical, nihilistic youth, not themselves
members of this underclass, but identifying with it, able to communicate with
it, and determined to use it as an instrument of violent, apocalyptic confron-
tation with a white society they have decided is irredeemably militaristic and
racist." Moynihan reproached liberals "because it is largely they who have been
in office and presided over the onset of both the war in Vietnam and the violence in American cities." He further excoriated liberals for failing to condemn African American radicalism and violence. "Liberals," he claimed,
"must somehow overcome the curious condescension that takes the form of
defending and explaining away anything, however outrageous, which Negroes, individually or collectively, might do."[51] Many liberals in the audience
were outraged. They noted that Moynihan caricatured liberals; for example,
he failed to provide an example of a liberal who excused "anything" African
Americans did. They also objected to Moynihan's presumption that liberals
had dominated domestic policy; they accurately pointed out that Kennedy
and Johnson enacted only watered-down liberal reforms.[52]

Moynihan remained committed to antipoverty reforms targeted at African Americans, but he couched such reforms in terms of conservative values of social stability and conventional values. Liberals recognized Moynihan's rightward turn. Robert Kennedy reportedly remarked about Moynihan in 1968, "He knows all the facts and is against all the solutions."[53] As many liberals shifted left, Moynihan argued that they should break right. His ADA talk concluded, "Liberals must see clearly that their essential interest is in the stability of the social order; and given the present threats to that stability, they must seek out and make much more make effective alliances with political conservatives who share their interest."[54] By proposing that liberals ally with conservatives to preserve social stability, Moynihan foreshadowed his entrance into the Nixon administration. He also signaled the rightward drift of a set of postwar liberals who came to be known as "neoconservatives."

Neoconservatives

In 1973, Moynihan Report defender Michael Harrington popularized the term "neoconservative" to refer to one-time liberal intellectuals Daniel Bell, Nathan Glazer, and Moynihan, who were turning against the welfare state.[55] The initial phase of neoconservativism in the late 1960s and early 1970s identified by Harrington should be distinguished from its later manifestations. In its first iteration, neoconservatives focused on domestic policy, particularly Great Society liberalism and the threat of social radicalism. Like Moynihan, they advocated modest income redistribution, but were hostile to government bureaucracy. The origins of neoconservatism are best understood as part of a late 1960s split within postwar liberalism. New social movements of the period, especially Black Power, the antiwar movement, and second-wave feminism, helped fracture postwar liberalism in two directions. The Democratic Party was riven by conflict that spilled from the streets onto the Chicago convention floor in 1968 and persisted when some of the party establishment declined to back the 1972 candidacy of George McGovern, who infused his campaign with the spirit of the new social movements. The intellectual strength of the Democrats' anti-McGovern wing came from postwar liberals who resisted the influence of the 1960s left and developed an insiders' critique of liberalism.

In addition to Moynihan, the most influential neoconservatives were James S. Coleman, Nathan Glazer, Gertrude Himmelfarb, Irving Kristol, Norman Podhoretz, and James Q. Wilson. Moynihan was particularly close to Glazer, his writing collaborator; Kristol, his one-time editor at the *Reporter*; and Wilson, his Harvard colleague. Neoconservatives gathered around two influential journals. In the late 1960s, Podhoretz steered *Commentary*, the organ of postwar Jewish liberalism, toward the right. *The Public Interest*, the journal Kristol and Bell founded in 1965 with the goal of using social science to evaluate social policy, quickly became a forum for criticizing the supposedly overreaching liberalism of the Great Society. Neoconservative intellectuals were remarkably well connected in government and the media and possessed considerable power to set the terms of national debate. They also shared a distinctive generational and political experience. Most were born in the 1920s, had socialist backgrounds, but became anti-Communist liberals after World War II. Neoconservatives were rooted in Cold War liberalism's suspicion of mass politics and embrace of technocracy and political pluralism. They idealized a stable postwar consensus, one they blamed the left for rupturing in the late 1960s.[56]

Neoconservatives were white, but mostly not WASPs, and they tended to view African Americans through a white ethnic lens. Most were Jews, though a few prominent neoconservatives, such as Moynihan and Michael Novak, were Catholics. Neoconservatives analogized African Americans to European immigrant groups in ways that overlooked that African Americans were hardly recent arrivals (even if many were recent migrants to cities) and that anti-black racism differed in degree and kind from discrimination previously faced by European immigrant groups. Moreover, white ethnics had historically benefited from the pervading color line that allowed them eventually to enjoy the privileges of whiteness.

Moynihan encouraged this misleading comparison. Following his report's publication, he likened the position of African Americans to that of Irish immigrants in the mid-nineteenth-century. For instance, in a 1967 *Newsday* article, "How the Liberals Failed the Negro," Moynihan indirectly explained recent African American uprisings by quoting Children's Aid Society of New York reports about the Irish around the time of the 1863 draft riots that warned of "the outcast, vicious, reckless multitude of New York boys, swarming now in every foul alley and low street" and "the existence . . . of a great, ignorant, and irresponsible class, who were growing up here without any permanent interest in the welfare of the community or the success of government."[57] One of the most original chapters of *Toward Equality* contended that African American equality was an "Irish problem" and not a "Jewish problem." A "fully competitive" minority group like Jewish Americans, Moynihan argued, needed "only [to] obtain the opportunity to enter competition in order to achieve its ends." However, legal equality was insufficient to achieve socioeconomic equality for groups such as nineteenth-century Irish Americans and contemporary African Americans. By writing about nineteenth-century Irish as a proxy for African Americans, Moynihan could use even more charged language than normal to describe black social pathology. For example, he claimed that the nineteenth-century Irish "spawned a generation of thugs, drunks, whores, derelicts, and worse." Like African Americans, he claimed, Irish Americans had suffered from matriarchal family structure: "The 'sainted Irish mother,'" he contended, "assumed her place in the succession of matriarchs who have borne the brunt, and perhaps ever so slightly perpetuated, the pathology of the slum."[58] Comparing African Americans to Irish Americans helped Moynihan defuse charges that his frank depiction of black social pathology was racist. After all, he applied the same descriptions to his own group (albeit at a considerable historical distance).

The immigrant-African American analogy was a staple of neoconservatism. The title of a 1966 *New York Times Magazine* article by Irving Kristol declared, "The Negro Today Is like the Immigrant Yesterday." Perhaps influenced by Moynihan, Kristol compared African Americans specifically to nineteenth-century Irish Americans. He began by imagining what Americans a century earlier might say about the "crisis of the cities" in the mid-nineteenth century. They would focus on "people who are themselves problems" marked by "disorderly" family life, "high rate of crime and delinquency" and a propensity to "create slums wherever they live."[59] Kristol suggested these imagined observations about the 1860s Irish applied equally to 1960s African Americans.

The contours of the immigrant-black analogy had been evident in Glazer and Moynihan's influential 1963 book, *Beyond the Melting Pot*. Introducing the book's 1970 edition, the authors updated their argument to challenge Black Power. Glazer and Moynihan pointedly stated that African Americans should not have "chosen" a "racial" identity that separated them from mainstream American values, but rather opted for an "ethnic" identification as had European immigrant groups: "In the Negro communities, we have seen a wholly admirable and impressive rise of self-assertion and pride. . . . But when it is combined with an effort to separate Negroes from the mechanism by which varied groups, in this most mixed of nations, participate in a common society and a common state, then we can only be saddened and frightened." While

Glazer and Moynihan rejected what they called "colorblindness" in favor of a "multiethnic" conception of American society, they bemoaned African Americans' failure as a group to assimilate more fully into American society. For this, they blamed Black Power advocates and a liberal new class of "intellectuals and the mass media" who encouraged black militancy.[60] Kristol similarly used the immigrant analogy to denounce Black Power. African Americans in New York, he claimed, "seemed, until recently, well on their way toward following the traditional immigrant route to a secure and honorable position in American society" until they were derailed by "an upsurge of black nationalism of such intensity as to be obsessive in character, and immensely self-destructive in effect."[61]

Neoconservatives offered intellectual justification to white ethnics who claimed that since they had advanced through hard work, no special privileges should be given to African Americans.[62] Glazer and Moynihan sympathized with working-class white ethnics who they believed were unfairly blamed for racism, at whose expense African American progress was frequently made, and whose problems were ignored by the liberal media. They claimed white ethnics had good reason to complain that blacks should work patiently for upward mobility: "'Do you expect Negroes to wait *that* long for a good job?' There is an answer to this, 'Everyone else has.' Unfortunately, many Negroes, and in particular militant leaders, are not aware of this."[63]

However, some white ethnics cringed when directly compared to blacks. Several Irish Americans wrote Moynihan in protest after he compared African Americans to earlier Irish immigrants in a 1967 *Time* cover article published shortly following the Newark riot. "Paddy and Sambo are the same people," declared Moynihan.[64] One letter-writer asserted that African Americans failed to advance because they lacked the personal morality of Irish Americans and other European immigrant groups: "The great difference between Paddy and Sambo is that practically all of our Paddys were brought up in homes in which they were subjected to both parental and religious training and discipline."[65] An outraged Irish-American woman treated Moynihan's comments as a slander against her hard-working grandmother, a single mother whom she proudly declared never accepted welfare. Moynihan replied, "[M]rs. Brady's sainted grandmother was abandoned by her husband and went to work supporting her children, just as do the negro women today. Paddy and Sambo were the same."[66]

The European immigrant analogy contained a qualified optimism about future African American progress. However, neoconservatives warned that such progress might be blocked by African American militancy and welfare dependency, both of which would hinder racial self-help. In 1965, Kristol offered "a few kind words" for Booker T. Washington and Uncle Tom: "one of the problems inherent in 'militancy' is . . . by concentrating exclusive attention on the proposition that all the ills of the Negro condition derive from white wickedness . . . it weakens the instinct for self-help and mutual aid *within* the Negro community."[67] The European immigrant-African American analogy implied that groups succeeded in American society based on their internal characteristics. If African Americans failed to achieve equality, neoconservatives maintained, it would not be due to racism. James Q. Wilson argued, "The argument over the details of the Moynihan Report . . . has to some extent obscured its most important implication . . . if all Negroes were turned white tomorrow, they would still have serious problems."[68] Kristol similarly explained, "Anyone who has taken the trouble to read the Moynihan Report cannot fail to be impressed by the truth of his claim that this unstable family situation makes it particularly difficult for the urban Negro both to cope with the disadvantages of his condition and to exploit the possibilities for achievement that do exist."[69]

In the late 1960s, neoconservatives advocated social reforms aimed at creating jobs for African Americans. Kristol, for example, endorsed Moynihan's idea of introducing twice-a-day mail delivery to create jobs for black men in the postal service.[70] Wilson advocated full employment and a guaranteed annual income.[71] Nevertheless, neoconservatives used the Moynihan Report to articulate a powerful critique of the liberal welfare state that led many of them to jettison their social-democratic beliefs during the 1970s. They trumpeted the report's finding that welfare cases rose in the early 1960s despite the rise in African American male employment. Moynihan thought these dual trends indicated welfare dependency and self-perpetuating pathology. In a 1973 essay, Wilson dubbed this finding "Moynihan's scissors" (referring to the diverging paths of unemployment and welfare), and argued that it lay at the heart of Moynihan's contribution. He claimed it partially explained rising rates of crime, unemployment, and heroin addiction in the "sick Sixties" and hailed Moynihan for noticing that "we were becoming two societies—one affluent and worried, the other pathological and predatory."[72]

By the early 1970s, Moynihan increasingly pointed to the broken link between male employment and family stability as the central finding of *The Negro Family*, though he rarely mentioned it in initial defenses of the report. In 1973, he claimed the report's "central statistical argument" was that unemployment in the early 1960s "started to go down and new AFDC cases to go up. If this continued, the report reasoned—if macroeconomic forces lost their apparent influence on social structure—there would form an urban under-class which, because of its racial identification, would lead to a new and wholly unexpected range of social conflict."[73] Moynihan even blamed welfare, rather than male unemployment, for black family instability: "The present situation seems to be of relatively recent origin . . . its explanation will be found in changing relationships between employment and income, and *especially in the presence of welfare income as an alternative to earnings*."[74]

Kristol cited Moynihan's "famous and brilliant memorandum on the Ne-gro family" in a 1971 essay, "Welfare: The Best of Intentions, the Worst of Results." Kristol articulated a by-then characteristic neoconservative theme: the negative unintended consequences of government action. He reviewed left-wing scholars Frances Fox Piven and Richard Cloward's book *Regulating the Poor*, which argued that government used welfare relief to stabilize the capitalist system and that welfare rolls rose during the 1960s as a response to political unrest. In contrast, Kristol argued that welfare emerged from the good intentions of liberals such as welfare rights advocates Piven and Cloward and that it destroyed family structure. "A liberal and compassionate social policy has bred all sorts of unanticipated and perverse consequences," Kris-tol opined. Specifically, it caused "the disorganization and demoralization of the Negro family." The Moynihan Report showed "that most of the new wel-fare recipients were in the Aid to Dependent Children category, that a grow-ing proportion of families in this category were black and fatherless, and that the disorganization of the Negro family seemed to have gathered a sociolog-ical momentum of its own—a momentum impervious to the effects of im-proving economic circumstances." Kristol complained that "a great deal many liberal-minded scholars" spent "all their energies attacking [Moynihan] rather than the problem."[75]

Kristol argued that anti-poverty programs created poverty. Because Moynihan had perceptively demonstrated "a connection between family disorganization and the influx of poor black female-headed families to wel-fare," Kristol supposed, "the existence of a liberal welfare program might itself have been responsible . . . for this family disorganization." Kristol blamed wel-fare, not unemployment, for undermining the place of African American men as family breadwinners: "welfare robs the head of the household of *his* economic function and tends to make of him a 'superfluous man.' Welfare . . . *competes* with his . . . earning ability; and the more generous the welfare program, the worse he makes out in this competition."[76] By Kristol's logic, empowering African American men required dismantling welfare.

As Kristol's concern for the patriarchal authority of African American men indicated, neoconservatives' defense of the male-headed nuclear family was a central element in their understanding of African American inequality. Using family structure to explain why some ethnoracial groups met greater success complemented the immigrant-black analogy. Neoconservatives contributed to growing concern among Americans about the decline of the nuclear family.[77] For example, a 1967 magazine editorial concluded about the Moynihan Report:

> Unhappily the entire thrust of intellectual thought today is toward the destruction of the family unit and the moral strength that has held it together. You cannot pick up a magazine, you cannot pick up a book, you cannot go to a movie or a play without observing immorality, violence, ridicule of the family as a viable unit, joyfully presented and enthusiastically applauded. How can you expect the low-income Negro to accept standards that the rest of society seems determined to reject?[78]

Neoconservatives praised the Moynihan Report not only for its understanding of racial inequality but for calling attention to a disturbing decline in the nuclear family. For instance, Glazer invoked black family instability to highlight the need to protect the "traditional family." "A funny thing happened on the way to developing a radical critique of the American family," Glazer quipped in a 1977 essay, "it has turned out that the old model was not so bad after all." As proof, Glazer cited the increasingly high "proportion of poor black children born illegitimate, raised by a single parent, and living on welfare" and its negative effects "on health, scholastic achievement, delinquency, [and] employment." However, he regretted, "a decade after the Moynihan Report first raised this issue, it is still not quite proper to talk about it directly and honestly."[79]

Neoconservatives furthered their incipient criticism of the welfare state by arguing that activist government inevitably undermined the family. In an influential 1971 article, Glazer pointed to family structure as one of the "Limits of Social Policy." He argued that welfare programs created dependency among beneficiaries and thereby undermined self-support: "every piece of social policy substitutes for some traditional arrangement . . . a new arrangement in which public authorities take over, at least in part, the role of the family, of the ethnic and neighborhood group, or of the voluntary association. In doing so, social policy weakens the position of these traditional agents, and further encourages needy people to depend on the government, rather than on the traditional structures, for help." He deduced, "the breakdown of traditional modes of behavior is the chief cause of our social problems."[80] Generous welfare programs, he suggested, undermined the traditional values of family and work.

In arguing in favor of "traditional" families, Glazer drew on an unlikely authority, the social critic Christopher Lasch, once prominently identified with the New Left. In a 1977 book, Lasch defended the nuclear family as a "haven in a heartless world"—a barrier against the intrusive state and the ruthless marketplace. Lasch invoked the Moynihan Report in his chapter, "The Attack on the Nuclear Family." Citing Moynihan and Rainwater, Lasch rejected the idea that the matrifocal African American family was a healthy adaptation to poverty. Middle-class defenders of the lower-class African American family, he claimed, tended to "idealize the matrifocal family, exaggerate the degree to which it is embedded in a rich network of kinship relations, and ignore evidence which plainly shows that blacks themselves prefer a family in which the male earns the money and the mother rears the young." Lasch's main concern was not African American families, but the eroding strength of the nuclear family ideal among all Americans, for which he partly blamed feminists. "The real objection to the Moynihan Report," he proclaimed, "is that it exaggerates the distance between the ghetto and the rest of American culture, which in some ways has come to resemble a pale copy of the black ghetto."[81] To be sure, Lasch's left-wing critique of the state and the market distinguished him from neoconservatives such as Glazer, who discounted Lasch's radicalism as the efforts of a "writer, struggling with his conservative instincts . . . trying to save his radical credentials by invoking the proper spells."[82] Nevertheless, Lasch echoed neoconservatives by using the Moynihan Report to defend the nuclear family ideal.

Are You a Racist?

The intellectual father of postwar conservatism, William F. Buckley, was delighted by Moynihan's neoconservative turn. Moynihan, Buckley declared in 1967, is "saying some of the most interesting things said these days in public life, most striking that the liberals have a good deal to learn from the conservatives with whom they should . . . make common cause." Buckley concurred with Moynihan that "the single most urgent problem at home is to abort the threatening union between the young Negro revolutionaries, who are few in number, and the class of Negro dispossessed and disenchanted."[83] The admiration was mutual. As Moynihan recalled, "Glazer and I began to notice that we were getting treated in [Buckley's] *National Review* with a much higher level of intellectual honesty [than in liberal publications]." "I was not a bigot," he remembered, "but all the good guys were calling me a racist, [while] here was this fellow Buckley saying these thoughtful things."[84] The Moynihan Report controversy helped forge an unlikely partnership between conservatives such as Buckley and budding neoconservatives. Conservatives who opposed the ideal of "equality" used the Moynihan Report to rationalize racial inequality.[85]

A rapprochement between Moynihan and Buckley would have seemed impossible at the start of the 1960s. A conservative Catholic, Buckley detested the Church's social teaching on labor rights and a living wage that had influenced Moynihan. In 1955, Buckley founded *National Review* to unite postwar conservativism out of disparate strands of moral traditionalism, economic libertarianism, and anti-Communism. Northern conservatives such as Buckley allied with Southern segregationists. Buckley argued for Southern states' rights to preserve racial segregation in the South and opposed the Civil Rights Act of 1964. In 1957, he justified Jim Crow on the basis that whites were "the advanced race."[86] Nevertheless, defending Southern segregation was a minor issue for Buckley compared to his overriding concern to defend free-market capitalism and the hierarchal class structure it produced against liberal egalitarianism. Jim Crow's demise allowed Buckley to discard the baggage of defending outright white supremacy and enabled him to craft new, ostensibly color-blind justifications of racial and class hierarchy. The Moynihan Report (shorn of its call for national action) and *Beyond the Melting Pot* aided Buckley's construction of a new conservative position on race.

Buckley discovered *Beyond the Melting Pot* when he ran for mayor of New York on the Conservative Party ticket in 1965 (the same election in which Moynihan ran for City Council President). The patrician Buckley learned that he could garner support from working-class white New Yorkers by appealing to their resentment of city programs such as welfare that they thought benefited African Americans and Puerto Ricans.[87] Drawing on Glazer and Moynihan, Buckley denied white responsibility for racial minorities' low economic positions. In an October 1965 speech, he called for public frankness regarding lower-class African American families: "There is . . . a special problem of illegitimacy and broken homes among Negroes in certain areas of New York." While he conceded that African American social pathology resulted partly from past discrimination, Buckley nevertheless insisted that African Americans had to practice self-help. As an economic conservative, Buckley wanted to halt momentum from the civil rights movement that might lead to social-democratic reforms. Citing *Beyond the Melting Pot*, Buckley asserted, "the situation in Harlem [is] dire and dreadful, and . . . the moment has come when, the government's competence in these matters having been largely exhausted, leaders of the Negro people must take on the responsibility of helping their own people and dispelling the illusion that what is left to do is primarily up to the white man to do."[88] When the *New York Times* chastised Buckley for appealing "to racism and bigotry," he charged the paper with hypocrisy for having praised Glazer and Moynihan for making identical arguments. For his part, Moynihan reportedly declared in a radio interview, "everything Mr. Buckley has said on the Negro question is a plagiarism taken straight out of my book, *Beyond the Melting Pot*."[89]

Buckley defended Moynihan and Glazer from charges of "racism" in a 1965 press release, "Are You a Racist?" "If every sociologist who puts down figures about illegitimacy rates or crime rates is marked down as a racist," Buckley reasoned, "then the entire data-collecting profession will inherit the word." Buckley defended racial generalizations: "If everyone who says the Negroes in New York breed more illegitimate children is a racist; if everyone who says the Irish have a better sense of humor than the Swedes is a racist; if everyone who says the I.Q. of the average Jew in New York is higher than that of the average Anglo-Saxon is a racist—then it will turn out that most people are 'racist.'"[90] Buckley's proclamation that those who advocated "states' rights" were not racists distanced him from Moynihan and Glazer. Yet like neoconservatives he restricted the term "racist" to refer only to explicit white supremacists. He diverted discussion to individual motives—who was and who was not a racist—and silenced discussion of unconscious racial prejudice and institutional racism.

Buckley also defended the Moynihan Report. In a syndicated 1967 newspaper column, Buckley hailed Moynihan's *Commentary* article, "The President and the Negro" as "imperative reading for liberals and conservatives alike." Buckley's piece "The Great, Lost Opportunity of 1965," was oddly titled since the possibility of liberal economic reforms appalled him.

Nevertheless, Buckley agreed with Moynihan's contention that "the family was the crucial unit in social progress." Moreover, Moynihan's narrative of left-liberal political correctness instinctively appealed to Buckley. "[H]yper-sensitive egalitarianism," Buckley concluded, "can be the worst enemy of frank discussion of how to move toward effective equality" for African Americans.[91] Buckley portrayed himself as committed to the "cause of Negro equality" and declared egalitarian liberals shackled by "ideological dogma" as enemies of African American advancement.

In "Are You a Racist?" Buckley defended as non-racist even those who insisted ethnoracial groups had different IQs, a hallmark of scientific racism. In the late 1960s, a few prominent scientists won attention by reviving the notion of biological disparities in intelligence to explain the low socioeconomic position of African Americans.[92] That they drew on the Moynihan Report was surprising, given that it explicitly rejected genetic explanations for African American inequality. However, by seeing racial inequality as primarily caused by defects among African Americans, the report opened a space for scientific racists to offer a biological alternative to Moynihan's sociological analysis.

The new scientific racists did not favor Jim Crow-style segregation and discrimination, but rather argued that African American's low socioeconomic status resulted from biological difference and that government efforts to secure equal results were misguided and unfair to whites. Because they did not support legal segregation, these scientists claimed not to be "racist" even as they advanced an old racist argument. Nobel Prize-winning physicist William Shockley led the campaign for attributing racial inequality to genetics. In a 1965 interview with *U.S. News and World Report*, he identified "heredity" as a key factor explaining poverty and crime among African Americans.[93] Shockley criticized Great Society programs, which he claimed inaccurately assumed that ethnic groups had equal genetic abilities. To prove that this was official government perspective, he quoted the Moynihan Report's statement, "Intelligence potential is distributed among Negro infants in the same proportion and pattern as among Icelanders or Chinese or any other group."[94] At first, then, the new scientific racists viewed the Moynihan Report as embodying the liberalism they sought to undermine. That changed by decade's end.

Shockley influenced Arthur Jensen, who published an influential and controversial 1969 article in the *Harvard Education Review*, "How Much Can We Boost IQ and Scholastic Achievement?" For Jensen, intelligence was mainly a matter of heredity, not environment (he speculated that it was 80 percent the former and only 20 percent the latter). Jensen cited the Moynihan Report as proof of African Americans' inability to "compete on equal terms." Jensen proposed that hereditary differences in intelligence explained the racial disparities Moynihan highlighted. Drawing on Moynihan's statistics, Jensen particularly worried that poorer African Americans, whom he assumed to be less intelligent, reproduced at a higher rate than wealthier African Americans: "The differential birthrate, as a function of socioeconomic status, is greater in the Negro than in the white population."[95] Here Jensen recalled Theodore White's warnings of "biological anarchy" in black ghettos. Jensen's argument recycled previously discredited ideas and rested on the questionable assumption that IQ tests accurately measured innate intelligence. Despite the dubious nature of his science, Jensen's argument received a wide hearing in academic and media circles because it offered a simple explanation for the persistence of racial inequality that absolved whites of responsibility.[96]

The Moynihan Report became further entangled with the revival of scientific racism in a notorious 1971 *Atlantic Monthly* article by Harvard professor Richard Herrnstein that popularized Jensen's arguments. Herrnstein defended class hierarchy in the United States, which, he argued, largely resulted from biological differences. "When people can freely take their natural level in society," he asserted, "the upper classes will, virtually by definition, have greater capacity than the lower."[97] Herrnstein rejected the notion that government could rectify social inequalities as based "on a false belief in the equality of human endowment."[98] Though Herrnstein was most concerned to defend capitalist class hierarchy, his argument that economic inequality resulted naturally from differences in human intelligence led him to consider racial differences in class position. His article's most controversial claim was that further scientific research could very well prove that African Americans were genetically inferior in intelligence.

Atlantic Monthly editors portrayed Herrnstein as taking up the mantle of earlier reports on African American inequality by Moynihan, Coleman, and Jensen. (Referring to Jensen's scholarly article as the "Jensen Report" likened it to these earlier government documents.) Jensen and Herrnstein, they implied, *answered* the questions raised by Moynihan and Coleman: "Both the Moynihan and Coleman reports grappled with the idea that something within the black community itself was holding back its economic and educational advance." They observed, "both reports noted that, for reasons not wholly understood, the removal of external barriers such as racist customs and laws did not always bring the promised improvement in economic and educational condition, presumably because of internal barriers—for example, family structure or cultural ambience."[99] The editors' confidence that "external barriers" to African American progress had already been removed led them to look for flaws in African Americans that explained their low socioeconomic position. They praised Jensen and Herrnstein because they "faced head-on the possibility that blacks and whites differed in inherited intelligence." For the editors of a major American magazine, it was a small step from the sociological arguments of Moynihan and Coleman to the biological ones of Jensen and Herrnstein.

Neoconservatives defended the new scientific racists. When student protestors heckled Herrnstein during his Harvard classes, neoconservatives rallied to his defense. Writing in *Commentary*, Norman Podhoretz retread arguments that supported Moynihan against his critics from the left by defending free inquiry against left-wing political correctness. Casting Herrnstein as a victim of liberal orthodoxy, Podhoretz pronounced, "Today the only ideas it seems to be the aim of a college education to disturb are those that conflict with the pieties which happen to prevail at the time within the 'liberal' culture." He concluded, "The upshot is an atmosphere which is no longer conducive to fearless inquiry or even to playful speculation and which, far from encouraging, positively obstructs the development of independence of mind and of the critical spirit."[100] Shockley and Jensen supporters portrayed criticism of their science as a free speech issue as had Moynihan's supporters. A letter in the *Washington Post* criticized misinformed attacks on Jensen: "It would be shameful to let the thing slide into another Moynihan affair."[101]

Moynihan helped promote Jensen's article even while disagreeing with it. He sent an excerpt to President Nixon. He briefed Nixon's cabinet on the article and helped establish Jensen's argument as a legitimate hypothesis in the media.[102] Regarding Jensen's thesis that African Americans were genetically inferior in intelligence, Moynihan advised Nixon, "I personally simply do not believe this is so, but the truth is that it is an open question."[103] Thus, Moynihan conferred scientific legitimacy on Jensen's hypothesis even while rejecting it. Moynihan sought to spin Jensen's data to convince Nixon to invest in early childhood education. Clearly, he rejected Nixon adviser Pat Buchanan's interpretation that Jensen offered a reason to abandon efforts to provide African Americans an "equal chance at the starting line."[104] In personal correspondence with Jensen, Moynihan told him that environmental factors, such as father absence, better explained the low educational achievement of black schoolchildren. Yet, noting white racists' misuse of Jensen's scholarship, Moynihan expressed empathy because, as the author of *The Negro Family*, he knew the "perils of scholarship in this present time."[105] That Moynihan flirted with Jensen's ideas illustrated the distance he had traveled from earlier in the decade, when he avowed that racial inequality could be solved by liberal social engineering.

Benign Neglect

In 1967, Barry Goldwater lauded Moynihan as one of "the intellectually honest . . . liberals [who] are beginning to change their attitude and are seeking some place else to hang their hat than upon the outworn post of the government-can-do-it-best philosophy."[106] Moynihan's neoconservative views appealed to Republicans. Representative Donald Rumsfeld, for instance, read into the *Congressional Record* articles by Moynihan questioning the use of racial "quotas" in university admissions.[107] Melvin Laird, chair of the House Republican conference, included Moynihan's "Where Liberals Went Wrong," in his edited volume *Republican Papers*, published for the 1968 election.[108]

In his 1968 presidential campaign, Nixon praised Moynihan as a "thoughtful liberal," foreshadowing his later invitation to Moynihan to join his administration.[109] Moynihan's mix of liberal social policies and conservative logic made him a perfect fit for Nixon, whose recruitment of advisers with differing ideological views reflected his grappling with the era's rapid political change. Nixon's domestic policies were so contradictory that he inspired a wide variety of images that persist today. Some consider him the pioneer of Reaganite Republicanism; others believe he was the last liberal to hold office.[110] For example, Nixon introduced affirmative action programs. But he also mobilized disaffected white voters against liberal elites—portrayed as overly generous to African Americans. His racially coded appeals to "law and order" sought voters who had backed George Wallace, the populist who defended racial segregation as Alabama governor.[111] At the same time, Nixon carefully distinguished himself from segregationists. His color-blind language was tailored to moderate suburban white voters who did not think of themselves as racists but who had no interest in rectifying residential segregation or paying taxes to alleviate African American poverty.[112]

Moynihan repackaged arguments he had developed since writing *The Negro Family* to convince Nixon that it was in the interest of social order to provide economic aid to lower-class African Americans. "The Negro lower class," he posited, "appears to be unusually self-damaging." Moynihan predicted a dire future of "black-white hatred, fear, and turmoil" including the territorial break-up of the U.S. itself if it failed to take action. Asking Nixon to ponder "what those half starved, malaria ridden, pajama clad Viet Cong have done to the armies of the American Republic," Moynihan posited that African American radicals posed a similar threat to the American government. He thus recommended that Nixon aim "to dissolve the great black urban lower class . . . that the militant middle class now uses as a threat to the larger society, much as the desperate bank robber threatens to drop the vial of nitroglycerin." Moynihan's portrayal of Black Power was hyperbolic at best. While Moynihan made another case for national action, it rested on quelling African American radicalism rather than acknowledging African Americans' legitimate demands for economic justice.[113]

Moynihan saw offering income support to poor African Americans as a means to "dissolve" them into stable working-class America and thus "dissolve" the threat of African American radicalism. When Moynihan became a Nixon adviser, he advocated a universal family allowance of the kind he had hoped *The Negro Family* might generate. The Family Assistance Plan (FAP) Nixon proposed was a liberal measure justified by conservative logic. Nixon initially understood FAP as Moynihan did: an antipoverty measure directed especially at African Americans. By replacing welfare (AFDC) with benefits to all low-income American families and standardizing payments across the nation, FAP would have moved American welfare policy to the left. However, Moynihan and Nixon justified FAP with rhetoric that pushed political discourse rightward. They presented FAP as shoring up the nuclear family (payments could go to families with fathers present) and the work ethic (payments could go to those with jobs). They did not advocate a guaranteed annual income as a matter of economic justice, as many liberals did and Moynihan had earlier. Moynihan presented FAP as part of a broader strategy of defusing perceived threats to social order.

Replicating his understanding of the Moynihan Report dispute, Moynihan blamed the left for FAP's defeat.[114] In fact, the welfare rights movement campaigned against FAP because of its low level of benefits (welfare recipients in Northern cities would have seen no rise in payments), punitive work requirements, and assumption that women needed men to escape poverty.

However, the plan largely failed because Nixon quietly withdrew his support and because of its contradictory mix of liberal policy and conservative justification. Though FAP offered universal benefits that would have destigmatized beneficiaries, Nixon alienated liberals when he labeled welfare recipients as lazy and undeserving. Many conservatives nonetheless recognized FAP as a guaranteed income program, an unwelcome expansion of the welfare state.[115]

Moynihan's best remembered contribution to the Nixon administration was his "benign neglect" memo written in early 1970 to assess Nixon's policies toward African Americans during his first year in office. Moynihan surveyed developments among African Americans, reprising familiar themes of "social pathology," "female-headed families," and "anti-social behavior among young black males." Unlike in *The Negro Family*, however, Moynihan highlighted middle-class African Americans' "extraordinary progress" in closing educational and income gaps with whites. Accordingly, Moynihan advised Nixon to initiate "a period in which Negro progress continues and racial rhetoric fades." Moynihan hoped that African American advancement could proceed without the contentious racial discourse of recent years. "The time may have come," he famously opined, "when the issue of race could benefit from a period of 'benign neglect.'"[116]

With "benign neglect" Moynihan coined a phrase as resonant and contentious as anything from *The Negro Family*. Moynihan did *not* mean that the federal government should ignore African Americans, a common misinterpretation. (He wanted FAP to alleviate African American poverty.) Rather, the expression reflected Moynihan's personal experience with how explosive a topic race could be: "The subject has been too much talked about." Moynihan urged Nixon to curb statements by his administration that might provoke African American radicals. He clearly had in mind incendiary statements by Vice President Spiro Agnew.

The "benign neglect" memo resembled the neoconservative narrative of the Moynihan Report controversy by pinpointing left-wing political correctness as the cause of racial disharmony. The main problem was not African American inequality, but intemperate discussions of race. The term "equality," which was central to *The Negro Family* and had registered the civil rights movement's demands for substantial economic reforms, did not appear in Moynihan's memo. Moynihan focused instead on "threats to the stability of society." He specifically urged the need to silence African American radicals and their liberal allies, whom he portrayed hyperbolically. Moynihan claimed that the Black Panthers were motivated by racial hatred and likened them to white supremacists. Yet he argued it was better to ignore their "provocations" rather than stamp them out with repression, which would only win them more liberal allies.

Nixon enthusiastically endorsed Moynihan's suggestions, circling the memo's section on "benign neglect" and writing "I agree" in the margin. He circulated Moynihan's memo to his cabinet. By emphasizing middle-class African Americans' success and urging Nixon to court a politically moderate "silent black majority," Moynihan seems to have inadvertently convinced Nixon to scrap programs to alleviate African American poverty such as FAP (which he secretly abandoned soon thereafter), and concentrate instead on programs such as affirmative action that could win the support of middle-class blacks. Spurred by Moynihan's memo, Nixon shifted to (as he put it), "helping and backing the strong [African Americans]—instead of putting all effort into raising the weak."[117]

Ironically, Moynihan's memo generated exactly the uproar it advised Nixon to avoid. The dispute over "benign neglect" not only replicated that over *The Negro Family*, it directly resulted from the earlier dispute. Civil rights leader James Farmer, a prominent critic of *The Negro Family*, leaked the memo to the press after encountering it in his role as assistant secretary of Health, Education, and Welfare (HEW) under Nixon. Farmer was predisposed to interpret the memo the same way he had seen the report: an excuse for government inaction.[118] The *New York Times* printed the memo on March 1, 1970; it was extensively reprinted, reported and debated thereafter. The press and critics widely interpreted the memo in terms of its author's flair for sparking racial controversy. A *Newsday* article quipped that if Moynihan recited "Mary Had a Little Lamb" in Central Park he would be "charged by somebody with inciting a riot."[119] A political cartoon depicted an armored truck delivering "Moynihan memos," a comment on the tendency of Moynihan's confidential reports to become public.[120]

Though "benign neglect" meant not talking about race, it is easy to see why civil rights activists interpreted Moynihan's memo as marking a national retreat from racial equality. They knew that the political transformation needed to address African American inequality could not occur while ignoring discussion of race. To many civil rights leaders, "benign neglect" seemed an apt description for Nixon's policies on African Americans. Activists were already angry about slowed school desegregation efforts, diluted voting rights, unenforced antidiscrimination measures, and the courting of political support from Southern conservatives. Some thought "benign neglect" a euphemism for policies better described as "malignant paternalism."[121]

Twenty-one civil rights leaders released a statement denouncing Moynihan's memo as a "flagrant and shameful political document." They misleadingly claimed that Moynihan advocated "'benign neglect' of the plight of black Americans." Nevertheless, signers legitimately thought the memo diverged from the goal of "achieving full equality." They asserted that the only way to avoid strengthening "black and white extremists" was "to try to solve the race problem," not to quiet discussions of race. They advocated substantial programs to tackle African American inequality, programs that Moynihan no longer supported. Many signers had been involved in the Moynihan Report controversy, including Bayard Rustin and sociologists Andrew Billingsley and Nathan Hare. Some signers had initially backed the Moynihan Report, including Dorothy Height and Whitney Young, whose National Urban League distributed the statement denouncing "benign neglect." Just five years earlier, Young defended the Moynihan Report as endorsing his domestic Marshall Plan program for ending African American poverty.[122]

Perhaps the most surprising name on the statement was that of Kenneth Clark, cited in the Moynihan Report and initially one of its staunchest defenders. Clark earlier saw Moynihan as the kind of white liberal ally African Americans needed to achieve racial equality. By 1970, however, Clark was embittered by the lack of national commitment to addressing the problems of African American ghettos, a lack perfectly encapsulated by "benign neglect." After the memo's release, Clark became a scathing critic of Moynihan. In his 1974 book, *Pathos of Power*, he excoriated him as the leading member of a "new breed of social scientist mercenaries" who "align themselves with those with power and against the aspirations of the powerless victims of flagrant and subtle inequities." He attacked Moynihan and other neoconservatives for "rationalizing political decisions which maintain inequities, inequality, and cruelties under such catch-phrases as 'benign neglect' or with the assertion that we do not know enough to change clearly unjust practices; they seek to make intolerable and clearly destructive inequities palatable."[123]

Moynihan's explanation of the origin of the phrase "benign neglect," offered following the memo's publication, may also have alarmed critics. He claimed he borrowed the phrase from an 1839 British parliamentary report by Lord Durham, a colonial governor of Canada who argued that a hands-off policy toward Canadians had encouraged their capacity for self-government. (As Moynihan later realized, Durham never used the phrase.)[124] "Benign neglect" thus evoked policy toward a group of people. The analogy implied that African Americans would best progress by relying on their own efforts without government aid, echoing the racial self-help reading of the Moynihan Report. Using a colonial analogy (albeit a Canadian one) was also bound to disturb some. A *Boston Globe* columnist surmised that the phrase gave "every black the impression of Mr. Nixon's adviser saying, 'Marvelous, these aborigines, really. They're getting along very well in the white man's world'."[125]

The benign neglect memo provoked further debate over who had the authority to advise on racial policy. A Berkeley, California, newspaper editorial, "Moynihan Rides Again," observed, "Moynihan's expertise in the field of race relations is about as up-to-date as the Earl of Durham's report."[126] U.S. Representative Louis Stokes, an African American, charged that the memo epitomized "the continuous ineptness that flows from white people relying upon white people to advise them of the affairs of black people."[127] An editorial in the Protestant journal *Christianity and Crisis* saw a common thread of technocratic elitism in the both the memo and *The Negro Family*: "The same relentless commitment to social engineering is present: 'we should do this for Negroes' slips repeatedly into 'we should do this with Negroes.'"[128]

As with the Moynihan Report, mainstream media voices defended Moynihan against what they characterized as misinformed and irrational attacks. Television news anchor Walter Cronkite commented on air in support of Moynihan against "impatient militants."[129] Conservatives attacked liberals for political correctness. One newspaper column, "Liberals Finally Place Knife in Moynihan's Back," proclaimed, "these fellows [liberals] will stop at nothing" to punish those "who have failed their litmus test."[130] The *Wall Street Journal* defended Moynihan's new "apostasy" and denounced liberals for their "special animosity" toward him. It praised Moynihan along with fellow neoconservatives Irving Kristol and Edward Banfield as social scientists "debunking much of the liberal creed."[131] Outspoken priest Andrew Greeley defended Moynihan in a column syndicated in the Catholic press. He alluded to the infamous turn-of-the-twentieth-century treason trials of French military officer Alfred Dreyfus: "*L'affaire* Moynihan is one of the best proofs we have had in a long tie of the immorality, not to say fascism of American liberals." Greeley further claimed that hatred of Irish Catholics by "puritan" liberals fueled attacks on Moynihan. "As for the liberal left," he reckoned, "the best thing that could be done for it would be neglect, and not particularly benign either."[132] Conservative media overall interpreted the "benign neglect" memo as an endorsement of racial self-help, similar to their interpretations of the Moynihan Report. A *Chicago Tribune* editorial defending Moynihan professed: "Now that the Negroes have full equality under the law and equal opportunities in education and employment, their future is up to them. . . . It is time for them to stop talking about 'black power,' to forget about race . . . and to do their utmost to take full advantage of their opportunities."[133]

For Moynihan, proposing "benign neglect" was a logical if hardly inevitable progression from his report, which contained the seeds of neoconservatism. Yet "benign neglect" was a significant departure from the "national action" he recommended a half-decade earlier. For neoconservatives, the Moynihan Report controversy demonstrated how even well-intentioned discussions of race could incite left liberals. They deflected the concern for racial inequality to political correctness. They paved the way for 1980s conservatives to appropriate the Moynihan Report—a liberal response to civil rights demands for equality—to launch a full-scale attack on the liberal welfare state.

EPILOGUE

A Mixed Legacy

The Moynihan Report's legacy is as mixed as its contents. It continued to incite a wide range of reactions after the 1970s. Nearly all interpretations of the report surfaced by the mid-1970s, indicating the crucial long-term impact the first decade after the 1964 Civil Rights Act had on American racial discourse. To trace the controversy past the 1970s is largely to witness the tedious rehashing of the same arguments. Nevertheless, the 1980s saw the controversy revitalized and reframed as public discussion of "the black family" increased to explain persistent racial inequality. As in the 1960s, interpreters divided over whether the report advocated national action or racial self-help. The balance, however, had shifted toward the latter. With the election of Ronald Reagan in 1980, the political climate moved decisively to the right. Drawing on ideas developed by neoconservatives in the wake of the Moynihan Report's release, conservative intellectuals mounted a frontal assault on liberalism.

The report also continued to appeal to liberals since the 1970s. When prominent sociologist William Julius Wilson revived the report's analysis of black social pathology to promote reforms to address race-based economic inequality in the 1980s, he declared he was "following in the footsteps of Moynihan."[1] Still, other liberals distanced themselves from Moynihan's path. In 1989, civil rights leader J. H. O'Dell compared the Moynihan Report's destructive effects on poor African Americans to the atomic bomb dropped on Nagasaki.[2] Even fifty years after its publication, the report remains a Rorschach test, inviting viewers to see in it what they want, as well as a litmus test, reflecting deep ideological cleavages.

The Conservative Appropriation

"We are all Moynihans now," proclaimed Republican cultural warrior William Bennett at a 1995 symposium celebrating the Moynihan Report's "blueprint" for a "world without welfare." On its thirtieth anniversary, Bennett praised *The Negro Family* as "prescient," excoriated its left-wing critics, and lauded Moynihan's "political courage."[3] The symposium occurred at an auspicious time for the right: in the 1994 mid-term elections, Republicans gained control of both houses of Congress and soon abolished the program commonly known as "welfare" (AFDC). Though it took place in 1995, the symposium captured conservative interpretations of the Moynihan Report emerging since the early 1980s that had significantly shifted public debate over the document. Reaganite conservatives used the Moynihan Report to argue that liberalism, not racism, caused racial inequality.

The symposium also capped a long effort by conservatives to capture the Moynihan Report for their ideological ends. Positive responses to the report by conservative journalists and intellectuals in the 1960s anticipated this appropriation. In addition, neoconservatives articulated themes later adopted by Reaganite conservatives: denouncing left-wing political correctness, pointing to African Americans' supposed cultural defects to explain racial inequality, discrediting social engineering, and defending the patriarchal nuclear family. Starting in the early 1980s, Reaganite conservatives amplified these ideas beyond what neoconservatives touted in the 1960s and 1970s. Bennett and other symposium participants offered a version of the Moynihan Report that promoted dismantling the welfare state to restore traditional "family values."

Bennett, former secretary of education under Reagan, applied the main lesson conservatives took from the Moynihan Report—that government programs could not solve social inequality—to launch a wholesale challenge to the liberal welfare state. His agenda dovetailed with that of the symposium's organizer, the American Enterprise Institute (AEI). A corporate-funded right-wing think tank that advocated government deregulation, the AEI rejected redistributionist government policies. Bennett identified flawed family structure as the main cause of social ills in American society: "The most serious problems afflicting our society today are manifestly moral, behavioral, and spiritual, and therefore remarkably resistant to government cures." For Bennett, the report conclusively demonstrated that breaking up patriarchal families produced social disorder. He hailed Moynihan for being "so right, so early, and at the very time when the assault on the nuclear family was in its early stages," and for calling attention to the rising rates of divorce and out-of-wedlock births among all Americans that Bennett believed constituted a "serious moral decline."[4] Bennett perversely suggested that the increase in single-parent families predicted by the Moynihan Report had a silver lining: the "accumulating decay" of family life, he avowed, "has undermined popular faith in government and reminded us of its limits." Combining nuclear family values with economic individualism, Bennett asserted that citizens must solve their own problems: "Government cannot force a man to be a good father to the child he sired, or make individuals take their professions of religious faith seriously, or cause the popular culture to become less vulgar." In Bennett's view, liberal government programs actively undermined families. His call for moral regeneration complemented attacks on the liberal welfare state as he demanded that government "stop subsidizing illegitimacy through welfare payments" and instead bolster the nuclear family through tax breaks and rescinding no-fault divorce laws.[5]

At a time when conservatives stepped up attacks on affirmative action programs designed to benefit historically oppressed minorities, Bennett merged praise for the Moynihan Report with color-blind rhetoric that denied racism mattered. "Today's major domestic problem," he asserted, "is family solidarity, not race."[6] Family structure offered Bennett a powerful alternative to racism as an explanation for persistent socioeconomic disparities between whites and African Americans. Bennett and other conservatives claimed to promote a race-neutral state that eschewed policies targeted at racial minorities. However, they ignored government policies that disproportionately harmed African Americans. Tellingly, Bennett overlooked how increasing rates of African American imprisonment undermined the male-headed black families he claimed to support. As President George H. W. Bush's "Drug Czar" from 1989 to 1991, Bennett presided over the "War on Drugs," which dramatically increased incarceration rates and especially targeted African Americans.[7]

Bennett articulated an interpretation of the Moynihan Report that had been developed since the early 1980s by conservative intellectuals, many of whom also participated in the 1995 symposium. Libertarian African American economist Walter Williams asserted, "The welfare state has done to the black family what slavery, Jim Crowism, and the rankest racism never could."[8] Charles Murray, who popularized the argument that the welfare state caused poverty in his influential 1984 book, *Losing Ground*, hailed the Moynihan Report. He blamed politically correct liberals for perverting public discourse and neglecting real social problems. It was tragic, Murray contended, that Moynihan "had been so right, and said so . . . and the warning had been so completely ignored." Recalling the controversy over Arthur Jensen's ideas in the late 1960s, Murray compared the Moynihan dispute to the "brouhaha" over his recently published bestseller with Richard Herrnstein, *The Bell Curve*, which argued that hereditary differences in intelligence explained racial inequality. Despite the ostensibly color-blind stance adopted by conservatives, updated versions of scientific racism retained considerable appeal on the right.[9]

Other symposium participants extolled the Moynihan Report's strong defense of the patriarchal family. Praising its "fresh" language of "[f]atherless families, broken homes, illegitimacy, and . . . 'tangle of pathologies,'" journalist Barbara Dafoe Whitehead called for reversing the "sex and divorce revolution."[10] Senator Joseph Lieberman, reflecting the appeal of conservative family ideals even among Democratic Party leaders, hailed Moynihan as "our prophet Patrick." "The report got Pat into a lot of trouble," Lieberman noted, "But of course he was right, and we have all paid a high price for ignoring his call to action." Lieberman advocated welfare reform to enforce nuclear family values and called for "restigmatizing births out of wedlock."[11]

Squaring the report with the Republican Party's 1994 platform required ignoring its strong focus on unemployment and Moynihan's continued centrist beliefs. Senator Moynihan's opposition to welfare abolition befuddled symposium participants. Bennett wished "that the career of Senator Patrick Moynihan, legislator, would have more closely resembled Professor Pat Moynihan, scholar."[12] Eugene Genovese, a Marxist historian of slavery who had once defended the "ill-fated Moynihan Report," continued to praise it now that he had shifted to the right. However, he rebuked Moynihan for bearing with "equanimity his party's surrender to the radical feminists, gay liberationists, and thinly disguised nihilists who are assaulting what remains of family structure."[13]

Two symposium participants in particular, George Gilder and Glenn Loury, had contributed to conservative appropriation of the report in the 1980s. For Gilder, the Moynihan Report was "so luminously true in all major particulars that it blinded nearly all who read it." Gilder repeated the oft-cited myth that political correctness silenced the report's ideas. "Moynihan had it right in 1965," Gilder claimed, "But the political culture, tragically, has rendered all his key insights nearly unspeakable."[14] Loury too thought, "By daring to suggest that dysfunctional family behavior among

poor blacks constituted an insuperable barrier to economic equality, Moynihan elicited an emotional, ideologically charged response."

For Gilder, the report's key contribution was "Moynihan's scissors": the
finding that family break-up and poverty had entered a self-perpetuating
cycle no longer connected to unemployment. This dynamic signaled "the
transformation of the welfare state from a remedy for poverty to the cause of
it." Gilder amplified the report's concerns regarding African American men's
inability to provide for families, but unlike Moynihan, identified liberalism
and feminism as the causes. He blamed feminists for "ravaging the lives of
families of the poor" by demanding economic opportunities for women that
should have been reserved for men. "Cuckolded by the welfare state and deprived of any disciplinary structure or needed family role," Gilder asserted, "young black men turned to the perennial male equalizers: greater
physical strength and aggression, rape, and violence."[15]

At the symposium, Gilder reprised arguments he first made in his influential 1981 book, *Wealth and Poverty*, which justified Reagan's policies of cut-
ting taxes on the rich and slashing social services for the poor. His argument
differed from the other major Reagan-era attack on the welfare state, Murray's *Losing Ground*, which posited that lower-class Americans who chose not
to marry or seek employment acted rationally in response to government programs' perverse incentives. In contrast, Gilder faulted the poor for their de-
ficient values and behaviors. Asserting men's superiority as workers, Gilder
stressed their responsibility as patriarchs and breadwinners. Gilder hailed the
"famous Moynihan Report" for highlighting "overemployment" of African
American women and the rising "number of female-headed black families,"
which together created "a wreckage of broken lives and families worse than
the aftermath of slavery." To Gilder, "family deterioration" was cause, not consequence, of poverty and unemployment. Welfare and feminism had destabilized African American families such that "liberalism . . . accounts for the
enduring poverty of blacks."[16]

A small but influential group of African American conservatives, including Supreme Court Justice Clarence Thomas and economists Glenn Loury
and Thomas Sowell, shared Gillder's critique of the liberal welfare state for
harming African Americans. While tapping into a long tradition of racial uplift, black conservatives' ideas proved especially valuable to white conservatives, who, if charged with racism, could respond that some blacks shared their
views.[17] Loury, a Harvard professor, appealed to the Moynihan Report to promote racial self-help. "There are worse things than blaming the victim," he

declared in an influential 1985 article in *The Public Interest.* "Many of the problems of contemporary black American life lie outside the reach of effective
government action," he opined, "and require for their successful resolution
actions that can be undertaken only by the black community itself." He pointed
to the state of African American families to clinch his argument: "These problems involve at their core the values, attitudes, and behaviors of individual
blacks. They are exemplified by the staggering statistics on pregnancies among
young, unwed black women, and the arrest and incarceration rates among
black men."[18]

Loury invoked the Moynihan Report controversy to assert the moral
bankruptcy of African American civil rights leaders who should have tried
to morally uplift lower-class blacks rather than protest racism: "Moynihan . . .
argued that the growth of single-parent families posed an emerging and
fundamental problem for blacks that would impede the ability of some to
advance in the post-civil rights era. . . . Yet, when Moynihan released his
study, he was savagely attacked for 'blaming the victim'." Notably, Loury misrepresented the positions of civil rights leaders in the 1960s: most expressed
concern for single-parent families and some supported Moynihan, though
none thought racial self-help alone could bring about racial equality. Pres-
suring civil rights leaders to turn from protest to uplift, Loury suggested
they "may be most usefully employed in efforts to confront the serious internal difficulties that beset our low-income black communities."[19] Loury articulated an increasingly common conservative argument that blamed civil
rights leaders for politicizing race.[20] Moynihan's 1970 "benign neglect"
memo accused the Black Panthers of fomenting racial conflict; Loury and
other conservatives made the same charge against mainstream civil rights
organizations in the 1980s. Because irresponsible civil rights leaders used
the report to distract from needed self-help measures, Loury lamented, African American families continued to deteriorate: "Those committed to the
silencing of Moynihan, and to the banishment of the topic of behavioural pathology in the ghetto from public discussion managed to have their way."[21]

Loury combined his call for racial self-help with an endorsement of nuclear "family values." He praised the Moynihan Report for its patriarchal ideals, but criticized Moynihan for failing to uphold them in the 1980s. The
Moynihan who wrote *The Negro Family* "admired the nuclear family and
thought its preservation essential" and "had a healthy respect for the central
role of male authority in the child-rearing process." However, Loury alleged
that the Democratic Party's "feminist and homosexual-rights constituency"

had co-opted Senator Moynihan. He criticized Moynihan for failing to disparage divorce, condemn "homosexual adoption," or "consciously attempt to strengthen the male role in the family."[22] Loury and other conservatives fought a losing battle to resurrect the patriarchal family as a shared American ideal. They were considerably more successful in discrediting the liberal welfare state. As media revival of the Moynihan Report in the 1980s demonstrated, conservative appropriation of the document helped shift public discourse of racial inequality to the right.

Year of the Black Family

Ebony dubbed 1986 "the year of the Black Family, or, more precisely, the year of public discussion of the Black Family."[23] In fact, media attention to the topic waxed since the start of the 1980s. The continued rise in single-parent households among African Americans led to the topic's revival, although single-parent households increased among all Americans. As in the 1960s, journalists saw family structure as causing African American economic inequality. Despite a growing African American middle class, black economic progress was hampered by mass unemployment, cuts to government services, residential segregation, and increasing incarceration rates.[24] While liberals once drove public discussion of African American families, conservatives' increasingly popular claims about welfare dependency now set the tone. Public concern about "the black family" duplicated earlier responses to *The Negro Family*, which gained a new lease on life. Journalists portrayed Moynihan as a tragic hero who predicted the breakdown of African American families. According to *Washington Post* writer David Remnick, Moynihan caught "swift hell" for his 1965 report but was now "being hailed as an embattled prophet redeemed."[25] The title of a 1985 *Newsweek* article said it all: "Moynihan: 'I Told You So'."[26]

Moynihan contributed to the discussion of the "black family" with his widely publicized Godkin lectures at Harvard University delivered in 1985, two decades after the Moynihan Report. He published the lectures the following year as *Family and Nation*. In the early 1980s, Moynihan broke with neoconservative friends Irving Kristol and Norman Podhoretz who continued their rightward trajectory into the Republican Party, and tacked back to the left as a Democratic senator from New York. Even so, his ideas continued to cut both left and right. For example, *Family and Nation* approvingly cited conservative Glenn Loury as well as liberal William Julius Wilson. Moynihan refuted claims by Charles Murray and Ronald Reagan that Great Society programs undermined family structure: "The charge that those who advocate a role for government in social issues ignore the responsibility of the individual is pernicious and wrong."[27] Nevertheless, he inspired little confidence in government reforms. Reflecting his lingering neoconservative suspicion of public policy's limits, he cited sociologist Peter Rossi's "iron law" that "the expected value for any measured effect of a social program is zero."[28] Moynihan still adhered to the nuclear family norm, even if he now embraced that ideal less openly. While feminism influenced him to abandon the language of "matriarchy," he still regarded female-headed families as sufficient markers of family pathology.

Moynihan devoted much of *Family and Nation* to a memoir of his report. Yet, while he once presented the uproar over his report as a "lost opportunity" for "national action," he now portrayed the controversy as a missed chance to confront openly the problems of African American families. This view complemented conservatives' criticizing African American leaders' focus on institutional racism rather than on problems in their communities. The modest reforms Moynihan proposed in *Family and Nation* fell well short of his calls for full employment and family allowances in the 1960s. Thus, Moynihan acceded in the broader conservative drift in interpreting his report.

Family and Nation helped fuel the media revival of the report whose twentieth anniversary it marked. As in the initial debate, journalists interpreted the report to advance either social reforms or racial self-help. In the increasingly conservative climate of the 1980s, media treatment shifted toward the latter. For example, in 1965, *Newsweek*, the most liberal major weekly magazine, suggested that the Moynihan Report presaged a domestic "Marshall Plan" program of government investment to benefit urban African Americans. In 1986, however, a *Newsweek* writer opined, "it's no longer only racism or an unsympathetic government that is destroying black America . . . the problem now lies in the black community itself, and its failure to pass on moral values to the next generation."[29] Though the author presented the need for racial self-help as novel, his interpretation of the Moynihan Report was over two decades old.

Following conservatives' lead, journalists alleged that civil rights leaders' failure to acknowledge problems outlined in the Moynihan Report had helped cause continued deterioration of African American families. For example,

Ann Hulbert's 1984 article in the center-left magazine, *New Republic*, attributed the declining numbers of African American nuclear families to the "taboo" placed on the subject following the Moynihan Report's publication. Civil rights leaders' "furor" over the report, she claimed, "was a display of distortion and misinterpretation rather than useful debate."[30] Hulbert applauded African American leaders who had recently held a Black Family Summit for moving to a strategy of racial self-help.

Some former critics of Moynihan reversed their positions in the 1980s. Eleanor Holmes Norton, who pioneered a Black Feminist critique of the Moynihan Report, wrote a widely noticed 1985 *New York Times* article, "Restoring the Traditional Black Family." Norton called on African American leaders to address a mounting "crisis" of African American families with roots in "the self-perpetuating culture of the ghetto." She cited the Moynihan Report controversy to explain why "until recently, many blacks have had an almost visceral reaction to mention of black family problems." Hints of Norton's earlier critique of the nuclear family remained in her comment that a "pervasively middle-class society . . . equates manhood with money," but she now emphasized African American men's inability "to earn a respectable living, to form households and assume the roles of husband and father." Norton supported government reforms, but suggested self-help was essential: "nothing can substitute for or have a greater impact than the full-scale involvement of the black community."[31]

Even when advanced by liberals, media discussion of the "black family" benefited conservatives. In 1986, Bill Moyers, the White House aide who presented Moynihan's "case for national action" to Lyndon Johnson, produced an award-winning and widely-viewed CBS television documentary, *The Vanishing Family: Crisis in Black America*. Attributing African Americans' problems to a change in "values," especially among irresponsible fathers allegedly missing from their children's lives, Moyers played into the hands of conservatives. One writer praised as a "conservative victory" the documentary's pinpointing of family "breakdown" as explaining the "persistence of poverty in inner cities."[32]

Not all journalists celebrated the Moynihan Report, however. The liberal magazine, *The Nation*, remained a consistent critic. In 1979, it devoted an entire issue to refuting Moynihan's neoconservative views, including those it saw expressed in *The Negro Family*. In 1985, journalist Andrew Kopkind reviewed Moynihan's Godkin Lectures for *The Nation* and repeated the charge by William Ryan in the same magazine twenty years prior: "rarely . . .

have victims been blamed so thoroughly for their misery."[33] Kopkind saw little difference between Moynihan and conservatives such as Gilder and Loury. Since the 1980s, many liberals critical of the report have interpreted it much as conservatives have: as advocating racial self-help and underwriting a Reaganite attack on the welfare state.

Ebony expressed ambivalence toward the Moynihan Report in its 1986 special issue, "The Crisis of the Black Family." The magazine's strategy of marshaling African American leaders, intellectuals, and its middle-class readership to strengthen black families complemented the report's 1980s defenders. However, *Ebony* editors decried the "lamentable" Moynihan Report, which they regarded as a symptom of mainstream white discussion that only ostensibly expressed concern about African Americans. "[F]lagrantly insincere public rites" of white concern with black families, they claimed, "have served the function historically of defending the system and proving that the victims are no-good hedonists who are responsible for their own misery." Drawing on Black Power critiques of sociological objectification, *Ebony*'s special issue about "the men, women, and children the statistics hide and defile" urged African Americans to seize authority to define their social problems.[34]

Several veterans of the Moynihan Report controversy participated in the *Ebony* issue. Joyce Ladner and Robert Staples, the two leading Black Sociology critics of the report, were cited as authorities in one article. Staples reprised his argument that African American families could not be understood in terms of "American middle-class White values."[35] In a separate article, Black Studies leader Lerone Bennett repeated his objection that the Moynihan Report stigmatized African Americans: "There is nothing wrong with us."[36] However, psychologist Alvin Poussaint's contribution, "Save the Fathers," recapitulated the report's analysis of family instability's origins in "unemployment among Black males" and the pressing need to restore African American men to breadwinner roles. Yet even while calling the Moynihan Report "prescient," Poussaint dismissed it as "disparaging."[37]

Like Black Sociology a decade earlier, the *Ebony* issue aspired to a unified front for African American self-definition. However, contributors divided over feminism. Poussaint, for example, argued that not only did the Moynihan Report stigmatize African Americans, so too did the film *The Color Purple*. (Based on the novel by leading African American feminist Alice Walker, the film portrayed domestic abuse in an African American family.) Contributors also split over the viability of racial uplift strategies. Several recommended self-help. Even articles that pointed to the economic and

political roots of black family problems were undermined by the special issue's framing. By structuring the issue around "the black family," *Ebony* met
conservatives on their preferred field of battle.

Moynihan Reincarnated

Sociologist William Julius Wilson hoped to reverse the conservative appropriation of the Moynihan Report though an act of intellectual jujitsu: to demonstrate that addressing African American nuclear family break-up required
structural economic reforms rather than dismantling the welfare state. Wilson sought to demonstrate that "behavior described as socially pathological
and associated with the ghetto underclass should be analyzed not as cultural
aberration but as a symptom of class and racial inequality."[38] In the 1980s, Wilson became the most important scholarly interpreter of poor, urban African
Americans; his work influenced Barack Obama, among others.[39] However, by
resuscitating the Moynihan Report as a liberal document in the 1980s,
Wilson invited a controversy similar to the one Moynihan had provoked.
One left-wing critic indulged a gothic fantasy that "Daniel Patrick Moynihan was reincarnated 15 years later in the form of William Julius Wilson."[40]

The subject of African American families was personal to Wilson in a way
it never was to Moynihan. Born in 1935, the son of a Pennsylvania coal miner
who died of lung disease at thirty-nine, Wilson saw class as the key to African American inequality.[41] Though Wilson was roughly the same generation
as Joyce Ladner, he distanced himself from the Black Sociology movement.
In a 1974 essay, he debunked Black Sociology for its lack of scholarly rigor
and dismissed its advocacy of a "black perspective" as unscientific. Yet Wilson thought the Moynihan Report had been "soundly and convincingly criticized by black sociologists."[42] Only later did Wilson turn to *The Negro Family*
for ammunition to argue that African Americans suffered primarily from low
class position rather than from racial discrimination.

Wilson was skeptical of the cultural nationalism of Black Power and identified instead with Bayard Rustin and Martin Luther King, Jr., who advocated
an interracial alliance to achieve economic justice. He placed himself in a tradition of social democrats who saw African American inequality primarily
in class terms and applauded the report for highlighting economic inequality's damaging effects on African American families. For example, Rustin,
once critical of the report, praised it while campaigning for Moynihan in his

1976 Senate primary race as revealing the "intolerable" problem of unemployment.[43] Leading socialist and Democratic activist Michael Harrington, a political ally of Wilson, defended the report into the 1970s as a "compelling . . . statement of moral obligation toward people who have suffered discrimination for centuries." Even as Harrington rebuked Moynihan for becoming a neoconservative, he supported the report as a brief for "full employment."[44]

Wilson's influential 1979 book, *The Declining Significance of Race*, argued the central importance of class to understanding African American inequality. To Wilson, the growing black middle class proved that racial discrimination no longer significantly limited African American success. Rather, the problems of a large urban "underclass" of poor African Americans resulted from "economic class position" rather than "day-to-day encounters with whites." Wilson blamed structural changes in the economy that decimated manufacturing and reduced job opportunities for unskilled African American men. He persuasively argued for "public programs to attack inequality on a broad class front." However, conservatives were attracted by his argument that racism no longer significantly featured in American social life. The book's misleading title and the simplistic dichotomy it drew between race and class obscured how the class positions of African Americans resulted from past and present racism.[45]

The Declining Significance of Race did not mention the Moynihan Report and contained only a brief section on family structure that referenced one of Moynihan's major critics, Carol Stack. However, African American sociologists who faulted Wilson for downplaying overt racism likened his book to Moynihan's report. The Association of Black Sociologists clearly had the report in mind when they challenged Wilson's receipt of an award from the American Sociological Association: "In the past reactionary groups have seized upon inappropriate analyses as a basis for the further suppression of blacks."[46] Charles V. Willie, a leader of the association and long-time critic of *The Negro Family*, alleged that Wilson was like Moynihan in diverting attention from "the system and its various forms of institutional oppression."[47]

Far from denying the charge that he resembled Moynihan, Wilson embraced it. In *The Truly Disadvantaged*, his highly influential 1987 sequel to *The Declining Significance of Race*, Wilson resurrected liberal social pathology discourse of the 1960s. He celebrated Moynihan, Kenneth Clark, and Lee Rainwater for "forthrightly examin[ing] the cumulative effects of racial isolation and class subordination on inner-city blacks." Wilson followed Moynihan in measuring "family deterioration" through "urban blacks' rising rates of broken marriages, female-headed families, out-of-wedlock births, and welfare dependency." He thought the report proved that "male joblessness" primarily explained black family instability.[48] However, Wilson did far more than simply reincarnate Moynihan. In fact, Wilson's analysis of the political economy that reinforced racial and class inequality was far more sophisticated and far-reaching than Moynihan's. For example, Wilson pointed to a changing urban geography that led to a spatial mismatch between job opportunities and poor African American neighborhoods.

Like 1960s pathologists, Wilson highlighted African American behavior to make a case for structural reform. Acknowledging that cultural traits "matter," Wilson rejected the "culture of poverty" thesis because it "implies that basic values and attitudes have been internalized and thereby influence behavior."[49] To Wilson, the point was not to directly change individual behaviors, but to alter the structures that created them. He dismissed as wholly inadequate the "so-called self-help programs" receiving "so much attention from the media and policymakers."[50] Consistent with his belief that class, not race, centrally caused African American inequality, Wilson dismissed affirmative action, which he claimed disproportionately benefited middle-class blacks. He argued instead for universal programs to boost employment and redistribute income, reasoning, "problems that fall heavily on much of the black population . . . require solutions that confront the broader issues of economic organization, and are not made more understandable by associating them directly or indirectly with racism."[51] Wilson labeled his proposals a "hidden agenda" because they would disproportionately benefit African Americans yet be presented in class terms, thus more likely to win support from whites. However, Wilson's strategy held the same flaws as Moynihan's 1960s call for universal programs to combat African American inequality. Presenting his programs as cures for African American pathology, as Moynihan had, Wilson ensured that Americans would perceive them in racial terms. Proclaiming a "hidden agenda" was self-defeating.

Like Moynihan and other pathologists, Wilson endorsed African Americans' assimilation of middle-class values. He complained, for example, about the dearth of "mainstream role models" for "ghetto youth" and worried that they lacked "the habit of waking up early to a ringing alarm clock." Wilson also promoted the male-breadwinner family model. He even created a "male marriageable pool index" that explained the high number of African American single-female families as due to the paucity of eligible male breadwinners. "[T]o be marriageable," Wilson asserted, "a man needs to be employed."

Hence, Wilson's policy proposals created jobs for black men in particular, as Moynihan's had. In seeking to reconcile his focus on African American men with his ostensible embrace of feminism, Wilson saw rising female-headed families among African Africans as indicating community breakdown caused by male joblessness, but viewed growing rates of divorce among whites as a positive sign of women's increasing independence that allowed for the easier "dissolution of a bad marriage."[52]

Wilson's identification with the Moynihan Report undermined his effort to shift debate about African American families toward structural economic reform. His account of the controversy resembled conservatives' attack on political correctness: "virulent attacks against Moynihan" based on "distortions and misinterpretations" had forestalled an honest discussion of black pathology. Wilson lambasted the "black solidarity" movement for celebrating the strengths of black families and for denouncing "the candid, but liberal writings on the inner city." He faulted liberals for their reluctance "to discuss openly or . . . even to acknowledge the sharp increase in social pathologies in ghetto communities." He ignored scholars such as Stack, who, while rejecting pathologism, identified serious social problems facing poor African Americans and who, like Wilson, had located their economic roots. Wilson's criticism of "civil rights leaders [who] were preoccupied with the affirmative action agenda of the black middle class" corresponded with the views of Loury and other conservatives.[53] Accepting the conservative narrative of the Moynihan Report controversy, Wilson solidified his standing as a legitimate participant in mainstream debate, where the pathology of "the black family" had become conventional wisdom. Yet Wilson undermined his book's thesis by implying that liberal failure to discuss race candidly, rather than structural changes in political economy, accounted for the deepening socioeconomic inequalities of poor urban African Americans.

Wilson provoked many of the same criticisms as had Moynihan. Writing in *The Nation*, African American socialist Adolph Reed, Jr., alleged that Wilson's focus on African Americans' cultural traits distracted attention from capitalist inequality. Reed also attacked Wilson for his "abominably sexist, not to mention atavistic" focus on creating jobs for African American men to the exclusion of programs bolstering the economic security of female household heads.[54] Reed's criticism of Wilson for "his antidemocratic, Reaganite frame of reference" echoed the left's response to *The Negro Family* by conflating conservative and liberal analyses of black family instability. However, by resurrecting the Moynihan Report, Wilson rendered available for conservative capture his otherwise compelling critique of the structural economic roots of African American inequality.

*   *   *

Almost a half-century after the Moynihan Report became public, the controversy reignited in March 2014, when Republican Representative Paul Ryan told William Bennett (now a radio show host) about a "tailspin of culture, in our inner cities in particular, of men not working and just generations of men not even thinking about working or learning the value and the culture of work."[55] Ryan's comments were immediately attacked by liberals. Democratic Representative Barbara Lee described them as a "thinly veiled racial attack" on blacks. Pinpointing the poor's alleged lack of work ethic, Ryan cited an age-old explanation for inequality rather than any specific idea from the Moynihan Report. Yet Ryan referred to a recent report of the House Budget Committee (which he chaired), *The War on Poverty: 50 Years Later*, which prominently cited *The Negro Family* as evidence for its claim that "the single most important determinant of poverty is family structure."[56] *The Negro Family*, written to convince Johnson to adopt more vigorous antipoverty measures, had become a reference point for conservative arguments that antipoverty programs caused poverty by undermining nuclear families and eroding the work ethic.

Because Ryan invoked the notion that urban African American men suffered from an inherited, self-perpetuating pathology, commentators immediately connected his remarks to Moynihan's famous report. Veteran conservative pundit George Will, a long-time admirer of Moynihan, cited the report as proof that cultural pathology caused economic inequality: "Moynihan's scissors," he recalled, conclusively showed that deviations from nuclear family structure caused poverty. To Will, the same left-liberal political correctness that deluged Moynihan drenched Ryan: "the usual acid rain of accusations—racism, blaming the victims, etc. He had sauntered into the minefield that a more experienced Daniel Patrick Moynihan—a liberal scholar who knew the taboos of his tribe—had tiptoed into five years before Ryan was born." Will blamed the left's failure to recognize the cultural and familial roots of poverty—what he called a half-century of "malice, ignorance, and intellectual sloth"—for the persistence of race-based economic inequalities despite the "astonishingly rapid receding of racism and discrimination."[57] For

Will as for other conservatives, the Moynihan Report explained enduring racial inequalities in a post-racist twenty-first-century America.

Writing for *Commentary*, neoconservative journalist Jonathan Tobin denounced liberals who lay "in wait not only to derail efforts to address the problems of the black family and urban poverty but to tar all those who speak about the issue as racists in the same way that Moynihan was attacked nearly 50 years ago." Tobin claimed that liberal "race baiters" turned a discussion about poverty and government policy into one about race, even though *he* likened Ryan's remarks to a report about African American families. Tobin followed the logic of "benign neglect": racial conflict resulted not from inequality but from the political correctness of left-liberals.[58] Ryan too protested that his comments had "nothing to do whatsoever with race," implying that his critics had introduced race to the dispute.[59]

Demonstrating the Moynihan Report's continued malleability, liberals cited it as support against Ryan. African American journalist Jamelle Bouie appealed to "the actual report" against "the imaginary report that conservatives wish Moynihan had written." Bouie claimed that Moynihan saw African American family instability as "a direct consequence of America's brutal treatment of African Americans" and "supported broad national action to . . . directly address the problem of family structure—a far cry from Paul Ryan's small government approach."[60] Ta-Nehisi Coates similarly cited *The Negro Family* in a contentious exchange with fellow liberal commentator Jonathan Chait about Coates's assertion that President Obama shared Ryan's view that African American inequality resulted from family and personal irresponsibility. Coates challenged the "entrenched belief among many liberals and conservatives that discussions of American racism should began somewhere between the Moynihan Report and the Detroit riots." Beginning discussion of racial inequality with *The Negro Family*, Coates thought, erased the longer legacy of racial oppression. Yet, Coates also claimed that an accurate reading of the Moynihan Report's discussion of slavery, Jim Crow, and unemployment revealed the deeper roots of present-day racial inequality.[61]

It is astonishing that the Moynihan Report incites controversy today and continues to attract figures across the political spectrum. Conservative appropriation and liberal nostalgia breathe life into it. It still serves as both a call to combat racial inequality and as a rationalization for its persistence. Because of its historical association with the mid-1960s, the report marks for many the emergence of the post-civil rights era.

Above all, it is still invoked because African American inequality remains with us today, as detailed in a recent Urban Institute report that highlighted "large socioeconomic gaps between blacks and whites."[62] It pointed to unacceptably high rates of unemployment for African American men; average annual incomes for African American workers that remain roughly three-quarter those of whites (and far greater wealth disparities); disproportionately poor education of African Americans; persistence of residential segregation by race; and the outrageous incarceration of African American men—nearly one in six of whom have been imprisoned—fueled by the cruel and futile War on Drugs.

Unfortunately, the Urban Institute report's title, "Revisiting the Moynihan Report," reveals how unproductive it is for contemporary critics to hitch their analysis to *The Negro Family*. For example, even while citing criticism of Moynihan's "patriarchal view of the world," they update the report's statistics on out-of-wedlock births, female-headed families, and educational disparities between black men and black women. These statistics only have clear meaning if one accepts the male-breadwinner family norm.[63] A flawed and ambiguous government report written fifty years ago is hardly the best starting point for discussing African American inequality today.

The enduring Moynihan Report controversy demonstrates that Americans struggle to disentangle race and class, but understanding and combating inequality in our own time requires that we do so. We need to recognize, as Moynihan did, that the Civil Rights Act did not ensure racial equality. However, we cannot see the damage done to African Americans by centuries of slavery, racism, and exploitation as resting in family and social structure; rather, it rests primarily in the expropriation of wealth and labor that has left a potent legacy our nation has never adequately addressed. Yet inequality is not solely a racial problem. The goal Moynihan advocated in his report—an "equality of results" in which American ethnoracial groups had roughly equal class distributions—was not the equality for which the civil rights movement fought. The proportionate representation of racial minorities among our nation's elite—even the election of an African American president—hardly changes the fact that our society overwhelmingly favors the wealthy and powerful at the expense of most Americans, especially the poor and working class. In that sense, dismissing Paul Ryan's comments simply as "racially offensive" misses his point: Ryan's main motivation was to discredit antipoverty programs. The dramatic increase of economic inequality is one of the central historical facts of the half-century since Moynihan wrote his report. By redirecting discussion to how family structure causes poverty, Ryan hoped to suppress a growing public debate about how the very rich possess such a large share of our wealth. It is an unfortunate and largely unintended consequence of the Moynihan Report controversy that Moynihan and many of his critics shifted debate about inequality away from political economy. Work, taxes, housing, and education explain inequality better than does family.[64]

On its fiftieth anniversary, the Moynihan Report should be neither celebrated nor condemned. Rather, we should see it as a complex historical artifact with a mixed legacy for our own time. At its best, *The Negro Family* called for national action to ensure social and economic equality for African Americans, not just the legal equality that had been ostensibly granted during the civil rights movement. At its worst, the report conflated racial equality with patriarchy. It encouraged Americans to focus on African Americans' cultural traits rather than political economy. It obscured how government reproduces racial and class inequality. Despite Moynihan's liberal intentions, it fed the delusion that racial self-help alone could effect racial equality. Advocates of economic and social justice have little to gain by appealing to a document that embodies not only the ambitions of 1960s liberalism but also all of its shortcomings.

NOTES

Introduction. Crisis of Equality

1. Barack Obama, *The Audacity of Hope* (New York: Random House, 2006), 254.

2. Ibid., 245. Obama also invoked the decline of African American nuclear families to advocate liberal reforms to "tackle the nexus of unemployment . . . so that the men who live there can begin fulfilling their responsibilities," 257.

3. David Remnick, "On and Off the Road with Barack Obama," *New Yorker*, January 27, 2014, 53.

4. Ta-Nehisi Coates, "The Champion Barack Obama," *The Atlantic*, January 31, 2014, http://www.theatlantic.com/politics/archive/2014/01/the-champion-barack -obama/283458/.

5. Ta-Nehisi Coates, "Revisiting the Moynihan Report," *The Atlantic*, June 18, 2013, http://www.theatlantic.com/national/archive/2013/06/revisiting-the-moynihan -report/276936/.

6. *The Negro Family: The Case for National Action* (Washington, D.C.: Office of Policy Planning and Research, U.S. Department of Labor, 1965), n.p.

7. Roderick A. Ferguson, *Aberrations in Black: Toward a Queer of Color Critique* (Minneapolis: University of Minnesota Press, 2004), 124. Laura Briggs finds the report synonymous with the image of "the 'welfare queen'." See Briggs, *Reproducing Empire: Race, Sex, Science, and U.S. Imperialism in Puerto Rico* (Berkeley: University of California Press, 2002), 3. Some historians criticize the Moynihan Report as an insulting depiction of African Americans. For example, Robin Kelley writes, "I have had kids tell me that my hair was so nappy it looked like a thousand Africans giving the Black Power salute, but never has anyone said to my face that my whole family—especially my mama—was a 'tangle of pathology.'" See Kelley, *Yo' Mama's Disfunktional: Fighting the Cultural Wars in Urban America* (Boston: Beacon, 1997), 2.

8. Alice O'Connor, *Poverty Knowledge: Social Science, Social Policy, and the Poor in Twentieth-Century U.S. History* (Princeton, N.J.: Princeton University Press, 2001), 203–10. My book draws on O'Connor's excellent study while contesting its interpretation of the Moynihan Report.

9. Lee Rainwater and William L. Yancey, *The Moynihan Report and the Politics of Controversy* (Cambridge, Mass.: MIT Press, 1967); James Patterson, *Freedom Is Not*

Enough: The Moynihan Report and Black Family Life from LBJ to Obama (New York: Basic Books, 2010). See also Peter-Christian Ainger, "What the Left and Right Both Get Wrong About the Moynihan Report," *The Atlantic,* April 16, 2014., http://www.the atlantic.com/politics/archive/2014/04/what-the-left-and-right-both-get-wrong-about -the-moynihan-report/360701/. Many social scientists currently studying African American inequality also interpret the Moynihan Report as unambiguously liberal. See the 2009 issue of *Annals of the American Academy of Political and Social Science,* "The Moynihan Report Revisited: Lessons and Reflections After Four Decades." Ironically, the editors' intention to establish that Moynihan's clear purpose was "to make an impassioned moral case for a massive federal intervention to break the cycle of black poverty" is undermined by the contribution of long-time Moynihan friend James Q. Wilson, a neoconservative who claimed the report's central message was the need to bolster "cultural support for marriage," which government could not do. See Douglas S. Massey and Robert J. Sampson, "Moynihan Redux: Legacies and Lessons," *Annals of the American Academy of Political and Social Science* 621 (2009): 6, and James Q. Wilson, "Pat Moynihan Thinks About Families," 33.

10. Patterson, *Freedom Is Not Enough,* xiv. For another prominent historical account that claims that misunderstanding caused the controversy, see Michael B. Katz, *The Undeserving Poor: From the War on Poverty to the War on Welfare* (New York: Pantheon, 1990), 24–28.

11. Nicolas Lemann, *The Promised Land: The Great Black Migration and How It Changed America* (New York: Knopf, 1991), 177.

12. In addition to Patterson, see Steve Estes, *I Am a Man!: Race, Manhood, and the Civil Rights Movement* (Chapel Hill: University of North Carolina Press, 2005), 107–30.

13. Stephan Thernstrom and Abigail Thernstrom, *America in Black and White: One Nation, Indivisible* (New York: Simon & Schuster, 1997), 172.

14. Conservatives' advocacy of racial self-help tapped into a racial uplift ideology with deep roots in African American tradition. Politically quiescent versions of racial uplift have always held strong appeal for whites. See Kevin K. Gaines, *Uplifting the Race: Black Leadership, Politics, and Culture in the Twentieth Century* (Chapel Hill: University of North Carolina Press, 1996).

15. Raymond Williams, *Keywords: A Vocabulary of Culture and Society* (New York: Oxford University Press, 1976).

16. Briggs, *Reproducing Empire,* 162–92.

17. *The Negro Family,* 42.

18. Merrillee A. Dolan, "Moynihan, Poverty Programs, and Women—A Female Viewpoint," manuscript, National Organization for Women Records, Schlesinger Library, Harvard University; Marisa Chappell, *The War on Welfare: Family, Poverty, and Politics in Modern America* (Philadelphia: University of Pennyslvania Press, 2010), 102–3, 170–71.

19. "Liberal" is used here to refer specifically to the views of post-World War II Americans. Liberalism is notoriously difficult to define because of its diversity and dynamism and its vastly different meanings in different periods and places. For an attempt at broader definition see Michael Freeden and Mark Stears, "Liberalism," in Michael Freeden, Lyman Tower Sargent, and Mark Stears, eds., *Oxford Handbook of Political Ideologies* (New York: Oxford University Press, 2013), 329–47.

20. Though many liberals were slow to make securing civil and political rights for African Americans a priority, nearly all agreed with the goal.

21. Allen J. Matusow, *The Unraveling of America: A History of Liberalism in the 1960s* (New York: Harper and Row, 1984), esp. 194–98.

22. For the view that liberalism fractured mainly because of its commitment to racial equality and that a "hostile outcry" against the Moynihan Report by leftists was instrumental, see Thomas Byrne Edsall with Mary D. Edsall, *Chain Reaction: The Impact of Race, Rights, and Taxes on American Politics* (New York: Norton, 1992), esp. 54.

23. This book builds on an excellent body of scholarship by historians who have analyzed this complex of mid-twentieth-century assumptions, typically described by the awkward phrase "racial liberalism." Walter Jackson and Daryl Scott, for example, have demonstrated how liberal support for racial equality was couched in assimilationist and racially paternalistic assumptions about African American culture. Ruth Feldstein, Marissa Chappell, and Robert Self have shown how liberal support for racial equality was inextricably tied to support for the patriarchal nuclear family (what Self calls "breadwinner liberalism"). See Walter A. Jackson, *Gunnar Myrdal and America's Conscience: Social Engineering and Racial Liberalism, 1938–1987* (Chapel Hill: University of North Carolina Press, 1990); Daryl Scott, *Contempt and Pity: Social Policy and the Image of the Damaged Black Psyche* (Chapel Hill: University of North Carolina Press, 1997); Ruth Feldstein, *Motherhood in Black and White: Race and Sex in American Liberalism, 1930–1965* (Ithaca, N.Y.: Cornell University Press, 2000); Marisa Chappell, *The War on Welfare: Family, Poverty, and Politics in Modern America* (Philadelphia: University of Pennsylvania Press, 2009); Robert Self, *All in the Family: The Realignment of American Democracy Since the 1960s* (New York: Hill and Wang, 2012).

24. However, I do not see late twentieth-century conservatism as the sole logical development from postwar liberalism. Rather, I argue that the liberalism embodied by the Moynihan Report had several possible permutations.

25. For a recent study, see Algernon Austin, *The Unfinished March: An Overview* (Washington, D.C.: Economic Policy Institute, 2013). See also Michael B. Katz, Mark J. Stern, and James J. Fader, "The New African American Inequality," *Journal of American History* 92 (2005): 75–108.

26. Eduardo Bonilla-Silva, *Racism Without Racists: Color-Blind Racism and the Persistence of Racial Inequality in the United States* (Lanham, Md.: Rowman & Littlefield, 2003).

Chapter 1. The Liberal Mindset

1. Daniel Patrick Moynihan, interview by Lee Rainwater and William Yancey, transcript, December 1, 1965, Box 464, Daniel Patrick Moynihan Papers.

2. Ibid.

3. John Herbers, "Moynihan Hopeful U.S. Will Adopt a Policy of Promoting Family Stability," *New York Times*, December 12, 1965.

4. Fred Powledge, "Amid Desperation, the Search for Meaning," *Life*, November 3, 1967, 75–76.

5. Thomas Meehan, "Moynihan of the Moynihan Report," *New York Times*, July 31, 1966.

6. On Moynihan's early life, see Godfrey Hodgson, *The Gentleman from New York: Daniel Patrick Moynihan, a Biography* (Boston: Houghton Mifflin, 2000), 25–48; and Douglas E. Schoen, *Pat: A Biography of Daniel Patrick Moynihan* (New York: Harper & Row, 1979), 1–48.

7. Moynihan, "A Modest Proposal" (speech, March 4, 1964), Box 61, Moynihan Papers.

8. Ibid.

9. Nathan Glazer and Daniel Patrick Moynihan, "Introduction to the Second Edition," in *Beyond the Melting Pot: The Negroes, Puerto Ricans, Jews, Italians, and Irish of New York City* (Cambridge, Mass.: MIT Press, 1970), xxxiv.

10. Moynihan to John P. Roche, March 15, 1967, Box 192, Moynihan Papers.

11. "Senior Prophecy," photocopy, Box 499, Moynihan Papers.

12. Moynihan to Barbara Deming, July 14, 1950, Barbara Deming Papers.

13. Moynihan to Dr. Hawkins, July 12, 1951, Box 51, Moynihan Papers.

14. Moynihan, "Correspondence," *New Statesman and Nation*, February 17, 1951, 186.

15. Landon R. Y. Storrs, *The Second Red Scare and the Unmaking of the New Deal Left* (Princeton, N.J.: Princeton University Press, 2012); Alan Brinkley, *The End of Reform: New Deal Liberalism in Recession and War* (New York: Knopf, 1995); Arthur M. Schlesinger, *The Vital Center: The Politics of Freedom* (Boston: Houghton Mifflin, 1949).

16. Schoen, *Pat*, 47, 59.

17. Moynihan, "The United States and the International Labor Organization, 1889–1934" (Ph.D. dissertation, Tufts University, 1960).

18. Hodgson, *Gentleman from New York*, 49–60.

19. Ira Katznelson, *When Affirmative Action Was White: The Untold Story of Racial Inequality in Twentieth-Century America* (New York: Norton, 2005).

20. Moynihan to Dr. Gross, June 29, 1960, Box 496, Moynihan Papers.

21. Addendum, Moynihan to "Clark," December 28, 1959, Box 15, Moynihan Papers.

22. Ibid.; Moynihan, "Epidemic on the Highways," *The Reporter*, April 30, 1959, 16–23.

23. Ralph Nader, *Unsafe at Any Speed: The Designed-in Dangers of the American Automobile* (New York: Grossman, 1965), 333; John Alfred Heitmann, *The Automobile and American Life* (Jefferson, N.C.: McFarland, 2009), 173.

24. "Remarks to the Members of the White House Council on Economic Issues, May 21, 1962," *Public Papers of the Presidents of the United States: John F. Kennedy* (Washington, D.C.: GPO, 1963), 203.

25. Moynihan, "The Professionalization of Reform," *Public Interest* 1 (1965): 8.

26. Ibid., 16.

27. Ibid., 5.

28. Moynihan, "A Modest Proposal."

29. Ibid.

30. Moynihan, "Three Problems of Poverty," *Catholic Mind*, June 1965, 8.

31. Karen Ferguson, *Top Down: The Ford Foundation, Black Power, and the Reinvention of Racial Liberalism* (Philadelphia: University of Pennsylvania Press, 2013), 23–74.

32. Moynihan, "The Professionalization of Reform," 16.

33. Nelson Lichtenstein, *State of the Union: A Century of American Labor* (Princeton, N.J.: Princeton University Press, 2002).

34. David L. Stebenne, *Arthur Goldberg: New Deal Liberal* (New York: Oxford University Press, 1996).

35. Alice Kessler-Harris, *In Pursuit of Equity: Women, Men, and the Quest for Economic Citizenship in 20th-Century America* (New York: Oxford University Press, 2001), 205.

36. Marisa Chappell, *The War on Welfare: Family, Poverty, and Politics in Modern America* (Philadelphia: University of Pennsylvania Press, 2010).

37. Moynihan to Glazer, April 7, 1960, Box 389, Moynihan Papers.

38. Moynihan, "The American Social and Economic Revolution: For Whose Benefit?" (speech at National Catholic Social Action Conference, August 14, 1964), Box 99, Moynihan Papers.

39. *Mater et Magistra*, promulgated May 15, 1961, as quoted in David J. O'Brien and Thomas A. Shannon, eds., *Catholic Social Thought: The Documentary Heritage* (Maryknoll, N.Y.: Orbis, 2010), 93.

40. Ibid., 96.

41. Buckley as quoted in O'Brien and Shannon, *Catholic Social Thought*, 83.

42. Moynihan, "Church and Synagogue in Boston Renewal" (address to Harvard Colloquium at Harvard Divinity School, January 1964), Box 97, Moynihan Papers.

43. Moynihan, "Poverty and Progress," *American Scholar* 33 (1964): 603.

44. Moynihan, "The Technological Revolution: What It Is Doing to People in Poverty," *Social Action* 30 (1964): 12.

45. Moynihan, "Toil and Trouble" (speech, November 30, 1964), Box 106, Moynihan Papers.

46. Moynihan, "Morality of Work and Immorality of Opportunity—Man's Inherent Right to Fulfill His Potential" (speech to National Vocational Guidance Association, San Francisco, March 25, 1964), Box 97, Moynihan Papers.

47. Margaret Mead and Frances Balgley Kaplan, eds., *American Women: The Report of the President's Commission on the Status of Women and Other Publications of the Commission* (New York: Scribner, 1965), 18; Kessler-Harris, *In Pursuit of Equity*, 213–34.

48. Jennifer Mittelstadt, *From Welfare to Workfare: The Unintended Consequences of Liberal Reform, 1945–1965* (Chapel Hill: University of North Carolina Press, 2005), 135–45.

49. Moynihan to Peterson, n.d., Folder 936, Esther Peterson Papers.

50. Moynihan, "Three Problems of Poverty," 12.

51. Sue Cronk, "Way Out of Poverty for a Man Is a Job," *Washington Post*, February 26, 1964.

52. Moynihan, "Memorandum for the Secretary," March 12, 1964, Box 71, Moynihan Papers.

53. Moynihan, "Poverty and Progress," 606.

54. Katz, *The Undeserving Poor.*

55. Michael Harrington, *The Other America: Poverty in the United States* (New York: Macmillan, 1962); Maurice Isserman, *The Other American: The Life of Michael Harrington* (New York: Public Affairs, 2000), 84.

56. "Statement of Daniel P. Moynihan Before the Subcommittee on Employment and Manpower," Box 61, Moynihan Papers; Moynihan, "Draft Rejectees: Nipping Trouble in the Bud," *The Reporter*, February 13, 1964, 22–24; Moynihan, "One-Third of a Nation," *New Republic*, June 19, 1982, 18–21.

57. "Nominations," Box 68, Moynihan Papers; "Administrative History of the Department of Labor," Box 1, Department of Labor, Administrative History, Lyndon Baines Johnson Library, 40–44.

58. President's Task Force on Manpower Conservation, *One-Third of a Nation: A Report on Young Men Found Unqualified for Military Service* (transmitted January 1, 1964), Box 398, Moynihan Papers, 1–2.

59. Ibid., 2.

60. Ibid., n.p.

61. Eli Ginzberg, *The Negro Potential* (New York: Columbia University Press, 1956).

62. On the War on Poverty, see Annelise Orleck and Lisa Gayle Hazirjian, eds., *The War on Poverty: A New Grassroots History* (Athens: University of Georgia Press, 2011); Michael K. Brown, *Race, Money, and the American Welfare State* (Ithaca, N.Y.: Cornell University Press, 1999), 206–77; Katz, *The Undeserving Poor*; James T. Patterson, *America's Struggle Against Poverty, 1900–1994* (Cambridge, Mass.: Harvard University Press, 1994); and Margaret Weir, *Politics and Jobs: The Boundaries of Employment Policy in the United States* (Princeton, N.J.: Princeton University Press, 1992).

63. Eileen Boris, "Contested Rights: The Great Society Between Home and Work," in Sidney M. Milkeus and Jerome M. Mileur, eds., *The Great Society and the High Tide of American Liberalism* (Amherst: University of Massachusetts Press, 2005), 115–44.

64. Michael L. Gillette, *Launching the War on Poverty: An Oral History* (New York: Oxford University Press, 2010), 107.

65. Brown, *Race, Money, and the American Welfare State*, 206–77; Molly C. Michelmore, *Tax and Spend: The Welfare State, Tax Politics, and the Limits of American Liberalism* (Philadelphia: University of Pennsylvania Press, 2012), 47–71.

66. As quoted in Patterson, *America's Struggle Against Poverty*, 131.

67. Moynihan, "Three Problems of Poverty," 11.

68. Moynihan, *Maximum Feasible Misunderstanding: Community Action in the War on Poverty* (New York: Free Press, 1969).

69. On the differences between the family allowance Moynihan advocated and the negative income tax preferred by other advocates of a guaranteed annual income, see Brian Steensland, *The Failed Welfare Revolution: America's Struggle over Guaranteed Income Policy* (Princeton, N.J.: Princeton University Press, 2008), 49–50.

70. Moyihan to Wirtz, November 9, 1964, Box 27, Moynihan Papers.

71. Nathan Glazer, "From Socialism to Sociology," in Bennett Berger, ed., *Authors of Their Own Lives: Intellectual Autobiographies from Twenty American Sociologists* (Berkeley: University of California Press), 190–209.

72. Glazer, "The Peoples of New York," Box 389, Moynihan Papers; Nathan Glazer, interview with the author, April 16, 2012.

73. Moynihan to Glazer, April 7, 1960, Box 389, Moynihan Papers.

74. Glazer and Moynihan, *Beyond the Melting Pot: The Negroes, Puerto Ricans, Jews, Italians, and Irish of New York City* (Cambridge, Mass.: MIT Press, 1963), 290.

75. Ibid., 291.

76. Ibid., 17.

77. Ibid., 302.

78. Ibid., vi.

79. Ibid., 23.

80. Ibid., 165, 200.

81. Moynihan to Glazer, n.d., Box 389, Moynihan Papers.

82. Matthew Frye Jacobson, *Roots Too: White Ethnic Revival in Post-Civil Rights America* (Cambridge, Mass.: Harvard University Press, 2006).

83. Moynihan to Glazer, February 3, 1961, Box 389, Moynihan Papers.

84. Glazer and Moynihan, *Beyond the Melting Pot*, 26.

85. Ibid., 239.

86. *The Negro Family*, 17.

87. "Life in the Frightening Corners," *Time*, July 28, 1967, 12.

88. Glazer and Moynihan, *Beyond the Melting Pot*, 41.

89. Ibid., 38.

90. Ibid., 49–50.

91. Ibid.

92. Ibid., 53.

93. Gunnar Myrdal, *An American Dilemma: The Negro Problem and Modern Democracy* (New York: Harper, 1944), 928.

94. Glazer and Moynihan, *Beyond the Melting Pot*, 53; emphasis added.

95. Ibid., 41.

96. Ibid., 79.

97. Ibid., 53.

98. Ibid., 52.

99. Ibid., 83.

100. Ibid.

101. Ibid., 84.

102. Oscar Handlin, "All Colors, All Creeds, All Nationalities, All New Yorkers," *New York Times Book Review*, September 22, 1963.

103. "In Praise of Pluralism," *Time*, October 18, 1963, 59.

104. Sylvia Rothchild, "Beyond the Melting Pot," *Jewish Advocate*, March 26, 1964.

105. "Beyond the Melting Pot," *U.S. News and World Report*, September 30, 1963, 100.

106. Mary McGrory, "Was the Melting Pot an American Myth?" *Washington Star*, September 22, 1963.

107. Moynihan "Memorandum for the President," May 4, 1965, Box 67, Moynihan Papers; see also Ellen D. Wu, *The Color of Success: Asian Americans and the Origin of the Model Minority* (Princeton, N.J.: Princeton University Press, 2013).

108. Glazer, interview.

Chapter 2. Negro Equality—Dream or Delusion?

1. A. Philip Randolph, "March on Washington Movement Presents Program for the Negro," in Rayford W. Logan, ed., *What the Negro Wants* (Chapel Hill: University of North Carolina Press, 1944), 137.

2. William P. Jones, *The March on Washington: Jobs, Freedom, and the Forgotten History of Civil Rights* (New York: Norton, 1963).

3. Moynihan, "Church and Synagogue in Boston Renewal" (address to Harvard Colloquium at Harvard Divinity School, January 1964), Box 97, Moynihan Papers

4. *The Negro Family: The Case for National Action* (Washington, D.C.: Office of Policy Planning and Research, U.S. Department of Labor, 1965), 2.

5. Draft of *The Negro Family*, Box 66, Moynihan Papers.

6. Moynihan, "Address Before National Civil Liberties Clearing House" (speech, March 19, 1964), Box 97, Moynihan Papers.

7. Jacquelyn Dowd Hall, "The Long Civil Rights Movement and the Political Uses of the Past," *Journal of American History* 91 (2005): 1251–53. For works examining civil rights organizations' economic programs see Jones, *The March on Washington*; Thomas F. Jackson, *From Civil Rights to Human Rights: Martin Luther King, Jr., and the Struggle for Economic Justice* (Philadelphia: University of Pennsylvania Press, 2007); and Donna Cooper Hamilton and Charles V. Hamilton, *Dual Agenda: Race and Social Welfare Policies of Civil Rights Organizations* (New York: Columbia University Press, 1997).

8. Moynihan, "Address Before the National Conference on Religion and Race" (speech in St. Louis, April 15, 1964), Box 98, Moynihan Papers; emphasis in original.

9. *The Negro Family*, 2.

10. Draft of *The Negro Family*.

11. Risa L. Goluboff, *The Lost Promise of Civil Rights* (Cambridge, Mass.: Harvard University Press, 2007).

12. Bayard Rustin, "From Protest to Politics," *Commentary*, February 1965, 25, 26.

13. Martin Luther King, Jr., *Why We Can't Wait* (New York: Signet, 1964), 11, 12, 151.

14. Nancy J. Weiss, *Whitney Young, Jr., and the Struggle for Civil Rights* (Princeton, N.J,: Princeton University Press, 1990).

15. As quoted in Jackson, *From Civil Rights to Human Rights*, 137.

16. Whitney M. Young, Jr., "Domestic Marshall Plan," *New York Times*, October 6, 1963.

17. Whitney M. Young, Jr., *To Be Equal* (New York: McGraw-Hill, 1964), 83, 247.

18. Ibid., 173.

19. As quoted in "Words of the Week," *Jet*, October 23, 1969, 34.

20. Brian Ward, *Just My Soul Responding: Rhythm and Blues, Black Consciousness, and Race Relations* (Berkeley: University of California Press, 1998).

21. Kevin Gaines, *Uplifting the Race: Black Leadership, Politics, and Culture in the Twentieth Century* (Chapel Hill: University of North Carolina Press, 1996).

22. Young, *To Be Equal*, 31.

23. Ibid., 163.

24. Young, as quoted in Louis Lomax, *The Negro Revolt* (New York: Harper, 1962), 211–12.

25. Moynihan, "Address before National Civil Liberties Clearing House."

26. Moynihan to Wirtz, September 30, 1963, Box 27, Moynihan Papers.

27. Moynihan to Wirtz, April 20, 1964, Box 190, Willard Wirtz Papers.

28. Myrdal, *An American Dilemma: The Negro Problem and Modern Democracy* (New York: Harper, 1944), lxxiii.

29. Ibid., 78.

30. Walter A. Jackson, *Gunnar Myrdal and America's Conscience: Social Engineering and Racial Liberalism, 1938–1987* (Chapel Hill: University of North Carolina Press, 1990).

31. James Baldwin, *The Fire Next Time* (New York: Dial Press, 1963).

32. Gunnar Myrdal, *Challenge to Affluence* (New York: Pantheon, 1963), 19.

33. Stephen Graubard, interview with author, May 7, 2010.

34. "Transcript of *The Negro in America* Planning Committee," Box 38, Moynihan Papers, ii, iii.

35. Ibid., 7.

36. "Transcript of the American Academy Conference on The Negro American: May 14–15, 1965," *Daedalus* 95 (1966): 312.

37. "Transcript of *The Negro in America* Planning Committee," 47.

38. Ibid., iii.

39. Moynihan, "Memorandum to Mr. Bill Moyers," May 19, 1965, Box 38, Moynihan Papers.

40. "Transcript of the American Academy Conference on the Negro American," 30.

41. Thomas F. Pettigrew, *A Profile of the Negro American* (Princeton, N.J.: Van Nostrand, 1964), 16.

42. Ibid., 17.

43. Ibid., 18.

44. Ibid., 169.

45. Charles E. Silberman, *Crisis in Black and White* (New York: Random House, 1964), 234.

46. Daryl Scott, *Contempt and Pity* (Chapel Hill: University of North Carolina Press, 1997).

47. Abram Kardiner and Lionel Ovesey, *The Mark of Oppression: A Psychosocial Study of the American Negro* (New York: Norton, 1951).

48. James B. Conant, *Slums and Suburbs: A Commentary on Schools in Metropolitan Areas* (New York: McGraw-Hill, 1961).

49. Silberman, *Crisis in Black and White*, 12.

50. Glazer and Moynihan, *Beyond the Melting Pot*, 64.

51. Moynihan, "Toward Equality," Box 415, Moynihan Papers.

52. Silberman, 16.

53. James Q. Wilson, *Negro Politics: The Search for Leadership* (Glencoe, Ill.: Free Press, 1960), 7.

54. Ibid., 7, 307.

55. Silberman, *Crisis in Black and White*, 12, 70, 231.

56. Robert Penn Warren, *Who Speaks for the Negro?* (New York: Random House, 1965), 170.

57. President Lyndon B. Johnson, "To Fulfill These Rights" (Commencement Speech at Howard University, June 4, 1965), http://www.lbjlib.utexas.edu/johnson/archives .hom/speeches.hom/650604.asp.

58. Moynihan, interview by Lee Rainwater and William Yancey, transcript, December 1, 1965, Box 464, Moynihan Papers, 5.

59. Graubard to Moynihan, December 10, 1964, Box 38, Moynihan Papers.

60. Moynihan, interview by Rainwater and Yancey, 10–11; Schoen, *Pat*, 88–90.

61. Paul Barton, "The Unknown Moynihan Report" (unpublished manuscript in author's possession); Paul Barton, interview with author, June 23, 2010; Melvin M. Tumin, *Desegregation: Readiness and Resistance* (Princeton, N.J.: Princeton University Press, 1959).

62. Moynihan to Gertrude Bancroft, May 25, 1964, Box 38, Moynihan Papers.

63. Moynihan to Antonia Handler Chayes, September 15, 1964, Box 24, Moynihan Papers.

64. Theodore M. Porter, *Trust in Numbers: The Pursuit of Objectivity in Science and Public Life* (Princeton, N.J.: Princeton University Press, 1995).

65. Sarah E. Igo, *The Averaged American: Surveys, Citizens, and the Making of a Mass Public* (Cambridge, Mass.: Harvard University Press, 2007).

66. Dorothy K. Newman and Morton S. Raff, "Memorandum: Unemployment and Family and Social Disorganization," October 21, 1964, Box 38, Moynihan Papers.

67. Lee Rainwater and William Yancey, *The Moynihan Report and the Politics of Controversy* (Cambridge, Mass.: MIT Press, 1967), 167–87.

68. As Moynihan acknowledged in the report, only some government data was specific to African Americans. Instead, many statistics grouped data into "white" and "nonwhite" categories. Moynihan interpreted "non-white" to mean "black" when he had no specific data on African Americans.

69. Paul Barton, "Memorandum for Mr. Daniel Moynihan," December 24, 1964, Box 429, Moynihan Papers.

70. Moynihan to Ashley Montagu, January 16, 1966, Box 388, Moynihan Papers.

71. Moynihan, "Memorandum," December 9, 1970, Box 251, Moynihan Papers.

72. E. Franklin Frazier, *The Negro Family in the United States* (Chicago: University of Chicago Press, 1966). First published in 1939, *The Negro Family in the United States* was best known in its revised and abridged 1948 edition reprinted in 1966.

73. As quoted in Harold Isaacs, *The New World of Negro Americans* (New York: John Day, 1963), 332.

74. On Frazier, see Anthony M. Platt, *E. Franklin Frazier Reconsidered* (New Brunswick, N.J.: Rutgers University Press, 1991); Jonathan Scott Holloway, *Confronting the Veil: Abram Harris, Jr., E. Franklin Frazier, and Ralph Bunche, 1919–1941* (Chapel Hill: University of North Carolina Press, 2001); Walter A. Jackson, "Between Socialism and Nationalism: The Young E. Franklin Frazier," *Reconstruction* 1 (1991), 124–34.

75. Frazier, *The Negro Family in the United States*, 243–44.

76. As quoted in Platt, *Frazier Reconsidered*, 17–18.

77. Frazier, *The Negro Family in the United States*, 225.

78. Melville J. Herskovits, *The Myth of the Negro Past* (New York: Harper, 1941); Walter A. Jackson, "Melville Herskovits and the Search for Afro-American Culture," in George W. Stocking, ed., *Malinowski, Rivers, Benedict and Others: Essays on Culture and Personality* (Madison: University of Wisconsin Press, 1986), 95–126.

79. Frazier, *The Negro Family in the United States*, 109.

80. Ibid., 259.

81. W. I. Thomas and Florian Znaniecki introduced the concept of "disorganization" in *The Polish Peasant in Europe and America* to describe difficulties Polish immigrants had maintaining traditional social norms in the urban environment of Chicago. See Eli Zaretsky, "Editor's Introduction," William I. Thomas and Florian Znaniecki, *The Polish Peasant in Europe and America* (Urbana: University of Illinois Press, 1984), 1–53.

82. Frazier, *The Negro Family in the United States*, 362.

83. E. Franklin Frazier, *The Negro Family in Chicago* (Chicago: University of Chicago Press, 1931), 117.

84. Frazier, *The Negro Family in the United States*, 294.

85. Ibid., 229.

86. Ibid., 230.

87. Ibid., 362.

88. Daniel Matlin, *On the Corner: African American Intellectuals and the Urban Crisis* (Cambridge, Mass.: Harvard University Press, 2014), 36–122; Ben Keppel, *The Work of Democracy: Ralph Bunche, Kenneth B. Clark, Lorraine Hansberry, and the Cultural Politics of Race* (Cambridge, Mass.: Harvard University Press, 1995).

89. Moynihan, interview with Rainwater and Yancey, 8.

90. Harlem Youth Opportunities Unlimited, *Youth in the Ghetto: A Study of the Consequences of Powerlessness and a Blueprint for Change* (New York, 1964), 156.

91. Kenneth B. Clark, *Dark Ghetto: Dilemmas of Social Power* (New York: Harper and Row, 1965), 70.

92. Ibid., 47.

93. Ibid., 10.

94. Ibid., 11.

95. Stokely Carmichael and Charles V. Hamilton, *Black Power: The Politics of Liberation in America* (New York: Random House, 1967)

96. Matlin, *On the Corner*, 86–89.

97. Barton, "The Unknown Moynihan Report," 20.

98. *The Negro Family*, 1.

99. Ibid., 3.

100. Ibid.

101. Nathan Glazer, "Negroes and Jews: The Challenge to Pluralism," *Commentary*, December 1964, 29–34.

102. *The Negro Family*, 3; emphasis in original.

103. Ibid.

104. Rustin, "From Protest to Politics," 27.

105. *The Negro Family*, n.p.

106. Ibid., 5.

107. Ibid.

108. Ibid., 14.

109. Stanley Elkins, *Slavery: A Problem in American Institutional and Intellectual Life* (Chicago: University of Chicago Press, 1959); August Meier and Elliott Rudwick, *Black History and the Historical Profession, 1915–1980* (Urbana: University of Illinois Press, 1986), 247–51.

110. Nathan Glazer, "The Differences Among Slaves," *Commentary*, May 1960, 455.

111. *The Negro Family*, 16.

112. Ibid.

113. Ibid., 17.

114. Ibid., 20.

115. Ibid., 21.

116. Ibid., 26.

117. Ibid., 29.

118. Draft of *The Negro Family*.

119. *The Negro Family*, 30.

120. Robert O. Blood and Donald M. Wolfe, Jr., *Husbands and Wives: The Dynamics of Married Living* (Glencoe, Ill.: Free Press, 1960), 20, 22.

121. *The Negro Family*, 25.

122. Ibid., 33.

123. Ruth Feldstein, *Motherhood in Black and White: Race and Sex in American Liberalism, 1930–1965* (Ithaca, N.Y.: Cornell University Press, 2000).

124. *The Negro Family*, 29; emphasis added.

125. Ibid.

126. Moynihan "Memorandum for the President," May 4, 1965.

127. Moynihan to Bill Moyers, January 21, 1965, Box 45, HU 2–1, LBJ Library.

128. Moynihan, "Memorandum for the President," May 4, 1965.

129. *The Negro Family*, 33.

130. "Transcript of the American Academy Conference on the Negro American: May 14–15, 1965," 295.

131. *The Negro Family*, 29.

132. Ibid., 16.

133. Ibid., 4.

134. Moynihan to Harry McPherson, September 22, 1966, Box 180, Moynihan Papers.

135. Draft of *The Negro Family*.

136. *The Negro Family*, 5, emphasis added.

137. Moynihan, "Memorandum for the President," May 4, 1965, emphasis in original.

138. James Q. Wilson, "The Sick Sixties," *Atlantic Monthly*, October, 1973, 92.

139. *The Negro Family*, 46.

140. Barton to Moynihan, September 14, 1967, Box 426, Moynihan Papers.

141. *The Negro Family*, 19.

142. Ibid., 47.

143. Moynihan, interview with Rainwater and Yancey, 11.

144. *The Negro Family*, 47.

145. Ibid.

146. Moynihan, "Employment, Income, and the Ordeal of the Negro Family," *Daedalus* 94 (1965): 769.

147. *The Negro Family*, 21.

148. Ibid., 43.

149. Ibid., 42.

150. Wirtz to Moyers, March 23, 1965, Box 290, Wirtz Papers.

151. Harry McPherson, *A Political Education: A Washington Memoir* (Boston: Little, Brown, 1972), 334–38.

152. Moynihan, "Memorandum for the President," May 4, 1965.

153. Ibid. Moynihan contradicted his overriding concern for lower-class African Americans by suggesting that middle-class African American families move to suburbs, which would deprive poorer African Americans remaining in urban areas of the role models he and other liberals believed they needed.

154. As quoted in Rainwater and Yancey, *The Moynihan Report*, 14.

155. Moynihan, interview with Rainwater and Yancey, 18. On the strategy of leapfrogging, see also David C. Carter, *The Music Has Gone Out of the Movement: Civil Rights and the Johnson Administration, 1965–1968* (Chapel Hill: University of North Carolina Press, 2009).

156. Moynihan to Wirtz, June 1, 1965, Box 67, Moynihan Papers.

157. Moynihan to Wirtz, June 4, 1965, Box 290, Wirtz Papers.

158. Moynihan was a gifted writer, but his speech draft was not his finest work. Some passages were particularly tin-eared. For example, discussing how rates of voting registration among blacks outpaced those of whites in Texas, Moynihan wrote: "Not, let me say, that both groups couldn't do with some improving, when you compare the figures with Tennessee, whose pretty girls we sing such disparaging songs about." See "The President's Address," Box 104, Moynihan Papers.

159. Johnson, "To Fulfill These Rights."

160. Moynihan, interview with Rainwater and Yancey, 14.

161. Richard Godwin, *Remembering America: A Voice from the Sixties* (Boston: Little Brown, 1988), 344.

162. Moynihan, "The President's Address."

163. Moynihan, interview with Rainwater and Yancey, 15–16.

164. Harry McPherson, interview by T. H. Baker, March 24, 1969, Harry McPherson Oral History Interview IV, transcript, Internet Copy, LBJ Library, 7.

Chapter 3. The New Racism

1. Harry McPherson to Moynihan, February 1, 1966, Box 463, Moynihan Papers.

2. Michele Wallace, *Black Macho and the Myth of the Superwoman* (New York: Dial, 1979), 11.

3. Moynihan to Ursula Niebuhr, February 28, 1966, Box 466, Moynihan Papers.

4. Gerald Horne, *The Fire This Time: The Watts Uprising and the 1960s* (Charlottesville: University of Virginia Press, 1995), esp. 3; Thomas Sugrue, *Sweet Land of Liberty: The Forgotten Struggle for Civil Rights in the North* (New York: Random House, 2009), 324–36.

5. *Report of the National Advisory Commission on Civil Disorders* (Washington, D.C.: GPO, 1968), 10.

6. David C. Carter, *The Music Has Gone Out of the Movement: Civil Rights and the Johnson Administration, 1965–1968* (Chapel Hill: University of North Carolina Press, 2009), 75–101; Kevin L. Yuill, "The 1966 White House Conference on Civil Rights," *Historical Journal* 41 (1998): 259–82; Morris Abram, interview by Michael L. Gillette, March 20, 1985, transcript, Morris Abram Oral History Interview I, Internet Copy, LBJ Library.

7. Harry McPherson, interview by T. H. Baker, March 24, 1969, interview IV, tape II, transcript, Harry McPherson Oral History, Internet Copy, LBJ Library.

8. Paul Le Blanc and Michael D. Yates, *A Freedom Budget for All Americans: Recapturing the Promise of the Civil Rights Movement in the Struggle for Economic Justice Today* (New York: Monthly Review Press, 2013); Lee White to President Johnson, August 10, 1965, Box 20, President's Appointment File, LBJ Library.

9. Elizabeth Wickenden, "Confidential Notes on the Planning Session for White House Conference," November 23, 1965, Box 5, Office Files of Lee White, LBJ Library.

10. John Lewis to A. Philip Randolph, December 14, 1965, Box 66, White House Conference, LBJ Library.

11. Carter, *The Music Has Gone Out of the Movement*, 75–101; Yuill, "The 1966 White House Conference on Civil Rights," 259–82.

12. Nicolas Lemann, *The Promised Land: The Great Black Migration and How It Changed America* (New York: Knopf, 1991), 175.

13. Douglas S. Massey and Robert J. Sampson, "Moynihan Redux: Legacies and Lessons," *Annals of the American Academy of Political and Social Science* 621 (2009): 9.

14. Moynihan, "Toward Equality," Box 415, Moynihan Papers. My account fits with Rainwater and Yancey's in *The Politics of Controversy*, which notes that Pomfret published his article with White House permission though they omit Moynihan's involvement and describe the report's release as a "leak." Lee Rainwater and Willam Yancey *The Moynihan Report* (Cambridge, Mass.: MIT Press, 1967), 137.

15. John Pomfret, "Capital Parley Planned," *New York Times*, July 19, 1965.

16. "New Crisis: The Negro Family," *Newsweek*, August 9, 1965, 32–35; Rowland Evans and Robert Novak, "The Moynihan Report," *Washington Post*, August 18, 1965. Moynihan takes credit for releasing the report to *Newsweek* in "Toward Equality," Box 415, Moynihan Papers. For his admission that he leaked the report to Novak, see Moynihan, "A Dahrendorf Inversion and the Twilight of the Family: The Challenge to the Conference," in Moynihan, Timothy M. Smeeding, and Lee Rainwater, eds., *The Future of the Family* (New York: Russell Sage, 2004), xvi.

17. Moynihan, interview with Rainwater and Yancey, 18.

18. Frank Erwin to John W. Leslie, July 21, 1965, Box 296, Wirtz Papers.

19. John Leslie to Frank Erwin, July 30, 1965, HU2 Box 3, LBJ Library.

20. Lee White to Bill Moyers, August 12, 1965, Box 5, Office Files of Lee White, LBJ Library.

21. Rainwater and Yancey, *The Moynihan Report*, 151.

22. John Leslie to Frank Erwin, July 30, 1965, HU2 Box 3, LBJ Library.

23. Moynihan, inteview with Rainwater and Yancey, 19.

24. Victory S. Navasky, "For Official Use Only," *Book Week*, January 2, 1966, 6.

25. "New Crisis: The Negro Family," 35.

26. Richard Rovere, "Letter from Washington," *New Yorker*, September 11, 1965, 130.

27. Michael Harrington, "Yes, $100 Billion," *New York Herald Tribune*, November 28, 1965.

28. Navasky, "For Official Use Only."

29. Daniel Patrick Moynihan, "A Family Policy for the Nation," *America*, September 18, 1965, 280–83.

30. "Growing Support for Family Allowances," *America*, September 18, 1965, 277.

31. Arthur T. Sheehan to the editor, *America*, October 9, 1965, 387.

32. "Los Angeles: And Now What?" *America*, August 28, 1965, 200.

33. Stephen Darst, "Question of Aid to Families by Federal Subsidy Raised," *St. Louis Review*, October 8, 1965.

34. "The Negro Family," *Catholic Family Leader* 5 (1965): 4.

35. "'Secret' Government Report 'The Negro Family' Now Available!" *The Citizen*, December 1965, 20–21.

36. Albert C. Persons, *Riot!* (Birmingham, Ala.: Esco, 1965), 4, 6.

37. "Concerned," "The Moynihan Report," *Arkansas Democrat*, September 22, 1967.

38. "Behind the Riots: Family Life Breakdown Sows Seeds of Race Violence," *Wall Street Journal*, August 16, 1965.

39. "New Stage in Civil Rights," *Wall Street Journal*, July 23, 1965.

40. Richard Wilson, "Frightening Negro 'Other World' to be Topic of Capitol Conference," *Los Angeles Times*, September 18, 1965.

41. Ralph de Toledano, "Family Decay a Major Factor in Riots," *Johnstown Tribune-Democrat*, August 24, 1965.

42. Ralph de Toledano, "Moynihan Report of 1965 Suppressed Due to Findings," *Huntsville News*, November 16, 1965.

43. Mary McGrory, "A President Talks Frankly to Negroes," *Washington Star*, June 6, 1965.

44. McGrory to Moynihan, September 24, 1966, Box 5, Mary McGrory Papers. Emphasis added.

45. Moynihan, interview with Rainwater and Yancey, 12; White to Moynihan, 23 April 1965, and White to Moynihan, May 5, 1965, Box 23, Theodore White Papers, Harvard University Archives.

46. Theodore White, *The Making of the President, 1964* (New York: Atheneum, 1965), 227.

47. "A Shift in the Wind in Washington," *U.S. News & World Report*, September 6, 1965, 27–32.

48. Wilson, "Frightening Negro 'Other World.'"

49. As quoted in Horne, *The Fire This Time*, 137, 39.

50. "New Crisis," 32.

51. G. C. Oden, "A Lesser People Might Have Died," *Pittsburgh Courier*, October 9, 1965.

52. Jacob Sherman, "The Controversial Moynihan Report," *Philadelphia Tribune*, December 21, 1965.

53. Jacob Sherman, "Breakdown of Negro Family Unit Blamed for All Our Troubles," *Philadelphia Tribune*, December 25, 1965.

54. "The Moynihan Report," *Chicago Defender*, December 6, 1965.

55. "A Man Around the House," *Ebony*, January 1966, 92.

56. "An Address by Martin Luther King," in Rainwater and Yancey, *The Moynihan Report*, 404. The speech was given in Westchester County, New York, October 29, 1965.

57. Ibid.

58. Martin Luther King, Jr., "The Negro Family: A Challenge to National Action" (speech, University of Chicago, January 27, 1966), Digital Archive, Martin Luther King, Jr. Center for Nonviolent Social Change, http://www.thekingcenter.org/archive/document/mlk-address-university-chicago.

59. Whitney M. Young, Jr., "White House Confab," *New York Amsterdam News*, October 2, 1965.

60. Whitney M. Young, Jr., "Broken Homes Result, Not Cause of Negro's Denial of Rights," *Philadelphia Tribune*, January 25, 1966.

61. See Box 41, Chicago Urban League Records.

62. Francis A. Kornegay to Moynihan, June 16, 1966, Box 162, Moynihan Papers.

63. Rainwater and Yancey, *The Moynihan Report*, 196.

64. "Suggestions for Content and Format: White House Conference of November 17–18, 1965," Box U:2844, National Association for the Advancement of Colored People Records.

65. Clarence Mitchell, "From the Work Bench," *Baltimore Afro-American*, December 4, 1965.

66. Carter as quoted in Rainwater and Yancey, *The Moynihan Report*, 201.

67. John D'Emilio, *Lost Prophet*, 414–30; Bayard Rustin to Lee White, 7 October 1965, Bayard Rustin Papers, Microfilm.

68. Moynihan to Rustin, November 2, 1966, Box 198, Moynihan Papers.

69. Bayard Rustin, "Why Don't Negroes . . . ," *America*, June 4, 1966, 798.

70. Bayard Rustin, "The 'Watts Manifesto' and the McCone Report," *Commentary*, March 1966, 29, 35.

71. James Farmer and George Wiley to Morris Abram and William T. Coleman, Jr., October 21, 1965, Reel 9, Congress of Racial Equality Papers [microform]: Addendum, 1944–1968.

72. James Farmer, "The Controversial Moynihan Report," *New York Amsterdam News*, December 18, 1965. See also James Farmer, "More on the Moynihan Report," *New York Amsterdam News*, December 25, 1965.

73. Rainwater and Yancey, *The Moynihan Report*, 197, 220; William Ryan to "Anyone Interested," October 8, 1965, Box 466, Moynihan Papers. William Ryan, "Savage Discovery: The Moynihan Report," *The Nation*, November 22, 1965, 380–84; William Ryan, "The New Genteel Racism," *The Crisis*, December 1965, 623–32. Despite its limited circulation, the impact of Ryan's memo may been as great as his published articles since it alerted important civil rights figures to the report.

74. On Ryan, see "A Conversation Between William Ryan and M. Brinton Lykes," in M. Brinton Lykes et al., *Myths About the Powerless: Contesting Social Inequalities* (Philadelphia: Temple University Press, 1996), 351–67.

75. Ryan to "Anyone Interested."

76. "A Conversation between William Ryan and M. Brinton Lykes," 352. *Nation* editor Carey McWilliams suggested Ryan develop his critique of the Moynihan Report into a book that identified several examples of "blaming the victim." For a history of the phrase "blaming the victim," which came to be used in contexts Ryan never intended, see Alyson M. Cole, *The Cult of True Victimhood: From the War on Welfare to the War on Terror* (Stanford, Calif.: Stanford University Press, 2007), 109–43.

77. Ibid., 351.

78. William Ryan, "Racial Imbalance, Socioeconomic Status, and School Advancement," May 8, 1964, Catherine East Papers.

79. "A Conversation Between William Ryan and M. Brinton Lykes," 351.

80. Ryan, "Racial Imbalance, Socioeconomic Status, and School Advancement."

81. Ryan to "Anyone interested"; Ryan, letter to the editor, *The Nation*, December 27, 1965, 525.

82. Rickie Solinger, *Wake Up Little Susie: Single Pregnancy and Race Before Roe v. Wade* (New York: Routledge, 1992), 65–8.

83. Ryan to "Anyone interested."

84. Anna Hedgeman, *The Gift of Chaos: Decades of American Discontent* (New York: Oxford University Press, 1977), 140; Jones, *The March on Washington*, 166.

85. Rainwater and Yancey, *The Moynihan Report*, 220; James F. Findlay, Jr., *Church People in the Struggle: The National Council of Churches and the Black Freedom Movement, 1950–1970* (New York: Oxford University Press, 1993), 169–89.

86. Findlay, *Church People in the Struggle*, 177–81; Rainwater and Yancey, *The Moynihan Report Controversy*, 211; "Resolution of New York Pre-White House Conference Planning Group," Box 466, Moynihan Papers.

87. Rainwater and Yancey, *The Politics of Controversy*, 236.

88. Benjamin Payton, "The President, the Social Experts, and the Ghetto: An Analysis of an Emerging Strategy in Civil Rights," Box 466, Moynihan Papers, 20.

89. Ibid., 18.

90. Ibid., 17.

91. Benjamin Payton, "New Trends in Civil Rights," *Christianity and Crisis*, December 13, 1965, 267.

92. Findlay, *Church People in the Struggle*, 185–87.

93. Ibid., 177.

94. Payton, "New Trends in Civil Rights," 266–69.

95. Robert W. Spike, "Fissures in the Civil Rights Movement," *Christianity and Crisis*, February 21, 1966, 20, 21.

96. Moynihan to Joseph Fichter, November 1, 1966, Box 147, Moynihan Papers.

97. Cox to Moynihan, December 31, 1965, Box 462, Moynihan Papers.

98. Mark Hulsether, *Building a Protestant Left*: Christianity and Crisis *Magazine, 1941–1993* (Knoxville: University of Tennessee Press, 1999), 114–26. Niebuhr recanted his resignation in fear that it would be mistaken as indicating his support for the Vietnam War, which the magazine opposed.

99. Farmer, "The Controversial Moynihan Report," 36; Farmer, "More on the Moynihan Report," 11.

100. William Ryan, "The Holy Work of Bruno Bettelheim," *Commonweal*, May 26, 1967, 286. Ryan also compared African American ghettos to concentration camps, employing the same analogy Moynihan borrowed from Stanley Elkins in the report.

101. Ryan, letter to the editor, *The Nation*, December 27, 1965, 525.

102. Rustin, "Why Don't Negroes," 798; Payton, "New Trends in Civil Rights," 269.

103. Farmer, "The Controversial Moynihan Report," 36.

104. Rainwater and Yancey, *The Moynihan Report*, 158; William B. Goodwin [senior editor, Harcourt, Brace] to Moynihan, September 27, 1965, Box 414, Moynihan Papers.

105. "Confetti," *Chicago Defender*, March 1, 1966.

106. "Political Pressures Charged in Mazique Divorce Appeal," *Washington Afro-American*, December 4, 1965.

107. Richard L. Coe, "Shaw Begins Rep at Arena," *Washington Post*, September 28, 1967.

108. Boxes 182, 184, 216, 217, 463, 464, 465, Moynihan Papers.

109. Margaret L. Cort to unknown ["Dear Father"], n.d., Box 184, Moynihan Papers.

110. Bill Southworth to Moynihan, August 15, 1967, Box 184, Moynihan Papers.

111. Jerome Goldstein to Moynihan, May 29, 1968, Box 184, Moynihan Papers.

112. "A Very Concerned Citizen" to Moynihan, n.d., Box 217, Moynihan Papers.

113. Abie Miller to Moynihan, April 19, 1966, Box 184, Moynihan Papers.

114. *The Negro Family*, n.p.

115. Albert S. Patterson to Secretary of Labor, September 14, 1965, Box 463, Moynihan Papers.

116. "One of your haters" to Moynihan, n.d., Box 465, Moynihan Papers.

117. Anonymous to Moynihan, n.d. (postmarked May 8, 1966, from Augusta, Kansas), Box 464, Moynihan Papers.

118. Anonymous to Moynihan, March 23, 1967, Box 216, Moynihan Papers.

119. Chalmers S. Murray to Moynihan, December 12, 1967, Box 182, Moynihan Papers.

120. H. R. Davies to Moynihan, October 10, 1966, Box 184, Moynihan Papers.

121. Jonathan Kozol to Herman Bookbinder, January 7, 1968, Box 147, Moynihan Papers.

122. Rufus Webb to Moynihan, March 31, 1966, Box 184, Moynihan Papers.

123. Letters to the editor, *Look*, June 28, 1966, 24.

124. Sollinger, *Wake Up Little Susie*, 54; Johanna Schoen, *Choice and Coercion: Birth Control, Sterilization, and Abortion in Public Health and Welfare* (Chapel Hill: University of North Carolina Press, 2005), 103–11.

125. Mrs. Peter R. Fleck to Moynihan, June 27, 1967, Box 189, Moynihan Papers.

126. Hazel M. Widney to Moynihan, August 5, 1967, Box 189, Moynihan Papers.

127. Letter to the editor, *Look*, June 28, 1966.

128. Moynihan to C. Dickerson Williams, November 4, 1968, Box 202, Moynihan Papers.

129. "Memorandum for the President," May 4, 1965.

130. Margaret Bright to Moynihan, August 8, 1966, Box 421, Moynihan Papers.

131. Frederick Jaffe to Harry McPherson, October 4, 1965, Box 421, Moynihan Papers.

132. Richard Titmuss to Moynihan, November 22, 1965, Box 464, Moynihan Papers.

133. Mario Obledo to Moynihan, August 3, 1967, Box 189, Moynihan Papers.

134. Paul Douglas Ware to Moynihan, October 24, 1966, Box 436, Moynihan Papers.

135. Ware to Moynihan, November 7, 1966, Box 436, Moynihan Papers.

136. Ware to Moynihan, March 18, 1968, Box 201, Moynihan Papers.

137. Dorothy M. White to Moynihan, October 7, 1966, Box 184, Moynihan Papers.

138. Mary E. Melane to Moynihan, March 15, 1966, Box 184, Moynihan Papers.

139. Robert Coles, *Children of Crisis: A Study of Courage and Fear* (Boston: Little, Brown, 1967), 145.

140. Ibid., 143.

141. Ibid., 144.

Chapter 4. The Death of White Sociology

1. Ralph Ellison, letter to the editor, *Harper's Magazine*, July 1967, 12.

2. Ronald W. Walters, "Toward a Definition of Black Social Science," in Joyce A. Ladner, ed., *The Death of White Sociology* (New York: Random House, 1973), 202.

3. Ellison, letter to the editor.

4. Abd-l Hakimu Ibn Alkalimat (Gerald McWorter), "The Ideology of Black Social Science," in Ladner, ed., *The Death of White Sociology*, 181.

5. Mrs. Frank J. Howard to Moynihan, September 23, 1967, Box 186, Moynihan Papers.

6. Charles Kadushin, *The American Intellectual Elite* (Boston: Little, Brown, 1974), 267.

7. Karen Ferguson, *Top Down: The Ford Foundation, Black Power, and the Reinvention of Racial Liberalism* (Philadelphia: University of Pennsylvania Press, 2013), 2.

8. See letter invitations in Box 465, Moynihan Papers.

9. Harmar Brereton to Moynihan, August 28, 1967, Box 156, Moynihan Papers.

10. "Press Release: Morning Papers of Friday, March 25, 1966," Box 463, Moynihan Papers.

11. Joint Center for Urban Studies, *The First Five Years: 1959 to 1964* (Cambridge, Mass.: 1964).

12. Wilson as quoted by Moynihan, "The Urban Negro *Is* the 'Urban Problem'," *Trans-action*, October 1967, 36.

13. Andrew Billingsley, *Black Families in White America* (Englewood Cliffs, N.J.: Prentice Hall, 1968), 159.

14. Alan Pifer to Moynihan, May 17, 1966, Box 148, Moynihan Papers; Moynihan, "Toward Equality as a Fact and a Result: A Program of Foundation Activity in Negro American Affairs," Box 148, Moynihan Papers.

15. "Life in the Frightening Corners," *Time*, July 28, 1967, 1.

16. Fred Powledge, "Idea Broker for the Race Crisis: A Troubled Nation Turns to Pat Moynihan," *Life*, November 3, 1968; Fred Powledge, "A Journalist's Apologia," *The Nation*, September 22, 1979, 241.

17. Moynihan to Robert Blauner, March 27, 1967, Box 147, Moynihan Papers.

18. Moynihan, "Toward Equality," Box 415, Moynihan Papers.

19. Moynihan, Foreword to W. E. B. Du Bois, *The Negro American Family* (Cambridge, Mass.: MIT University Press, 1970), viii.

20. Thomas Pettigrew to Carey McWilliams, July 13, 1966, Box 466, Moynihan Papers.

21. Thomas Pettigrew, interview with author, June 3, 2014.

22. Clark to Moynihan, February 2, 1966, Box 462, Moynihan Papers.

23. Clark to Lee Rainwater, May 12, 1966, Box 120, Kenneth Bancroft Clark Papers.

24. "The Negro Family: Visceral Reaction," *Newsweek*, December 6, 1965, 40.

25. Daniel Matlin, "Who Speaks for Harlem? Kenneth B. Clark, Albert Murray, and the Controversies of Black Urban Life," *Journal of American Studies* 46 (2012): 875–94.

26. William Yancey, interview with author, July 27, 2013; Moynihan to McPherson, November 28, 1964, Box 466, Moynihan Papers.

27. Yancey, interview. Unfortunately, the notes Yancey took during the interviews he conducted are no longer extant.

28. Rainwater and Yancey, *The Moynihan Report and the Politics of Controversy* (Cambridge, Mass.: MIT Press, 1967), xi.

29. Ibid., 302.

30. Ibid., xi.

31. *The Moynihan Report and the Politics of Controversy* emerged from a broader 1960s project by social scientists to better publicize their work. The book was funded by *Trans-action* magazine, co-founded by Rainwater in 1963 to enlist social scientists to write for a generally educated public.

32. Lee Rainwater and David J. Pittman, "Ethical Problems in Studying a Politically Sensitive and Deviant Community," *Social Problems* 14 (1967): 358.

33. Yancey, interview.

34. Kenneth Clark to Stephen Graubard, October 8, 1965, Clark Papers.

35. Lee Rainwater, "Crucible of Identity: The Negro Lower-Class Family," in Kenneth Clark and Talcott Parsons, eds., *The Negro American* (Boston: Houghton Mifflin, 1966), 165.

36. Lee Rainwater, *Behind Ghetto Walls: Black Families in a Federal Slum* (Chicago: Aldine, 1970), 387.

37. Ibid., 4.

38. Rainwater, "Crucible of Identity," 164.

39. Rainwater, *Behind Ghetto Walls*, 5.

40. Ibid., 405–6.

41. Rainwater and Yancey, *The Moynihan Report*, 294.

42. Ibid., 12.

43. Ibid., 238. Emphasis removed.

44. Honorary Negro card, Box 191, Moynihan Papers.

45. Irving Louis Horowitz to Moynihan, September 11, 1967, Box 172, Moynihan Papers.

46. Moynihan to Members of the Seminar on Poverty, December 13, 1966, Box 136, Moynihan Papers.

47. Letter [no heading], March 14, 1968, Box 177, Moynihan Papers. See also Jane Riddell, "4 Roxbury Agencies Hit MIT-Harvard Unit," *Boston Globe*, December 5, 1967; Fred Pillsbury, "Should Research or Roxbury Get Funds?" *Boston Globe*, December 11, 1967.

48. Stokely Carmichael, "We Are Going to Use The Term 'Black Power' And We Are Going to Define it Because Black Power Speaks to Us" (text of July 28, 1966 speech), in John H. Bracey, August Meier, and Elliott Rudwick, eds., *Black Nationalism in America* (Indianapolis: Bobbs-Merrill, 1970), 472.

49. Stokely Carmichael and Charles V. Hamilton, *Black Power: The Politics of Liberation in America* (New York: Random House, 1967). On Black Power, see Peniel E. Joseph, *Waiting 'til the Midnight Hour: A Narrative History of Black Power in America* (New York: Henry Holt, 2006); Jeffrey O. G. Ogbar, *Black Power: Radical Politics and*

African American Identity (Baltimore: Johns Hopkins University Press, 2004); William L. Van Deburg, *New Day in Babylon: The Black Power Movement and American Culture, 1965–1975* (Chicago: University of Chicago Press, 1992); and Clayborne Carson, *In Struggle: SNCC and the Black Awakening of the 1960s* (Cambridge, Mass.: Harvard University Press, 1981).

50. Stokely Carmichael, "We Are Going to Use the Term 'Black Power'," 471–72.

51. As quoted in Carson, *In Struggle*, 216.

52. Ibid. 219.

53. "Abuse and Debate," *Washington Post*, January 25, 1969.

54. Steve Estes, *I Am a Man!: Race, Manhood, and the Civil Rights Movement* (Chapel Hill: University of North Carolina Press, 2005), 123.

55. LeRoi Jones, *Black Music* (New York: Morrow, 1967), 190.

56. Julius Lester, *Look Out Whitey! Black Power's Gon' Get Your Mama* (New York: Dial Press, 1968), 53, 54.

57. Walt Shepperd, "The New Paternalists," *Nickel Review*, November 1967, clipping, Box 189, Moynihan Papers.

58. Daniel H. Watts, "The Negro Is Obsolete," *Liberator*, December 1965, 3.

59. Abdul Basit Naeem, "Says U.S. Publication Gives Substance to Statements Made by the Messenger," *Muhammad Speaks*, April 1, 1966; Abdul Basit Naeem, "U.S. Booklet Admits Negro Plight Worse, Notes Muslim Enlistments," *Muhammad Speaks*, April 8, 1966.

60. "Crisis of the Black Family in the U.S.A. Today," *Muhammad Speaks*, January 27, 1967.

61. Ibid.

62. "Black Families at the Crossroads," *Muhammad Speaks*, February 3, 1967.

63. "Minister Farrakhan Views Statements Made by Dr. Moynihan in Interview," *Muhammad Speaks*, March 3, 1967.

64. Ellison, letter to the editor, 13.

65. Ellison, *Shadow and Act* (New York: Random House, 1964), 303–17.

66. Ellison, "'A Very Stern Discipline': An Interview with Ralph Ellison," *Harper's Magazine*, March 1967, 90.

67. Ibid., 76. See also Matlin, "Who Speaks for Harlem?" and Richard H. King, *Race, Culture, and the Intellectuals, 1940–1970* (Baltimore: Johns Hopkins University Press, 2004), 290–303.

68. Ladner, *The Death of White Sociology*, xxi.

69. Joyce Ladner to author, December 3, 2013.

70. Martha Biondi, *The Black Revolution on Campus* (Berkeley: University of California Press, 2012); Derrick E. White, *The Challenge of Blackness: The Institute of the Black World and Political Activism in the 1970s* (Gainesville: University Press of Florida, 2011); Jonathan Scott Holloway, "The Black Scholar, the Humanities, and the Politics of Racial Knowledge Since 1945," in David Hollinger, ed., *The Humanities and the*

Dynamics of Inclusion Since World War II (Baltimore: Johns Hopkins University Press, 2006), 217–46.

71. James E. Blackwell and Morris Janowitz, eds., *Black Sociologists: Historical and Contemporary Perspectives* (Chicago: University of Chicago Press, 1974), vii.

72. Robert Staples, *Introduction to Black Sociology* (New York: McGraw-Hill, 1976).

73. Ladner, *The Death of White Sociology*, xiii. The quote is from Lerone Bennett's "The Challenge of Blackness." See Lerone Bennett, Jr., "The Challenge of Blackness," in Bennett, *The Challenge of Blackness* (Chicago: Johnson Publishing, 1972), 33–43; quote on 35–36.

74. John Henrik Clarke, ed., *William Styron's Nat Turner: Ten Black Writers Respond* (Boston: Beacon Press, 1968).

75. Nathan Hare, "The Challenge of a Black Scholar," in Ladner, *The Death of White Sociology*, 75.

76. Albert Murray, "White Norms, Black Deviation," in Ladner, *The Death of White Sociology*, 101, 105. Murray's contribution to *The Death of White Sociology* was a selection from his influential book, *The Omni-Americans: New Perspectives on Black Experience and American Culture* (New York: Outerbridge & Dienstfrey, 1970).

77. Charles V. Hamilton, "Black Social Scientists: Contributions and Problems," in Ladner, ed., *The Death of White Sociology*, 474.

78. Sidney M. Willhelm, "Equality: America's Racist Ideology," in Ladner, ed., *The Death of White Sociology*, 148.

79. Ladner, *The Death of White Sociology*, xxvi.

80. Ibid., xxvii

81. Ira Katznelson, "White Social Science and the Black Man's World," *Race Today*, February 1970, 48.

82. Holloway, "The Black Scholar."

83. Alkalimat, "The Ideology of Black Social Science," 173–89.

84. Gerald A. McWorter, "Deck the Ivy Racist Halls: The Case of Black Studies," in Armstead L. Robinson et al., eds., *Black Studies in the University: A Symposium* (New Haven, Conn.: Yale University Press, 1969), 59.

85. Abd-l Hakimu Ibn Alkalimat (Gerald McWorter), "The Ideology of Black Social Science," 178.

86. Murray, "Black Norms, White Deviation," 112.

87. Alkalimat, "The Ideology of Black Social Science," 173; Rhett S. Jones, "Proving Black Inferior: The Sociology of Knowledge," in Ladner, ed., *The Death of White Sociology*, 116.

88. John D. McCarthy and William L. Yancey, "Uncle Tom and Mr. Charlie: Metaphysical Pathos in the Study of Racism and Personal Disorganization," *American Journal of Sociology* 76 (1971): 669.

89. Drake, "Some Suggested Areas of Research in the Negro in Chicago," Box 40, St. Clair Drake Papers.

90. "Statement by St. Clair Drake, Professor of Anthropology on Moynihan Commencement Speaker Controversy . . . Mar. 12, 1975," Box 40, Drake Papers.

91. Drake as quoted in Biondi, *Black Revolution on Campus*, 188. In this quote, Drake referred to an offer he received to direct the Black Studies program at Harvard.

92. Drake, "Statement by St. Clair Drake."

93. "To the Senior Class Presidents of Stanford University From a Group of Faculty Members of the Department of Sociology," March 7, 1975, Box 40, Drake Papers.

94. Drake to "Dick" (no date), Box 40, Drake Papers.

95. Drake, "Statement by St. Clair Drake."

96. Drake, Untitled (speech, 1975), Box 40, Drake Papers.

97. The Black Graduating Seniors, "We Protest," Box 40, Drake Papers.

98. Andrew Billingsley, "Foreword" to Robert B. Hill, *The Strengths of Black Families* (New York: Emerson Hall, 1972), xv.

99. Andrew Billingsley, "Black Families and White Social Science," *Journal of Social Issues* 26 (1970): 137. Originally published in *Journal of Social Issues*, Billingsley's essay was collected in *The Death of White Sociology*.

100. Ibid., 130.

101. Robert Staples and Alfredo Mirandé, "Racial and Cultural Variations Among American Families: A Decennial Review of the Literature on Minority Families," *Journal of Marriage and Family* 42 (November 1980): 888.

102. Marie F. Peters, "Notes from the Guest Editor," *Journal of Marriage and Family* 40 (November 1978): 655.

103. Ibid.

104. Hylan Lewis, "The Family: Resources for Change," Box 462, Moynihan Papers.

105. Warren D. TenHouten, "The Black Family: Myth and Reality," *Psychiatry* 33 (May 1970), 171.

106. Andrew Billingsley and Amy Tate Billingsley, "Negro Family Life in America," *Social Science Review* 39 (September 1965): 310, 319.

107. Billingsley, *Black Families in White America*, 198.

108. Ibid., 153.

109. Whitney M. Young, Jr., *Beyond Racism: Building an Open Society* (New York: McGraw-Hill, 1969), 58.

110. Ibid., 57.

111. Hill, *The Strengths of Black Families;* "Ellen" to Moynihan, August 2, 1968, Box 150, Moynihan Papers.

112. Walter R. Allen, "Black Family Research in the United States: A Review, Assessment, and Extension," *Journal of Comparative Family Studies* 9 (Summer 1978): 167–89.

113. Young, *Beyond Racism*, 60.

114. Billingsley, *Black Families in White America*, 97.

115. Billingsley, "Black Families and White Social Science," 138

116. Robert Staples, "Towards a Sociology of the Black Family: A Theoretical and Methodological Assessment," *Journal of Marriage and Family* 33 (1971): 119–38.

117. Robert Staples, ed., *The Black Family: Essays and Studies* (Belmont, Calif.: Wadsworth, 1971).

118. Robert Staples, interview with author, October 15, 2013.

119. Robert Staples, "The Black Scholar in Academe," *Black Scholar*, November 1972, 44.

120. Robert Staples, "A Response to Clemmont Vontress," *Black Scholar*, November 1971, 42.

121. As quoted in Gary Wills, "All of Us Can Be Proud of Story 'Roots' Tells," *Baltimore Sun*, February 7, 1977.

122. Kathryn E. Delmez, "'Real Facts, By Real People': Folklore in the Early Work of Carrie Mae Weems," in Kathryn E. Delmez, ed., *Carrie Mae Weems: Three Decades of Photography and Video* (New Haven, Conn.: Frist Center for the Arts in association with Yale University Press, 2013), 11–12.

123. Meier and Rudwick, *Black History and the Historical Profession*, 251.

124. Eugene Genovese, *Roll, Jordan, Roll: The World the Slaves Made* (New York: Pantheon, 1974), 450.

125. Herbert Gutman, *The Black Family in Slavery and Freedom, 1750–1925* (New York: Pantheon, 1975), xvii.

126. Laurence Glasco to author, December 4, 2013.

127. Moynihan to Gutman, August 16, 1968, Box 431, Moynihan Papers; Glasco to author.

128. Moynihan, Foreword to Du Bois, *The Negro American Family*, ix.

129. Gutman to Moynihan, October 8, 1968, Box 431, Moynihan Papers.

130. Moynihan's collaborator, Nathan Glazer, made exactly this point after the publication of Gutman's book. See Glazer, "The Gutman Thesis," *New York Times*, September 29, 1976.

131. Gutman, *The Black Family*, 446.

132. Genovese, *Roll, Jordan, Roll*, 450.

133. Gutman, *The Black Family*, xvii.

134. Ibid., 465.

135. Staples, *The Black Family*, 3.

136. Billingsley, *Black Families in White America*, 9. On the general tendency of commentators in this period to compare lower-class African Americans to middle-class whites, see Jerald E. Podair, *The Strike That Changed New York: Blacks, Whites, and the Ocean Hill-Brownsville Crisis* (New Haven, Conn.: Yale University Press, 2002).

Chapter 5. Feminism and the Nuclear Family Norm

1. June Jordan, "Memo to Daniel Pretty Moynihan," in Jordan, *New Days: Poems of Exile and Return* (New York: Emerson Hall, 1974), 6.

2. Moynihan, "Toward Equality," Box 414, Moynihan Papers.

3. Bayard Rustin, "Why Don't Negroes . . . ," *America*, June 4, 1966, 796.

4. "The Moynihan Report," *Christian Century*, December 15, 1965, 1532.

5. Moynihan, "Toward Equality," Box 414, Moynihan Papers.

6. Wallace, *Black Macho and the Myth of the Superwoman* (New York: Dial, 1979), 110.

7. As quoted in Susan Hartmann, *The Other Feminists: Activists in the Liberal Establishment* (New Haven, Conn.: Yale University Press, 1998), 180. See also Susan Mayeri, *Reasoning from Race: Feminism, Law, and the Civil Rights Revolution* (Cambridge, Mass.: Harvard University Press, 2011), 9–40.

8. Pauli Murray to editors of *Newsweek*, Sept. 4, 1965, Folder 601, Esther Peterson Papers.

9. *The Negro Family*, 16.

10. Betty Friedan, *The Feminine Mystique* (New York: Norton, 1963), 137.

11. Nancy MacLean, *Freedom Is Not Enough: The Opening of the American Workplace* (Cambridge, Mass.: Harvard University Press, 2006); Stephanie Gilmore, *Groundswell: Grass-Roots Feminist Activism in Postwar America* (New York: Routledge, 2013).

12. *The Negro Family*, 34.

13. "1965 Convention Call," Box 16, Series 2, National Council of Negro Women Records.

14. Moynihan to Esther Peterson, December 30, 1965, Folder 601, Peterson Papers.

15. Landon R. Y. Storrs, "Red Scare Politics and the Suppression of Popular Front Feminism: The Case of Mary Dublin Keyserling," *Journal of American History* 90 (2003): 491–524.

16. Mary Dublin Keyserling, "Gains and Problems," November 11 address before "Conference on The Negro Woman in the U.S.A.: New Roles in Family and Community Life," Box 4, Folder 111, Mary Dublin Keyserling Papers.

17. Wickenden, "Confidential Notes on the Planning Session for White House Conference."

18. Catherine East to Rev. Nemzer, May 15, 1966, Catherine East Papers.

19. Martha Griffiths to Willard Wirtz, August 24, 1967, Box 170, Moynihan Papers.

20. Moynihan to Griffiths, Box 170, Moynihan Papers.

21. Alice Echols, *Daring to Be Bad: Radical Feminism in America* (Minneapolis: University of Minnesota Press, 1989).

22. Merrillee A. Dolan, "Moynihan, Poverty Programs, and Women—A Female Viewpoint," manuscript, National Organization for Women Records; Marisa Chappell, *The War on Welfare: Family, Poverty, and Politics in Modern America* (Philadelphia: University of Pennyslvania Press, 2010), 102–3, 170–71.

23. Aileen Hernandez to Dolan, December 15, 1970, Box 48, NOW Records.

24. Hernandez to Dolan, January 21, 1971, Box 7, NOW Records.

25. Merrillee A. Dolan, "Merrillee A. Dolan, Early New Mexico Activist," http://www.vfa.us

26. Dolan, "Moynihan, Poverty Programs, and Women."

27. Mrs. Linda Driver to Moynihan, "A White Man's Myth Explored: The Moynihan Report (An Open Letter to Mr. D.P. Moynihan from Mrs. L. Driver)," n.d., Box 462, Moynihan Papers.

28. Barbara Ehrenreich, *The Hearts of Men: American Dreams and the Flight from Commitment* (Garden City: Anchor, 1983), esp. 107.

29. Marcus Raskin, "Editorial," *Ramparts* 4 (1965), 3. Raskin is listed as the author of this editorial in Moynihan, "The President and the Negro: The Moment Lost," *Commentary*, February 1967, 38.

30. Walt Shepperd, "The New Paternalists," *Nickel Review*, November 1967.

31. Albert Murray, *The Omni-Americans: New Perspectives on Black Experience and American Culture* (New York: Outerbridge & Dienstfrey, 1970), 34.

32. Robert Staples, "Towards a Sociology of the Black Family: A Theoretical and Methodological Assessment," *Journal of Marriage and Family* 33 (1971): 134.

33. Robert Staples, "What Is Black Sociology," in Joyce Ladner, ed., *The Death of White Sociology* (New York: Random House, 1973), 170.

34. Robert Staples, "The Myth of the Impotent Black Male," *Black Scholar,* June 1971, 8.

35. See Kevin Mumford's excellent article, "Untangling Pathology: The Moynihan Report and Homosexual Damage, 1965–1975," *Journal of Policy History* 24 (2012): 53–73.

36. Moynihan, "Toward Equality as a Fact and a Result: A Program of Foundation Activity in Negro American Affairs," Box 148, Moynihan Papers, 80.

37. John Corry, "An American Novelist Who Sometimes Teaches," *New York Times*, November 20, 1966.

38. Staples, "The Myth of the Impotent Black Male," 5.

39. Robert Self, *All in the Family: The Realignment of American Democracy Since the 1960s* (New York: Hill and Wang, 2012), 219–47.

40. Moynihan, "Toward Equality as a Fact and a Result," 58, 61–62.

41. "Life in the Frightening Corners," *Time*, July 28, 1967, 12.

42. James E. Westheider, *Fighting on Two Fronts: African Americans and the Vietnam War* (New York: New York University Press, 1997), 35; Christian G. Appy, *Working-Class War: American Combat Soldiers and Vietnam* (Chapel Hill: University of North Carolina Press, 1993), 32–33.

43. Raskin, "Editorial," 4.

44. Joel Kovel, *White Racism: A Psychohistory* (New York: Pantheon, 1970), 39.

45. Ibid., 217.

46. Westheider, *Fighting on Two Fronts*, 12–13, 20, 35; Kimberley L. Philipps, *War! What Is It Good For? Black Freedom Struggles and the U.S. Military from World War II to Vietnam* (Chapel Hill: University of North Carolina Press, 2012), 188–227.

47. Stokely Carmichael, "We Are Going to Use The Term 'Black Power' And We Are Going to Define it Because Black Power Speaks to Us," in John H. Bracey, August Meier, and Elliott Rudwick, eds., *Black Nationalism in America* (Indianapolis: Bobbs-Merrill, 1970), 472.

48. "On Destruction of Black Youth," *Muhammad Speaks*, February 17, 1967.

49. "Minister Farrakhan Views Statements Made by Dr. Moynihan in Interview," *Muhammad Speaks*, March 3, 1967.

50. "Of Crime and a White Man's War," *Muhammad Speaks*, February 10, 1967.

51. "On Destruction of Black Youth."

52. Elijhah Muhammad, *Message to the Blackman in America* (Chicago: Muhammad Mosque of Chicago 2, 1965), 58.

53. Wallace, *Black Macho and the Myth of the Superwoman*, 110.

54. Ibid., 31.

55. Frances Beale, "Double Jeopardy: To Be Black and Female," in Toni Cade, ed., *The Black Woman: An Anthology* (New York: New American Library, 1970), 92.

56. Joanna Clark, "Motherhood," in Cade, ed., *The Black Woman*, 71.

57. Patricia Hill Collins, *Black Feminist Thought: Knowledge, Consciousness, and the Politics of Empowerment* (Boston: Unwin Hyman, 1990).

58. Kimberly Springer, *Living for the Revolution: Black Feminist Organizations, 1968–1980* (Durham, N.C.: Duke University Press, 2005); Deborah Gray White, *Too Heavy a Load: Black Women in Defense of Themselves* (New York: Norton, 1999), 212–56.

59. Johnnie Tillmon, "Welfare Is a Women's Issue," *Ms.*, Spring 1972, 111. See also Premilla Nadasen, *Welfare Warriors: The Welfare Rights Movement in the United States* (New York: Routledge, 2005); Kornbluh, *The Battle for Welfare Rights: Politics and Poverty in Modern America* (Philadelphia: University of Pennsylvania Press, 2007).

60. Chappel, *War on Welfare*, 53.

61. Lloyd Shearer, "Negro Problem: Women Rule the Roost," *Parade*, August 20, 1967, 4.

62. Eldridge Cleaver, *Soul on Ice* (New York: McGraw-Hill, 1967), 61.

63. Ibid., 168.

64. As quoted in Paula Giddings, *This Is When and Where I Enter: The Impact of Black Women on Race and Sex in America* (New York: Morrow, 1984), 318. See also Jacqueline Jones, *Labor of Love, Labor of Sorrow: Black Women, Work, and the Family from Slavery to Present* (New York: Basic, 2010), 256–65 and Daniel Matlin, "Lift Up Yr! Self: Reinterpreting Amiri Baraka (LeRoi Jones), Black Power, and the Uplift Tradition," *Journal of American History* 93 (2006): 91–116.

65. Inez Smith Reid, *"Together" Black Women* (New York: Emerson Hall, 1972), 59–60.

66. Robert Staples, "The Myth of the Black Matriarchy," *Black Scholar* January–February 1970, 8.

67. Ibid., 12.

68. Ibid., 16n.

69. Ibid., 16.

70. Linda La Rue, "The Black Movement and Women's Liberation," in Beverley Guy-Shaftall, ed., *Words of Fire: An Anthology of African-American Feminist Thought* (New York: Dial, 1995), 169.

71. Jean Carey Bond and Patricia Peery, "Is the Black Male Castrated?" in Cade, ed., *The Black Woman*, 114.

72. Ibid., 115.

73. Margaret Wright, "I Want the Right to be Black and Me," in Gerda Lerner, ed., *Black Women in White America* (New York: Pantheon, 1972), 607.

74. Bond and Peery, "Is the Black Male Castrated?" 116–17.

75. As quoted in Deborah Gray White, *Too Heavy a Load*, 245.

76. Bond and Peery, "Is the Black Male Castrated?" 116–17.

77. Mary Ann Weathers, "An Argument for Black Women's Liberation as a Revolutionary Force," *No More Fun and Games: A Journal of Female Liberation* 1 (1969), http://library.duke.edu/rubenstein/scriptorium/wlm/fun-games2/argument.html.

78. Beale, "Double Jeopardy," 91.

79. Eleanor Holmes Norton, "For Sadie and Maude," in Robin Morgan, ed., *Sisterhood Is Powerful: An Anthology of Writings from the Women's Liberation Movement* (New York: Random House, 1970), 357.

80. Joyce A. Ladner, *Tomorrow's Tomorrow: The Black Woman* (Garden City, N.Y.: Doubleday, 1971), 269.

81. Ibid., 267.

82. Jacqueline J. Jackson, "But Where Are All the Men," *Black Scholar*, December 1971, 34.

83. Ladner, *Tomorrow's Tomorrow*, 272.

84. Ibid., 273.

85. Ibid., 233. However, Ladner complained that only after whites adopted African American norms would out-of-wedlock births become socially acceptable in mainstream America: "Conceivably, there will be no 'illegitimate' children and 'promiscuous' women in ten years if there are enough middle-class white women who decide that they are going to disavow the societal canons regarding childbirth and premarital sexual behavior. But this has to occur before the stigmatizing labels that are now attached to Blacks are destroyed."

86. Ibid., 46.

87. Norton, "For Sadie and Maude," 355.

88. Wallace, *Black Macho*, 120.

89. bell hooks, *Ain't I a Woman: Black Women and Feminism* (Boston: South End Press, 1981), 79. Though hooks did not mention the Moynihan Report in her text, an index entry for the Report refers readers to a long discussion of "matriarchy."

90. E. Frances White stresses diversity and disagreement among Black Feminists in *Dark Continent of Our Bodies: Black Feminism and the Politics of Respectability* (Philadelphia: Temple University Press, 2001), 25–80.

91. Moynihan, "Memorandum," December 9, 1970, Box 251, Moynihan Papers.

92. Oscar Lewis, *Five Families: Mexican Case Studies in the Culture of Poverty* (New York: Basic Books, 1959); Lewis, *La Vida: A Puerto Rican Family in the Culture of Poverty* (New York: Random House, 1966).

93. Oscar Lewis, *Children of Sanchez: Autobiography of a Mexican Family* (New York: Random House, 1961), xxiv.

94. Susan M. Rigdon, *The Culture Façade: Art, Science, and Politics in the Work of Oscar Lewis* (Urbana: University of Illinois Press, 1988), 87–106.

95. Carol Stack, "Writing Ethnography Against Public Reasoning" (unpublished paper in author's possession); Carol Stack, interview with author, August 23, 2013.

96. Stack, interview.

97. Elliot Liebow, *Tally's Corner: A Study of Negro Streetcorner Men* (Boston: Little, Brown, 1967); Handwriting, Stanley Hart to Moynihan, January 25, 1967, Box 179, Moynihan Papers.

98. Charles A. Valentine, *Black Studies and Anthropology: Scholarly and Political Interests in African American Culture* (Reading, Mass.: Addison-Wesley, 1972), 1.

99. Stack, interview.

100. Charles A. Valentine, *Culture and Poverty: Critique and Counter-Proposals* (Chicago: University of Chicago Press, 1968), 147.

101. Ibid., 35.

102. Ibid., 34.

103. Richard H. King, *Race, Culture, and the Intellectuals: 1940–1970* (Baltimore: Johns Hopkins University Press, 2004), 266–303.

104. Ladner, *Tomorrow's Tomorrow*, 53.

105. Valentine, *Culture of Poverty*, 148; David A. Hollinger, "Cultural Relativism," in Theodore M. Porter and Dorothy Ross, eds., *The Cambridge History of Science*, vol. 7, *The Modern Social Sciences* (New York: Cambridge University Press, 2003), 711–20; Richard Handler, "Boasian Anthropology and the Critique of American Culture, *American Quarterly* 42 (1990): 252–73.

106. Corry, "An American Novelist Who Sometimes Teaches," 180.

107. Carol B. Stack, *All Our Kin: Strategies for Survival in a Black Community* (New York: Harper and Row, 1974), 71.

108. Ibid., 9.

109. Jacqueline S. Mithun, review of Stack, *All Our Kin*, *Journal of Black Studies* 8 (1977): 119.

110. Stack, *All Our Kin*, 73.

111. Ibid., 22.

112. Ibid., 22.

113. Robert Coles, "Learning About Life in the Black Ghetto," *Boston Globe*, April 7, 1974.

114. Stack, *All Our Kin*, 24.

115. Ibid., 124.

116. Ibid., 43.

117. Ibid., 43.

118. Valentine, *Culture and Poverty*, 147.

119. Stack, *All Our Kin*, 38.

120. Roger D. Abrahams, *Positively Black* (Englewood Cliffs, N.J.: Prentice Hall, 1970), 5, 22.

121. Stack, *All Our Kin*, 25.

122. Robin Marie Averbeck, "'Want in the Midst of Plenty': Social Science, Poverty, and the Limits of Liberalism" (Ph.D. dissertation, University of California Davis, 2013), 224–33.

123. Frances Fox Piven and Richard A. Cloward, *Regulating the Poor: The Functions of Public Welfare* (New York: Pantheon, 1971), xvi.

Chapter 6, From National Action to Benign Neglect

1. Moynihan to Nixon, January 9, 1969, Box 449, Moynihan Papers.

2. Moynihan to Nixon, January 16, 1970, Box 261, Moynihan Papers.

3. Stephan Thernstrom and Abigail Thernstrom, *America in Black and White* (New York: Simon & Schuster, 1997), 172.

4. See Paul Berman, ed., *Debating P.C.: The Controversy over Political Correctness on College Campuses* (New York: Dell, 1992).

5. Moynihan, "The President and the Negro: The Moment Lost," *Commentary*, February 1967, 35, 41.

6. Ibid., 33, 32.

7. Ibid., 32, 33, 43.

8. Ibid., 43, 32, 40, 38, 42.

9. Moynihan, "Toward Equality," Box 413, Moynihan Papers.

10. Moynihan to Podhoretz, October 22, 1966, Box 216, Moynihan Papers.

11. Moynihan, "Toward Equality," Box 415, Moynihan Papers.

12. Moynihan, "The President and the Negro," 33.

13. Moynihan to McPherson, n.d., Box 216, Moynihan Papers.

14. Moynihan, "The President and the Negro," 44; emphasis added.

15. William Ryan, "Letters to the Editor," *Commentary*, June 1967, 6.

16. Bayard Rustin, "Letters to the Editor," *Commentary*, June 1967, 10.

17. Epstein to Moynihan, February 3, 1967, Box 164, Moynihan Papers.

18. "... And a Crisis of Confidence," *New York Times*, February 16, 1967.

19. Moynihan, interview by Rainwater and Yancey, 23.

20. "A Mother Can't Do a Man's Job," *Newsweek*, August 22, 1966, 41.

21. Richard J. Margolis, "Let Sleeping Dragons Lie," *New Leader*, June 19, 1967, 24.

22. Foley to Moynihan, December 3, 1965, Box 462, Moynihan Papers.

23. Riesman to Moynihan, February 28, 1966, Box 192, Moynihan Papers.

24. Michael Novak, "Race and Truth," *Commentary,* December 1976, 54, 55, 54.

25. Ibid., 57, 58. In response, Gutman mocked Novak for defending "the Moynihan Report and its author as if the Republic itself were under siege" and quipped that the title of his article ("Race and Truth") "reads better in the original German." See Gutman, "Black History Seduced and Abandoned," *The Nation*, September 22, 1979, 235.

26. Steven R. Weisman, ed., *Daniel Patrick Moynihan: A Portrait in Letters of an American Visionary* (New York: Public Affairs, 2010), 199–202.

27. Handwritten note (n.d.), Box 417, Moynihan Papers. The handwriting is probably that of Jason Epstein, the book's editor.

28. Moynihan, "The Professors and the Poor," in Moynihan, ed., *On Understanding Poverty* (New York: Basic Books, 1969), 19.

29. Moynihan, "The Academy Seminar on Poverty" (speech, American Academy of Arts and Sciences, Cambridge, Mass., 1967), Box 207, Moynihan Papers.

30. Moynihan, "The Professors and the Poor," 39.

31. Moynihan, "The Academy Seminar on Poverty."

32. "Crisis Inside the Black Family," *Muhammad Speaks*, February 24, 1967.

33. Moynihan, *Maximum Feasible Misunderstanding: Community Action in the War on Poverty* (New York: Free Press, 1969), 82.

34. Ibid., xi.

35. Ibid., 192.

36. Gary Wills, *Nixon Agonistes: The Crisis of the Self-Made Man* (Boston: Houghton Mifflin, 1970), 524–27.

37. Moynihan, *Maximum Feasible Misunderstanding*, 99, 190.

38. James S. Coleman et al., *Equality of Educational Opportunity* (Washington, D.C.: U.S. Department of Health, Education, and Welfare, 1966).

39. For details on the seminar, see Moynihan to Ted Sizer, May 15, 1967, Box 150, Moynihan Papers.

40. Frederick Mosteller and Daniel Patrick Moynihan, *On Equality of Educational Opportunity* (New York: Vintage, 1972), 20.

41. Moynihan, "The Politics of Stability," *New Leader*, October 9, 1967, 9.

42. James S. Coleman, "Equal Schools or Equal Students?" *Public Interest* 1 (1966): 73–74.

43. Mosteller and Moynihan, *On Equality of Educational Opportunity*, 56.

44. Coleman to Moynihan, December 8, 1966, Box 150, Moynihan Papers.

45. Coleman to Cater, August 1, 1967, Box 149, Moynihan Papers.

46. Coleman to Moynihan, May 25, 1967, Box 150, Moynihan Papers.

47. Moynihan, "Toward Equality," Box 415, Moynihan Papers.

48. Ibid.

49. Ibid.

50. Moynihan, "Toward Equality as a Fact and a Result: A Program of Foundation Activity in Negro American Affairs," Box 148, Moynihan Papers, 82.

51. Moynihan, "The Politics of Stability," *New Leader*, October 7, 1967, 6, 9.

52. See the comments in *ADA World Magazine* following its publication of "The Politics of Stability," February 1968, 3M–4M.

53. As quoted in George Plimpton, ed., *American Journey: The Times of Robert Kennedy* (New York: Harcourt Brace, 1970), 185.

54. Moynihan, "The Politics of Stability," 7.

55. Michael Harrington, "The Welfare State and Its Neoconservative Critics," *Dissent* 20 (1973): 435–54.

56. The work that best captures neoconservatism as a variant of postwar liberalism is Peter Steinfels, *The Neoconservatives: The Men Who Are Changing America's Politics* (New York: Simon and Schuster, 1979). On the different phases of neoconservatism, see Justin Vaisse, *Neoconservatism: The Biography of a Movement* (Cambridge, Mass.: Harvard University Press, 2010).

57. Moynihan, "How the Liberals Failed the Negro," *Newsday*, August 5, 1967, 11W.

58. Moynihan, "Toward Equality," Box 413, Moynihan Papers.

59. Irving Kristol, "The Negro Today Is Like the Immigrant Yesterday," *New York Times*, September 11, 1966.

60. Glazer and Moynihan, *Beyond the Melting Pot* (Cambridge, Mass.: MIT Press, 1970), xxi, xxii, xvi.

61. Irving Kristol and Robert Weaver, "Who Knows New York," *Public Interest* 16 (1969): 47.

62. Thomas J. Sugrue and John D. Skrentny, "The White Ethnic Strategy," in Bruce E. Schulman and Julian E. Zelizer, eds., *Rightward Bound: Making America Conservative in the 1970s* (Cambridge, Mass.: Harvard University Press, 2008), 171–92; Matthew Frye Jacobson, *Roots Too: White Ethnic Revival in Post-Civil Rights America* (Cambridge, Mass.: Harvard University Press, 2006).

63. Glazer and Moynihan, *Beyond the Melting Pot*, lvi.

64. "Life in the Frightening Corners," *Time*, July 28, 1967, 12.

65. Ward B. Arbury to Moynihan, August 15, 1967, Box 189, Moynihan Papers.

66. Mrs. Bernard W. Brady to Moynihan (n.d., 1967), Box 189, Moynihan Papers; Moynihan, "Memo to Anne Brown," Box 189, Moynihan Papers.

67. Irving Kristol, "A Few Kind Words for Uncle Tom," *Harper's Magazine*, February 1965, 98.

68. James Q. Wilson, "The War on Cities," in Robert A. Goldwin, ed., *A Nation of Cities* (Chicago: Rand McNally, 1968), 27.

69. Irving Kristol, "The Negro in the City," in Goldwin, ed., *A Nation of Cities*, 58.

70. Kristol, "The Negro Today," 142.

71. Wilson, "The War on Cities," 27.

72. James Q. Wilson, "The Sick Sixties," *Atlantic Monthly*, October 1973, 92.

73. Moynihan, *The Politics of a Guaranteed Annual Income: The Nixon Administration and the Family Assistance Plan* (New York: Random House, 1973), 328. Many years later, Moynihan told journalist Nicolas Lemann that he wrote the report *because* of his finding that welfare rates were rising despite falling male unemployment. See Lemann, *The Promised Land*, 174.

74. Moynihan, "The Schism in Black America," *Public Interest* 27 (1972): 17. Emphasis added.

75. Kristol, "Welfare: the Best of Intentions, the Worst of Results," *Atlantic Monthly*, August 1971, 47, 46.

76. Ibid., 47.

77. Natasha Zaretsky, *No Direction Home: The American Family and the Fear of National Decline, 1968–1980* (Chapel Hill: University of North Carolina Press, 2007).

78. "The Riots and Daniel Patrick Moynihan," clipping, Box 191, Moynihan Papers.

79. Nathan Glazer, "The Rediscovery of the Family," *Commentary*, March 1978, 49, 50.

80. Nathan Glazer, "The Limits of Social Policy," *Commentary*, September 1971, 54.

81. Christopher Lasch, *Haven in a Heartless World: The Family Besieged* (New York: Basic Books, 1977), 159, 165. See also Zaretsky, *No Direction Home*, 183–221.

82. Glazer, "Rediscovery of the Family," 53.

83. William F. Buckley, "Moynihan at the ADA," *National Review*, October 17, 1967, 1108.

84. As quoted in John B. Judis, *William F. Buckley, Jr.: Patron Saint of the Conservatives* (New York: Simon and Schuster, 1988), 327.

85. On antiegalitarianism as the hallmark of conservatism, see Corey Robin, *The Reactionary Mind: Conservatism from Edmund Burke to Sarah Palin* (New York: Oxford University Press, 2011).

86. As quoted in Judis, *William F. Buckley*, 138.

87. Ibid., 244–52.

88. William F. Buckley, Jr., "On Stirring Against Race-Part II," remarks to Conservative Party, October 7, 1965, in Buckley, *The Unmaking of a Mayor* (New York: Viking, 1966), 154, 156.

89. "October 21, 1965 letter addressed to WFB," ibid., 153.

90. Buckley, "Are You a Racist?" press release, April 15, 1965, Box 131, Moynihan Papers.

91. William F. Buckley, Jr., "The Great, Lost Opportunity of 1965," *Boston Globe*, July 28, 1967.

92. William H. Tucker, *The Science and Politics of Racial Research* (Urbana: University of Illinois Press, 1994), 180–268; Daniel Kevles, *In the Name of Eugenics: Genetics and the Uses of Human History* (Cambridge, Mass.: Harvard University Press, 1995), 279–81; Jerry Hirsch, "To 'Unfrock the Charlatans,'" *Sage Race Relations Abstracts* 6 (1981): 1–66.

93. As quoted in Hirsch, "To 'Unfrock the Charlatans'," 5.

94. Tucker, *The Science and Politics of Racial Research*, 188; *The Negro Family*, 35.

95. Arthur R. Jensen, "How Much Can We Boost IQ and Scholastic Achievement?" *Harvard Education Review* 39 (1969): 95.

96. Tucker, *The Science and Politics of Racial Research*, 180–268.

97. Herrnstein, "I.Q.," *Atlantic Monthly*, September 1971, 57, 64.

98. R. J. Herrnstein, "On Challenging an Orthodoxy," *Commentary*, April 1973, 62.

99. Ibid., 44.

100. Norman Podhoretz, "The New Inquisitors," *Commentary*, April 1973, 8.

101. William F. Brazziel, "The Jensen Article on Intelligence," *Washington Post*, March 21, 1969.

102. John Neary, "A Scientist's Variations on a Disturbing Racial Theme," *Life*, June 12, 1970, 580.

103. "Memorandum from Daniel P. Moynihan to the President re: Race Relations," March 19, 1969, EX HU 2 Equality, White House Central Files, Nixon Library.

104. Pat Buchanan, as quoted in Tucker, *The Science and Politics of Racial Research*, 208.

105. Moynihan to Jensen, March 20, 1969, Box 286, Moynihan Papers.

106. Barry Goldwater, "Goldwater Column Bows Out," *Los Angeles Times*, December 31, 1967.

107. Donald Rumsfeld to Moynihan [n.d.], Box 192, Moynihan Papers.

108. Moynihan, "Where Liberals Went Wrong," in Melvin R. Laird, ed., *Republican Papers* (New York: Praeger, 1968), 129–42.

109. As quoted in Tevi Troy, *Intellectuals and the American Presidency: Philosophers, Jesters, or Technicians* (Lanham: Rowman & Littlefield, 2002), 80.

110. David Greenberg, *Nixon's Shadow: The History of an Image* (New York: Norton, 2003).

111. See Dan T. Carter, *From George Wallace to Newt Gingrich: Race in the Conservative Counterrevolution, 1963–1994* (Baton Rouge: Louisiana State University Press, 1998).

112. Matthew D. Lassiter, *The Silent Majority: Suburban Politics in the Sunbelt South* (Princeton: Princeton University Press, 2006); Dean J. Kotlowski, *Nixon's Civil Rights: Politics, Principle, and Policy* (Cambridge, Mass.: Harvard University Press, 2001); Hugh Davis Graham, "Richard Nixon and Civil Rights: Explaining an Enigma," *Presidential Studies Quarterly* 26 (1996): 93–106.

113. Moynihan to Nixon, March 19, 1969.

114. Moynihan, *Politics of a Guaranteed Income*. First introduced to Congress in August 1969, the last version of the FAP bill stalled in October 1972.

115. Brian Steensland, *The Failed Welfare Revolution: America's Struggle over Guaranteed Income Policy* (Princeton, N.J.: Princeton University Press, 2008); Kornbluh, *The Battle for Welfare Rights*, 127–60.

116. Moynihan to Nixon, January 16, 1970.

117. Nixon as quoted in Kevin L. Yuill, *Richard Nixon and the Rise of Affirmative Action: The Pursuit of Racial Equality in an Era of Limits* (Lanham, Md.: Rowman and Littlefield, 2006), 173; see 171–73 for Nixon's reaction to Moynihan's memo.

118. James Farmer, *Lay Bare the Heart: An Autobiography of the Civil Rights Movement* (New York: Arbor House, 1985), 324–26. It was not publicly known then that Farmer was the source of the leak. Farmer received the memo from an anonymous source in Vice President Spiro Agnew's office (the source may have hoped Farmer would publicize it to discredit Moynihan after he implicitly criticized Agnew for his inflammatory racial rhetoric). Farmer's suspicion of Moynihan grew during an early 1970 meeting when Moynihan failed to satisfy concerns about Arthur Jensen's influence on the administration. Farmer claimed that Moynihan commented seriously, "what your people need are some of our genes" (326). It is impossible to corroborate Farmer's claim, but it does not match Moynihan's other statements at the time.

119. "Moynihan Draws Anger . . . As Usual," *Newsday*, March 2, 1970, 2.

120. *Miami News*, March 13, 1970, clipping, Box 255, Moynihan Papers.

121. Roger Wilkins as quoted in Walter Trohan, "Thoughts on Note from Moynihan," *Chicago Tribune*, March 5, 1970; Lassiter, *Silent Majority*, 242–46.

122. "Text of Statement by Rights Groups and Individuals on Moynihan's Comments," *New York Times*, March 6, 1970.

123. Kenneth B. Clark, *Pathos of Power* (New York: Harper and Row, 1974). Clark felt so betrayed by Moynihan that he endorsed Moynihan's conservative opponent James Buckley (brother of William) in the 1976 New York Senate race.

124. Weisman, ed., *Daniel Patrick Moynihan*, 395.

125. Martin F. Nolan, "On the Theory of 'Benign Neglect'," *Boston Globe*, March 5, 1970.

126. "Moynihan Rides Again," *Berkeley Post*, March 5, 1970.

127. "Moynihan Regrets His Suggestion of 'Benign Neglect' on the Race Issue," *Washington Post*, March 3, 1970.

128. John David Maguire, "'Benign Neglect' or Malignant Concern?" *Christianity and Crisis*, April 13, 1970, 66.

129. "CBS Evening News with Walter Cronkite" (transcript), March 11, 1970, Box 255, Moynihan Papers.

130. William S. White, "Liberals Finally Place Knife in Moynihan's Back," *Corning Leader*, March 7, 1970.

131. "Mr. Moynihan's Apostasy," *Wall Street Journal*, clipping, Box 255, Moynihan Papers.

132. Andrew M. Greeley, "Column for Donald Quinn," Box 255, Moynihan Papers.

133. "'Benign Neglect'," *Chicago Tribune*, March 3, 1970.

Epilogue. Following in Moynihan's Footsteps

1. William Julius Wilson, *The Truly Disadvantaged: The Inner City, the Underclass, and Public Policy* (1987; Chicago: University of Chicago Press, 2012), 149.

2. J. H. O'Dell, preface to Carl Ginsburg, *Race and Media: The Enduring Life of the Moynihan Report* (New York: Institute for Media Analysis, 1989), vii.

3. William J. Bennett, "Reflections on the Moynihan Report," *American Enterprise*, January/February 1995, 30.

4. Ibid., 30.

5. Ibid., 31, 32.

6. Ibid., 31.

7. Michelle Alexander, *The New Jim Crow: Mass Incarceration in the Age of Colorblindness* (New York: New Press, 2010).

8. "Sex, Families, Race, Poverty, Welfare: A Symposium Revisiting the Moynihan Report at Its Thirtieth Anniversary," *American Prospect*, January/February 1995, 33. The symposium's sole dissenter was Lee Rainwater, who complained that the liberal measures he believed the report advocated were absent from contemporary discourse about African American families.

9. Ibid., 34.

10. Ibid., 33.

11. Ibid., 35.

12. Bennett, "Reflections on the Moynihan Report," 29.

13. "Sex, Families, Race, Poverty, and Welfare," 37.

14. Ibid., 36, 37.

15. Ibid., 36, 37.

16. George Gilder, *Wealth and Poverty* (New York: Basic, 1981), 151, 12, 118, 141.

17. Michael L. Ondaantje, *Black Conservative Intellectuals in Modern American* (Philadelphia: University of Pennsylvania Press, 2010), esp. 34–37. Loury found a welcome forum for his work in the leading neoconservative journals, *Public Interest* and *Commentary*, which editors Irving Kristol and Norman Podhoretz took into Reagan's camp. By 1986, Loury was the Reagan administration's "favored black spokesperson" and was to have been appointed deputy to Secretary of Education Bennett before personal scandal derailed his nomination.

18. Glenn C. Loury, "The Moral Quandary of the Black Community," *Public Interest* 79 (1985): 10.

19. Ibid., 14.

20. Angela D. Dillard, *Guess Who's Coming to Dinner Now: Multicultural Conservatism in America* (New York: New York University Press, 2001), 64–67.

21. Glenn C. Loury, "The Family, the Nation, and Senator Moynihan," *Commentary*, June 1986, 23.

22. Ibid., 24.

23. "The Controversy," *Ebony*, August 1986, 34.

24. Michael B. Katz, Mark J. Stern, and James J. Fader, "The New African American Inequality," *Journal of American History* 92 (2005): 75–108.

25. David Remnick, "The Family Crusader, Belying Labels, Drawing Crowds, and Loving It All," *Washington Post*, July 16, 1986. An informative, though polemical, account of widespread media embrace of the Moynihan Report in the 1980s is provided in Ginsburg, *Race and Media*.

26. "Moynihan: 'I Told You So'," *Newsweek*, April 22, 1985, 30.

27. Moynihan, *Family and Nation: The Godkin Lectures, Harvard University* (San Diego: Harcourt Brace, 1986), 175.

28. Ibid., 74.

29. "Bill Moyers Examines the Black Family," *Newsweek*, January 7, 1986, 236.

30. Ann Hulbert, "Children as Parents," *New Republic*, September 10, 1984, 16.

31. Eleanor Holmes Norton, "Restoring the Traditional Black Family," *New York Times*, June 2, 1985.

32. Kathryn Edin and Timothy J. Nelson, *Doing the Best I Can: Fatherhood in the Inner City* (Berkeley: University of California Press, 2013), 2–3; Adam Meyerson, "One Hundred Conservative Victories," *Policy Review*, April 1, 1989.

33. Andrew Kopkind, "Maximum Feasible Revisionism," *The Nation*, April 20, 1985, 468.

34. "The Controversy," 34.

35. Lynn Norment, "Resolve Tensions Between Black Men and Women," *Ebony*, August 1986, 153.

36. Lerone Bennett, Jr., "The 10 Biggest Myths About the Black Family," *Ebony*, August 1986, 129.

37. Alvin F. Poussaint, "Save the Fathers," *Ebony*, August 1986, 46. Poussaint is perhaps best known for co-authoring with comedian Bill Cosby the 2007 book, *Come On People: On the Path from Victims to Victors* (Nashville, Tenn.: Thomas Nelson, 2007).

38. Wilson, *The Truly Disadvantaged*, 14.

39. Thomas J. Sugrue, *Not Even Past: Barack Obama and the Burdens of Race* (Princeton, N.J.: Princeton University Press, 2010), 74–80.

40. Stephen Steinberg, "The Liberal Retreat From Race," *New Politics* 5 (1994).

41. William Julius Wilson, interview with author, February 17, 2014; William Julius Wilson, "Reflections on a Sociological Career that Integrates Social Science with Social Policy," *Annual Review of Sociology* 37 (2011): 1–18; Jack Niemonen, *Race, Class,*

and the State in Contemporary Sociology: The William Julius Wilson Debates (Boulder, Colo.: Lynn Rienner, 2002).

42. William J. Wilson, "The New Black Sociology: Reflections on the 'Insiders and Outsiders' Controversy," in James E. Blackwell and Morris Janowitz, eds., *Black Sociologists: Historical and Contemporary Perspectives* (Chicago: University of Chicago Press, 1974), 335.

43. Citizen's Committee for Moynihan, "Daniel P. Moynihan: A Look at the Record," Box 33, Bayard Rustin Papers. Rustin even defended the "benign neglect" memo as an argument "that progress toward racial equality would proceed more rapidly if more attention were paid to the economic issues affecting blacks and less attention paid to the divisive and emotional issues of race."

44. Michael Harrington, "The Welfare State and Its Neoconservative Critics," *Dissent* 20 (1973): 440.

45. William Julius Wilson, *The Declining Significance of Race* (1979; repr. Chicago: University of Chicago Press, 2012), 1, 154.

46. "Statement of the Association of Black Sociologists," in Charles Vert Willie, *The Caste and Class Controversy* (Bayside, N.Y.: General Hall, 1979), 178.

47. Willie, *Caste and Class Controversy*, 9.

48. Wilson, *The Truly Disadvantaged*, 49, 21, 105.

49. Ibid., 61.

50. Ibid., 158.

51. Ibid., 61, 158.

52. Ibid., 60, 83.

53. Ibid., 15, 20, 150, 6, 15.

54. Adolph Reed, Jr., "The Liberal Technocrat," *The Nation*, February 6, 1988, 170, 168.

55. Arthur Delaney, "Paul Ryan Laments Inner-City Culture of Not Working," *Huffington Post*, March 12, 2014.

56. *The War on Poverty: A House Budget Committee Report* (2014), 4.

57. George F. Will, "The Left's Half-Century of Denial over Poverty," *Washington Post*, March 21, 2014.

58. Jonathan S. Tobin, "In Trashing Ryan, Liberals Forget Moynihan," *Commentary*, March 14, 2014, http://www.commentarymagazine.com/2014/03/14/in-trashing-ryan-liberals-forget-moynihan/.

59. Paul Ryan, "'Inner City' Remarks Had Nothing to Do with Race," *Huffington Post*, March 13, 2014.

60. Jamelle Bouie, "The Imaginary 'Moynihan Report,'" *Daily Beast*, March 14, 2014.

61. Ta-Nehisi Coates, "Black Pathology and the Closing of the Progressive Mind," *Atlantic*, March 21, 2014, http://www.theatlantic.com/politics/archive/2014/03/black-pathology-and-the-closing-of-the-progressive-mind/284523/.

62. Gregory Acs et al., *The Moynihan Report Revisited* (Washington, D.C.: Urban Institute, 2013), 2.

63. Ibid., 12.

64. Though the Moynihan Report controversy highlights the dangers of discussing racial and economic inequality primarily in terms of the family, lower-class families certainly merit analysis. However, statistical generalizations that assume the meaning of a female-headed household cannot suffice. For an excellent recent ethnographic study of lower-class fathers, both white and African American, that upends conventional understandings of "absent" fathers, see Edin and Nelson, *Doing the Best I Can*.

ARCHIVAL COLLECTIONS CONSULTED

Chicago Urban League records, Special Collections and University Archives, University of Illinois at Chicago.

Kenneth Bancroft Clark Papers, Manuscript Division, Library of Congress.

St. Clair Drake Papers, Manuscripts, Archives and Rare Books Division, Schomburg Center for Research in Black Culture, The New York Public Library.

Catherine East Papers, Schlesinger Library, Radcliffe Institute, Harvard University.

Martha Elliot Papers, Schlesinger Library, Radcliffe Institute, Harvard University.

Lyndon Baines Johnson Presidential Library Collections.

Mary Dublin Keyserling Papers, Schlesinger Library, Radcliffe Institute, Harvard University.

Mary McGrory Papers, Manuscript Division, Library of Congress.

Daniel Patrick Moynihan Papers, Part I, Manuscript Division, Library of Congress.

National Association for the Advancement of Colored People Records, Manuscript Division, Library of Congress.

National Council of Negro Women Records, National Archives for Black Women's History.

National Organization for Women Records, Schlesinger Library, Radcliffe Institute, Harvard University.

National Urban League Records, Manuscript Division, Library of Congress.

Richard M. Nixon Presidential Library Collections.

Esther Peterson Papers, Schlesinger Library, Radcliffe Institute, Harvard University.

Bayard Rustin Papers, Manuscript Division, Library of Congress.

Theodore M. White Papers, Harvard University Archives.

Willard Wirtz Collection, Department of Labor Records, National Archives.

INDEX

ACKNOWLEDGMENTS

Having the time and resources to write this book was an incredible privilege. Even so, it was a challenge that sometimes seemed insurmountable. I could not have made it to the finish line without the support of my family, friends, and colleagues. One of the pleasures of completing it is that I am now able to thank them in print.

This manuscript benefited enormously from the feedback of friends and colleagues. The peer reviews from Howard Brick, Patricia Sullivan, and an anonymous reviewer were models of their kind: incisive and constructive. I am very grateful to those who commented on drafts: Eileen Boris, Felicia Kornbluh, Nelson Lichtenstein, Kevin Mumford, and Daryl Scott. Special thanks to those who read the entire manuscript: Dan Horowitz, Richard King, Dan Matlin, and Ellie Shermer. James Patterson's generosity is especially noteworthy given our interpretive differences. I also benefited from the expert research assistance of Scott Kamen, Steve Harris-Scott, and Eva Payne.

I was very lucky to have found a press as supportive as the University of Pennsylvania Press and an editor as skilled as Robert Lockhart. Bob enthusiastically supported the project from an early stage, offered productive feedback on its main ideas and on chapter drafts, and, along with managing editor Alison Anderson, expertly shepherded the book through the editorial process so that it could be published in time for the Moynihan Report's fiftieth anniversary.

I thank those who shared their memories of the controversy with me: Paul Barton, Laurence Glasco, Nathan Glazer, Stephen Graubard, Joyce Ladner, Thomas Pettigrew, Carol Stack, Robert Staples, William Julius Wilson, and William Yancey. Archivists are historians' best friends, and I thank all the archivists who aided my research, especially Bruce Kirby and his colleagues at the Library of Congress Manuscript Division and Allen Fischer at the LBJ library.

I especially appreciated the opportunity to spend the 2011–2012 academic year as a Visiting Scholar at the American Academy of Arts and Sciences, not only for the time it gave me to work on this project, but for the stimulating feedback from my fellow scholars and our adviser, Mary Dunn. I was also fortunate to receive funding from a Moody Grant from the Lyndon Baines Johnson Foundation, a Small Research Grant from the British Academy, and grants at Trinity College Dublin from the New Lecturer's Fund, Arts and Social Science Benefaction Fund, and Grace Lawless Lee Fund. I also thank Mark Pigott, whose philanthropy established my post at Trinity.

I am fortunate to work in a university and department that values historical research despite steep cutbacks in funding. I benefited from supportive colleagues, especially David Ditchburn who facilitated my year-long sabbatical at the American Academy as department head. I am especially grateful to Trinity students who took my "Race and Ethnicity in American Social Thought" class. They demonstrated that the Moynihan Report can incite passionate debate decades later in a different nation and confirmed the virtues of research-led teaching for both research and teaching.

I thank the June Jordan Estate for allowing me to quote in full her poem, "Memo to Daniel Pretty Moynihan." I am extremely grateful to the Glushko Samuelson Intellectual Property Clinic at American University, especially to Brandon Butler, Alexandra Chaffin, and Jonathan Perez. I also thank Robert English.

As always, the support of my parents, Bill and Susan Geary, my brother, Patrick, and my in-laws, Jim and Margaret Sutton, has been invaluable. Susan edited the entire manuscript. I dedicate this book to her and to Bill, who both lived through the period in which this book takes place.

I would have to write another book to list all the ways that my wife, Jennie Sutton, contributed to this one. The irony of starting our own family while I was writing a book about the family was not lost on us. Our loving memory of Joie will always remain bound up with this book. Over our son Oscar's first two years, he found that his father spent much of his time in the office "making donuts." Oscar made no specific contribution to this project. Truth be told, he cannot understand why anyone would write a book lacking copious pictures of trains or trucks. Still, he and Jennie provided the best possible distractions from writing any author could imagine.